Inside Television's First War

Inside Television's First War

A Saigon Journal

Ron Steinman

UNIVERSITY OF MISSOURI PRESS
COLUMBIA AND LONDON

Library of Congress Cataloging-in-Publication Data

Steinman, Ron, 1934–
    Inside television's first war : a Saigon journal / Ron Steinman.
        p. cm.
    Includes index.
    ISBN 0-8262-1419-3 (alk. paper)
        1. Steinman, Ron, 1934–   . 2. Vietnamese Conflict, 1961–1975—Television and the
    conflict.   3. Vietnamese Conflict, 1961–1975—Journalists—Biography.   4. War
    correspondents—United States—Biography.   I. Title.
    DS559.46.S74   2002
    959.704'3—dc21   2002075440

Designer: Kristie Lee
Typesetter: Bookcomp, Inc.
Printer and Binder: Thomson-Shore, Inc.
Typefaces: Minion and Nimbus Sans

**To all who worked in the Saigon Bureau
and helped make this book possible**

Contents

Inside Television's First War

Introduction

I BECAME THE SAIGON bureau chief for NBC News in April 1966 and served for twenty-seven months until July 1968, thus becoming a part of the history of the war in Vietnam. The reports generated by my bureau and all the other news bureaus, broadcasters, wire services, magazines, and newspapers defined the war then and for generations of Americans to come. We did not know the effect the war would have on the future when we covered it. When my tour in Vietnam ended, I thought of writing this book but I did not have the time to sit, write, and reflect on the war. I never doubted I would one day write about my days and nights in the Saigon bureau, but the opportunity eluded me for years. After Saigon, I went to Hong Kong as Southeast Asia bureau chief. I continued to cover the war from Hong Kong with repeated trips to Saigon. I also saw much of Korea, Japan, the Philippines, Thailand, and Cambodia as I learned my way around the Asian crescent. In 1969 I was given a new and exciting assignment as London bureau chief. The Troubles had started in Northern Ireland and that country was in flames, its social fabric in tatters, death and destruction common. During my four years based in London, I spent more than a year in Belfast covering the seemingly never-ending violence. There were problems in the Middle East, with trips to Israel to cover the tensions there. In Paris, the Vietnam peace talks kept me busy as my bureau filed daily progress reports on the size and shape of the table the participants would sit around, including, of course, who would participate once they started talking, if ever. I returned to Vietnam often between 1969 and 1972 to help run the Saigon bureau.

When the war finally ended in 1975, the idea of writing "the book," as I called it, again preoccupied me. The war in Vietnam had been television's first war. There were many books about strategy, tactics, diplomacy, and politics in the war, but none about how television journalists covered this major story of the twentieth century. There were no books on how a television news bureau worked. I had the material and the memories. It was my book to write, but I was not ready. My life as a working journalist gave me no time.

1

In the mid-1970s I returned to New York from my assignment in London. Though now an executive—general manager of news specials—I remained a working journalist engrossed in covering stories, particularly Watergate and the space program. At NBC News I oversaw the ninety-minute special programs we often broadcast on Friday nights, a summation and hoped-for clarification of the week's Watergate hearings. One day in my fifth-floor office at the network's headquarters in Rockefeller Center, I received an unexpected call from the NBC News archives in Fort Lee, New Jersey.

"Are you Ron Steinman?"

"Yes."

"We have a lot of boxes here with your name on them."

"My name?"

"Your name. You the Ron Steinman from Vietnam?"

"Yes, by way of Brooklyn."

"Then this is all you. You want us to dump the boxes or send them to you?"

"What's in the boxes?"

"Stuff. Your stuff. Cables from you. Cables to you. Letters. Let me see . . . names like Reuven Frank, Mac Johnson, others. Expense reports. Internal memos. Like I said, stuff."

"How many boxes?"

"Four, no, five big boxes. The legal size. Packed with paper."

"Sure. Send them to me at 30 Rock. They might be useful in the future."

I had no idea at the time how useful. The material in the boxes proved to be worth more than I could guess. Not only did they contain memos with handwritten notes, but they also held almost every cable I had sent from Saigon to New York when I was bureau chief. I had saved every piece of paper I generated and stored them away. These boxes had my daily logs, coverage reports, situation reports, political and military analyses, and a record of the bureau's expenses. I had sent most of this material by telex or mailed it to producers and editors in New York. These files had the details of what we planned to cover, who covered what and where, and notes on the people who worked in the bureau. Along with my files, to my surprise and gratification, headquarters in New York had also saved almost everything generated there. We then lived in a paper world. In today's computer era, having "hard copies," a paper record such as this, is probably impossible. I had a windfall, material that I still was not certain how to use.

In 1975, I became the Washington producer for the *Today* show. I still could not find the time to put my Saigon memories and experiences on paper. In the

1980s, I produced daily news programs and continued to cover stories. I worked as a senior producer on *Today* and in the news specials unit, where I covered politics, developed programs, and produced documentaries. In the news business, events take precedence over contemplation. One assignment led to another. My feet were hardly on the ground before I would be off covering something new. Politics. Conventions. Summits. By then, the war in Vietnam had been over for more than ten years. Thoughts of my book receded. I knew there would be many books in the years ahead on a subject that had so deeply affected American life. The world did not need another book about Vietnam, I thought.

My perspective changed in 1985 when I returned to Vietnam with an NBC News team to cover the tenth anniversary of the fall of Saigon. Every day during our stay, we did live inserts for the *Nightly News*. We broadcast *Today* live every morning for a week from the grounds and rooms of the former Presidential Palace in Saigon. For our control room, we used a deserted concrete guardhouse outside the palace. It felt strange to see our equipment placed against walls pocked with bullets; during the war, we often had to wait in that damp room for Vietnamese security to pass us through to President Thieu's office. In memory of the day Saigon fell, we produced a live special broadcast on April 30, 1985.

While in Saigon, I collected more material, made more notes, had new experiences, talked with many Vietnamese, and wandered the streets of the city I once called home. I was again covering Vietnam, now more than a decade after the war.

When I returned to New York, I started writing. However, I had a problem: too much material, too many notes. Again, I put the project aside. But journalists and academics I knew encouraged my efforts to get the book published. Over the next six years, I committed more memories to paper. I knew that what I had done as bureau chief at a special moment in broadcast history could not be duplicated. What the bureau's correspondents, cameramen, and soundmen did was also unique. My book, a tribute to everyone who covered the war, would be a trip back in time. In the late 1960s portable videotape did not exist, and we captured images of the war on sixteen-millimeter film. Personal computers and fax machines did not exist. Satellites were in their infancy. We were innovative, yet primitive by today's standards.

Covering the war in Vietnam was hugely different from the way we cover any story today, especially a war. We found our story in the field, in jungles, in rice paddies, and along the beaches and mountain ranges where we knew we could fill the screen with American soldiers in trying situations. The story moved too fast for an outside entity to run our operation. We had to move quickly, without waiting for the assignment desk in New York to say "go." We decided what to cover because we were the ones on the ground and we knew the story better than anyone, especially someone in a dry, well-lit office thousands of miles away. To our advantage, communications with headquarters were terrible, which meant less interference. Today, network headquarters usually has control over coverage of events. Communications by satellite, computer, and telephone are far superior and bureau chiefs in distant places have less authority. Getting on the air live and first often takes priority over good journalism, a major problem of broadcast news today. We participated in a way of life and a way of journalism during those busy years that none of us will ever see again. It is sad to think that most journalists today will never know the sustained high, the rush, that accompanies reporting under such intense, let-it-all-fly conditions.

Until the mid–nineteenth century, the modern war correspondent did not exist. When one of the London papers wanted to report a war, it arranged to have military officers or English nationals who were in the fight or observing the action—amateurs to journalism—write letters to the paper. These letters had the wonder of the new about them but were long and rambling, dominated by detail that only those with great patience could endure to read. These dispatches were journalism of a sort, but nothing like what would come. When the *Times of London* hired William Howard Russell to cover the Crimean War (1853–1856), reporting on war changed forever. Though Russell and his fellow full-time reporters showed great courage in reporting from the front lines, technically they had to know only how to put their pen to paper and get their stories on the next fast packet to Great Britain, no small feat.

In Vietnam, television correspondents had to know much more about their craft, because it had become far more complicated. By the time reporters went to war, the overt trappings of their craft had become second nature. After all, most were children of television and, as such, had an unconscious, though learned, understanding of the medium. They knew how to stand, how to sit, how to hold a microphone, and how to conduct an interview for the camera. They knew how to "write to picture," how many words per second to speak, and how to do the "stand-up": how to look like you're not in danger though you are and, conversely, how to look like you are in danger when you are not. If a correspondent lacked these basic skills, his reports would be weak, his composure unsteady, his ability to talk to his audience a failure. Fortunately, though such reporters existed, they were in the minority.

But few reporters who arrived in Vietnam had the training it took to be a war correspondent. Covering war is nothing like covering the local gardening club or the progress of a bill through the House or Senate. Unfortunately, news agencies did not have the money and staff to afford the luxury of sending only those experienced in war to cover war. Vietnam was the first major American ground war since Korea and few, if any, of the broadcast journalists who covered Korea later made their way to Southeast Asia. NBC News recruited young reporters, many of whom were working at local stations, the farm system for the networks. Eager to succeed but anxious about falling bombs and flying bullets, most did well.

Boot camps for war correspondents did not exist. Would they have worked? No. Only experience can teach journalists how to report on war. We had veteran reporters such as Wilson Hall, Dean Brelis, and Paul Cunningham alongside the novices and I would like to think they sometimes led by example. But training by doing prevailed. Good journalists learn to parachute with little notice into the unknown. By virtue of tenacity, guts, skill, training, and intelligence—and often with the help of an apt local guide—they manage surprisingly well at the start of their tour to survive, then grow wings and fly.

Journalists who cover military issues can find themselves spending too much time trying to understand budgets. They concern themselves with investigating cost overruns, soldiers' pay and housing, and weapons systems. All are valid and worthy pursuits. Their best education in war, however, is under fire. Exposure to danger matters more than what anyone can learn in the classroom. Textbooks provide templates for proper procedure: the who, why, what, and where of the story. But the doing—that is, the coverage itself—becomes so compelling, and often overpowering, that instinct rules rather than learned lessons. My reporters had varying strengths and levels of commitment to their craft. Some learned their trade faster than others. Some, however, never learned the skills to successfully operate in a war zone like Vietnam, with its ever-shifting, unstable fronts, its ambushes and frequent terror.

Though some of the reporters who worked for me had served in the army or marines and several had covered other wars, most had no previous military experience. They all tried, though, and the lack of a full understanding of the military mind and its often arcane culture rarely got in the way of doing a good job. In the thousands of television stories and radio reports that we sent from the bureau to the American people, there were few mistakes of substance, though military purists might disagree. We learned to treat the military with respect and never to assume that anyone wearing a uniform was one-dimensional. We understood they could think for themselves when orders from higher-ups superseded good sense.

While many of us knew next to nothing about the military, its customs and culture, none of us knew anything about the Vietnamese people, *their* customs and culture. But we had to learn everything we could, and fast, to survive. I found ignorance of Vietnamese values and customs to be shockingly high among senior officers. Perhaps I expected too much, as these men only reflected the policy from Washington, and our legislators and the executive branch proved equally delinquent. The U.S. command dismissed the enemy's goals as either simplistic or naive, rarely understanding that they believed truth was on their side. This made it a strange war by any yardstick.

We did not always believe what we heard from people in the government, whether in or out of uniform. They had an agenda and we did not. They had orders and we had curiosity. Many of us found it difficult to believe everything they said or, sometimes, preached. It resulted in a constant tug of war between truth and propaganda when we dealt with government officials. The situation in Vietnam demanded continuous intellectual pushing and shoving if we were to get the story we knew existed. Covering the whole war, we sometimes knew more about a story than an officer confined to a specific tactical zone. We were not always correct in our conclusions, but we tried mightily to get to the truth.

The military thought, as do professionals in any business, that we journalists could never understand their work, especially when it involved danger. However, once you're under fire from shelling or small arms, or witnessing a terrorist attack, that old saw dies quickly.

So how do you learn to cover war? In some ways, you never do. But you learn by doing, by asking many questions, and by coming to grips with fear. Knowing that fear is real often provides enough protective covering when the unexpected takes place, which it always does. To survive, you learn when to duck and how to identify the whistling sound of mortars and the angry belch of a 105-mm howitzer. You learn to distinguish the crack of a Viet Cong AK-47 from the pop of a Chinese recoilless rifle and the friendly sound of an M-16. You learn to cross your fingers and to wear, if available, a steel helmet on your head and a flak jacket to protect your chest, heart, and back. Helicopter pilots routinely lined the floor of their thin-shelled aircraft with flak jackets. More than once, enemy rounds struck and pierced the floor of a helicopter in which I was a passenger. Fortunately, though the "bird" bucked from the impact, the rounds never made it any closer to those of us inside because of those extra jackets.

Even when there is no combat and no shots sound, there is little theorizing. Lessons for the future are rarely considered. Our bar talk concerned our lack of sleep, our horrible living conditions, the heat, the monsoon rains, the bad food, and the terrible wine. We may have swapped stories, but rarely did we discuss specifically how to cover the war. Reporters talked about how misunderstood they were by producers and editors at home, and how they missed their loved ones. They talked about their next drink, their last meal, and occasionally about women. They did not think of journalism as anything other than a way of life, one that they wouldn't substitute for anything. I believed then that, more than the skills needed to cover the war, instinct honed by experience would guide the reporter through most, if not all, situations. I still hold that belief as gospel. To succeed in covering any war—especially a story as diverse as Vietnam, with its many images, in pictures and words, giving the look of a splintered windshield—it's important to be active first and to intellectualize second.

But covering war is more than seeing and experiencing action. There is the culture, the history, the food, the climate. By learning how the local people live, you become a better reporter and help yourself to avoid injury or, worse, death. At least, that is the hope. It can also help you make sense of the mystery surrounding the story you are covering. Vietnam remained ever enigmatic. There were too many areas where meaning stayed unclear, motives vague, and goals clouded. The goal of the correspondent and the all-important cameraman—and, through them, my goal as well—was to clarify the puzzle, if possible, and dig through the morass without violating the principles of the trade. Once the story was complete, it was up to the gatekeepers at the various stages of production to ask the right questions in the quest for accuracy.

The public expects reporters to cover everything that happens—that is, all the stories we can find. But in war, many stories may have obscure origins and be difficult to explain. Today, many who hold top management positions at the media conglomerates also expect journalists to entertain as they inform. Fortunately, that attitude played hardly any role in the Vietnam era. Doubtless, much of what we reported from Vietnam influenced our audience: people at home and in government, the military, foreign allies, and our enemies. In the late 1960s and in the 1970s, communications was still in its infancy as far as speed was concerned, and events with new twists sometimes overshadowed the events documented in our pieces. Yet, our stories remained valid and usually had enough heart to receive substantial airplay because they explained the reasons behind the events.

Though the networks covered the war in the early 1960s, it took a backseat to other news, as if the press lords did not have the time, energy, or perhaps the stomach to focus on the war full-time. In Vietnam the buildup was slow, almost ignored until late 1965 when the number of American troops started edging into the hundreds of thousands, culminating in more than half a million by early 1966.

Until the emergence of CNN in the 1980s, there were fewer channels demanding fresh news. News did not command the air twenty-four hours a day; news broadcasts had fixed times. Fixed schedules made for "appointment television." Viewers knew they could see morning television starting at 7:00 A.M. The network evening newscasts were on at either 6:30 or 7:00. Listeners could find radio newscasts every hour throughout the day. Breaking news, if warranted, came into the home at odd times, but these stories were always special. We never broadcast anything frivolous, because we wanted the audience to know they could trust us to give them what we considered important. The television news business in that era had different motives, and I like to think we were better, more focused, less tabloid.

There were only three television networks, but we were not any less competitive. I knew our competition, their strengths and weaknesses, and I sometimes covered stories with that in mind. If CBS had a weak correspondent on a particular military action, I might try, if I had one available, to put a stronger team in the field. Rarely were we head to head covering the same squad or even platoon. Thousands of men were fighting or hunting for the enemy, but for us, most of the action took place on a very small scale. This allowed us to cover stories, or parts of them, where we were alone, the competition not in sight. Perhaps we were even exclusive (a much overused term) to an entire battle.

We hoped that what we covered served a larger purpose than simply attracting and holding an audience. On the other hand, we were never so naive as to assume we could do without the audience, so we didn't tone down our coverage or ignore the obvious. Combat, the battle itself, action, is what is obvious in war and the easiest story to cover. But when we covered combat just for the sake of combat, it served only to stir the prurient in us. It edged easily toward pornography. Showing only combat is a poor substitute for covering other news in a war zone (though there is nothing more serious than death). It limits the growth of the correspondent and his crew, and is thus a disservice to the audience. In the end, the audience appreciates that there is little difference from one combat story to another except the nature of the horror. Of course, battle footage, with guns firing and men wounded and killed, did serve a purpose. The people sitting safely and snugly at home had the opportunity to see the ultimate, inherent futility of the war.

There is a continuing debate about the so-called moral detachment of the journalist, especially in war, where destruction and violence prevail. Is there a right and wrong here? How much should journalists be involved in the stories they tell? Does the choice of a sound bite and pictures, and the placement of those pictures against the narration, unduly influence the direction the story takes? When a reporter gives too much thought to the morals and ethics of the story-telling, the result can reek from the personal rather than be naturally strong from its inherent value. We must never underestimate the audience's ability to recognize feigned or imposed morality. Such imposition can bring a story from the potentially airy height of pure reportage down to the muddy waters of personal involvement. There are those who believe reporters can and should show moral and social responsibility without their report suffering. I have difficulty with that idea. I watched Buddhist monks immolate themselves in defiance of the Thieu government. I found what these men and women did abhorrent. But I would not allow my staff to editorialize and say, how horrible a waste of life. By playing the story straight, describing what happened and showing the pictures of the charred bodies, we did not compromise the story, the reporters, or the monks, their beliefs and actions. Because we could not expect families at home in America to fathom anyone taking his own life that way, we simply presented the facts, no more, no less. We maintained the art of storytelling by staying true to the event, to what the reporter and his camera team observed and recorded. Whatever occurred in the mind and heart of the viewer because of the report was a bonus and, perhaps, a salve to the reporter's psyche. The risk was always that the correspondent might err too much on one side and thus cloud his interpretation and unduly influence that of his audience. Reporters can't help but raise moral issues and taking a stand when confronted with anything abhorrent. But we should take seriously our role as purveyors of truth and clarity. The minute we try to serve another muse, however tantalizing, we are no use to our audience.

Slowly, the book took shape. Ideas became words and sentences. Friends read sections of the manuscript and encouraged me to complete it. Eventually I had a book not about politics or war or the politics of war but about how we at NBC News, Saigon, covered the war during my years running the bureau. It is about how I saw broadcast journalism—television and, yes, radio—and the internal politics of journalism in war as we coursed through uncharted territory, television's first living-room war.

In Vietnam, reporting for television was like nothing anyone had done previously. Television as the dominant mass medium did not exist in World War II. Newspapers, magazines with their wonderful still photographs, and radio dominated coverage. The occasional newsreel at the movie theaters featured government-released film of the war. When our troops entered Korea, where we sometimes euphemistically called the war a "conflict," television remained in its infancy and there were few combat film photographers. Again, radio, newspapers, magazines, and newsreels containing official war film supplied the coverage. Broadcast journalists in the Vietnam War wrote a new set of rules that are still emerging and are far from being perfected today; in the language of journalism, they are in "rewrite." These journalists combined eyewitness reporting, oral history, analysis, and even elements of legend and myth. My hope is that we will continue to fuse these diverse elements every way we can to allow them their rightful place in the world of reporting.

I have tried to describe what we did from day to day to cover the war and how we interacted with each other, with American and Vietnamese civilians and military personnel, and with New York headquarters. The book tells the behind-the-scenes story of how the war influenced young journalists and why some folded under stress and broke down while others remained strong. We were covering the biggest story of our lives. Nowhere is this more apparent than in the chapters that describe the bureau's heroic efforts in the 1968 Tet Offensive. Nothing I've covered since has been more gratifying or more frustrating than the Vietnam War. Now I have written the book I wanted, one I believe no one else could have written and that I hope will benefit all who read it.

1

A Changed City

OF ALL THE APRILS in my life, few had the significance or lasting meaning of those I spent in Vietnam.

It all started innocently in the bar of the Amsterdam Hilton in November 1965. I was producing a one-hour documentary for NBC on the Dutch royal family and how a soothsayer had infiltrated palace life through a relationship with Queen Wilhelmina. We were tentatively calling the film *The Royal Soap Opera.* Reuven Frank, our executive producer, was filming another documentary in Vienna and had come to Amsterdam on a break to see how my team was doing. That night, as we were all having a drink in the main bar of the hotel, Reuven heard his name being paged. He left to take a phone call from New York. Several minutes later he returned and announced that his boss, William McAndrew, president of NBC News, had offered him the position of executive vice president of the news division. He told us he had accepted the position with the proviso that he be allowed to complete the documentaries in production. In a moment of genuine largesse, he announced that this was our opportunity to ask him for any job we coveted. He made no promises, but said he would do everything he could to see our wishes come true.

I responded that I wanted to go to Saigon and run the news bureau there. There was silence from everyone. It was an audacious request. Everyone thought me mad for making it. I was thirty-one, unattached, and wanted to advance my already rising career. After graduating Lafayette College with a degree in history and kicking around for a few years in a variety of meaningless jobs, I had taken a position in the mail room at NBC. Soon I became a copyboy in the news division. In those days, the late 1950s, the news we received came clicking into our wire machines from the Associated Press, the International News Service, the United Press, and Reuters. Each machine held a roll of heavy, twelve-inch-wide paper. We copyboys would tear the paper into six-foot strips and then remove the carbons before we distributed the copy to the resident desk editor and the writers and editors in the newsroom. Our hands were always dirty, our backs and arms aching from lugging the boxes of paper, our legs tired from running the copy. Soon I graduated to the night assignment desk. Then, for one year, I had a job in Washington as David Brinkley's assistant. I came back to New York as a writer on the fifteen-minute *Huntley-Brinkley Report,* the network's major newscast. I will never forget the weeks I spent writing the ten-second announcement of the Dow Jones closing stock prices until I got it right and was able to move onto bigger, more complex stories. I quickly graduated to *Chet Huntley Reports,* a half-hour weekly television magazine show that aired Friday nights at 10:30. As a field producer, news editor, and writer, I often created the only long piece for the show on any given Friday. I traveled for the show to Guatemala, Brazil, and throughout the United States. By 1964, I was producing and developing hour-long documentaries on every conceivable subject. It was not enough. I needed something else, something fresh, invigorating, and challenging. Only one thing would do: the war in Vietnam. It was heating up and I did not see it ending soon. It was the place for a young journalist to be. I was not a correspondent, so I would not get there that way, but I was a good news editor and I thought I could run the Saigon bureau. I could, as they said in the military, get my ticket punched, earn my stripes, and move on from there to do almost anything I wanted.

However, I had some problems. I would be going to a foreign country halfway across the world, where almost everyone spoke a language other than English. And I had never run a bureau. The largest number of people I had supervised was three: a correspondent, a cameraman, and a soundman. Reuven knew that, and he and the others smiled sympathetically at me. We finished dinner without saying anything more about it. Several weeks later, after completing filming on the documentary about the Dutch royal family, I returned to New York.

My next assignment was with an old friend, George Murray. NBC made a decision to cover the war in Vietnam from the comfort of 30 Rockefeller Plaza, our headquarters in New York. George and I developed and ultimately produced *Vietnam Weekly Review,* a half-hour program devoted to the war that tried—through the eyes of correspondent Garrick Utley and with film from the battlefield, maps, and a military sand table—to put Vietnam into perspective each week. As its chief writer, for the time being I was as close to Vietnam as I believed I wanted to be.

■ ■ ■

It was February 1966. The death toll for American troops was increasing weekly. I was working long hours on the new program and living in an apartment on the Upper West Side. One day a call came from Reuven Frank, asking me to visit him in his office. I went dutifully, wondering what he wanted. He gestured for me to sit and I did, in the chair next to his desk.

"When can you go to Saigon?" he asked.

Not "can you go," but "when can you go." The tour of the current Saigon bureau manager was about to end, he told me. I had not thought about the assignment for many months, but in truth it was probably never far from my mind.

I did not hesitate. "As soon as you want," I replied.

"Then get started. See Jim White about money. Talk to everyone here you have to. Get your affairs in order, and let me know when you're ready to leave. I'll make the announcement."

"Thanks," I said. "It should take me . . . maybe six weeks."

"Don't be longer," he cautioned.

We shook hands and I left his office to start making preparations.

When I went to Saigon in April 1966 to become chief of the most unusual news bureau in the world, I did not know how the war would decimate Vietnam. I did not understand that it would change the characters of nations and the life of every person who became part of it, myself included. I did not know what to expect and had, naturally, a fear of the unknown, but I believed if I moved in a straight line, with purpose and resolve, problems would take care of themselves.

In 1966, I flew to Vietnam on a direct flight. But twenty years later, when I returned for six weeks as senior producer of *Today*'s tenth-anniversary coverage of the fall of Saigon, Bangkok was the first stop. At the airport in Bangkok, I bought several quarts of Johnny Walker Black Label Scotch and several cartons of Rothman's 555 cigarettes, the English cigarette smoked by Ho Chi Minh and revered in a mystical way by the Vietnamese. I no longer smoked but I planned to use the cigarettes and liquor to open closed doors, as small tokens of friendship, and perhaps as bribes and tips. On the short Air France flight between Bangkok and Ho Chi Minh City, I was served Charles Heidsieck Brut Rose, an excellent 1979 pink champagne. The first-class steward gently poured it into fluted glasses with a touch of pride. I drank with the delight of the prescient, realizing that when I landed in Vietnam nothing would be the same as it had been years ago. I was jolted back to reality by an announcement in French and English: "The taking of photographs from the air over Vietnamese territory or on the ground at Tan Son Nhut Airport is strictly prohibited."

Welcome to Vietnam, I thought. Welcome home. Some things never seem to change. The Communist government in the 1980s was as paranoid as the dictatorship that ran South Vietnam during the war. The announcement was the same one I had heard every time I landed at this airport from 1966 to 1968 and all the times I traveled to Vietnam from London through 1972. The same prohibitions prevailed and apparently the same fears.

We started our descent into Saigon soon after leaving Bangkok. It was gradual, slow and revealing, enough to make me hold my breath in anticipation. The fields below were so close that I felt I could reach down and touch them. I wanted to grab some mud from a rice paddy and smell its damp Mekong earthiness. Nothing moved on the ground. Nowhere was there any sign of life. The Mekong River, the waterway that cuts a wide swath through the southern delta of Vietnam, had been intensely overcrowded during the war but was now curiously empty. No sampans, rowboats, fishing boats, flatboats, or barges were in sight. The fields and rice paddies were too quiet to be real. Everything on the ground looked neat and carefully cultivated, precise and so unlike the devastated country I once knew so well.

The approach to Ho Chi Minh City was gentle, the landing slow and easy. The terrain once again reminded me of the *National Geographic* photographs that I had gazed at in awe as a child. Only there were no water buffalo, a staple of the magazine and a vivid pastoral memory of the war. Coasting toward the airport, I saw bomb craters as big as suburban American swimming pools. These pockmarked the landscape and held water, not chlorinated but brackish green and unhealthy. Rarely were they used for recreation, and only sometimes for fishing. Many farms and villages had been regularly bombed—sometimes hourly—and no longer existed. As the airplane prepared to land, it passed over more badly damaged fields, some with fewer craters, but big craters nevertheless. During the war, American generals with too much ammunition believed, or rather hoped, they were hitting Viet Cong guerrillas beyond the lines. When artillery officers were setting the distance for their cannon, their bombs plowed huge holes into the ground. They told me they "walked" the shells across the indistinguishable landscape until they landed on a target—sometimes, sadly, any target. Shells marched steadily toward their target, sometimes yard by yard, until they reached their destination. Officers bombed whole sections on their maps, one grid at a time. That method caused them to sometimes destroy quiet hamlets populated by innocent civilians. This destruction was wasteful and conquered nothing.

It was strange to land again at Tan Son Nhut Airport after so many years. I felt I had entered an alien world. It was April 1985 and I was in the new Vietnam. Almost nothing moved. The runways were barely active, in startling contrast with the war years, when Tan Son Nhut was the busiest airport in the world. Looking out my window I observed rows of obsolete military airplanes, mostly C-130s once belonging to the U.S. Air Force. There were also old Air Vietnam two- and four-engine passenger jets, their windows broken, paint peeling, bodies badly rusting. Pieces of wings and tails were strewn on the ground, surrounding the decaying fuselages. These airplanes had no grace or beauty even when they were whole; now they were empty hulks. Beside the main runway, overgrown grass and weeds dominated the other landing strips, the asphalt fractured. The runways looked as if they were hardly used, which I learned was the case. During the worst of times, when the airfield was under constant bombardment and regularly fought over, American military engineers managed to keep the runways in moderately good condition. Now, the Vietnamese kept operational only what they needed. It was strange to see empty half-moon revetments. Their sandbag walls once protected the powerful U.S. fighters and bombers that attacked Viet Cong and North Vietnamese troops.

Inside the vast terminal building, the process of checking my visa was slow and inefficient. Few immigration inspectors were present and they did their work without enthusiasm. Their steel-gray uniforms had not changed in twenty years, but were worn and unpressed. During the war, they were fresh and crisp. We often wondered in the 1960s how the inspectors managed to look good despite the lack of facilities. Going through customs was worse than in the past. An official handed me two identical forms that looked as if they were fresh from the local paper mill. The off-white sheets were of such poor quality that I was afraid to let the pages swing freely. I thought the dense, humid air might make them fall apart. The paper was difficult to write on, with hundreds of pieces of wood and debris embedded in each sheet. Worse, there was no carbon paper, so I had to mark each page separately, mimicking a photocopy. If the forms did not match up, the officials would refuse to accept them. I listed the money I carried in exact denominations, down to the pennies in my pocket. Any bit of U.S. currency had value to the Vietnamese. I carefully listed my tape recorder, my audio cassettes, my camera with its extra lenses and film, my watch, a gold wrist chain I wore, and anything else I considered of value. If I were to try to depart the country without any of the hard goods declared on entry, I would be subject to delays, fines, and possible arrest. In contrast, at the height of the war, with its rampant corruption, anyone could bring anything into the country if they made the right payoffs to clear the way.

When I completed the forms, I had to wait for my baggage to arrive at the terminal. There was no rush to unload the airplane, and there were no porters to carry the bags. I had to carry my own luggage to the customs table and submit my forms and baggage for inspection. I hoped the inspectors would not search my bags too carefully. I was breaking the law on arrival. I was carrying many bottles of costly antibiotics for my brother-in-law, a former South Vietnamese army officer who had been locked away in a reeducation camp since 1975. The inspectors would know immediately that the medicine was intended either for sale at a huge profit or for one of their fellow citizens. They would know that I couldn't use that quantity of antibiotics during so short a stay. I also carried important papers for my brother-in-law to help get him out of prison and out of the country so that he might finally join his wife and daughter in Maryland.

If I was caught, I would not get into the country and my employers at NBC News would be furious. It would mean they had sent me all that way at great expense for nothing. I would be unable to do my job and the other NBC staffers would have extreme difficulty doing their jobs. I held my breath as a young official in an ill-fitting uniform went through the correct motions. He explored my bags, looking at one layer, than another layer. He read my completed forms. He looked through my bags again. He reread my forms as if they had some hidden meaning. I tried to hurry him by exhibiting typical American impatience. It seemed to shake him up enough to want to get me out of his sight and on my way. Either he was as inexperienced as I thought or he did not care what I brought into the country. Whatever the case, he asked me no questions, gestured that I should close my bags, chalked them, and sent me on my way. It was nothing like the old days when, if the inspectors were in the wrong mood, they did a very tough search.

Not only did the young inspector miss the papers and photos of the prisoner's family and the plastic containers of prescription medicine, but he also overlooked eight bottles of Extra Strength Tylenol, probably the most coveted over-the-counter drug I could bring to Vietnam. I planned to give out the pain-relief capsules as tips and favors, especially for information. Many Vietnamese sold them one at a time to their friends and on the black market, which, I learned, still operated on almost every street corner in the city, every bar and restaurant, and every hotel and shop. Some people emptied the grains from a 500-milligram Tylenol capsule and cut the medicine with sugar. They returned half the mixture to the capsule and wrapped the other half in paper, doubling their sales by selling the contents of one capsule twice. A bottle of one hundred Extra Strength Tylenol capsules was worth three months' salary to the average Vietnamese. That one bottle could buy rice and canned milk for his children. It could help eliminate the struggles of everyday life. The Communist government, then ten years in power, had not solved the difficulty of daily survival. Many people in the South still had to resort to subterfuge to achieve anything more than a minimal existence.

Having made it through customs free and clear, I walked through the building, dragging my bags behind me. It was March, early in the monsoon season, and the day was hot and sultry. (Of course, Vietnam was hot, wet, and humid even in the dry season.) Other than the heat, there was nothing to remind me of the way things had been in the late sixties. Then, confusion dominated life in Saigon. People were always hurrying somewhere. But Tan Son Nhut Airport in the postwar era was relatively quiet. Even so, considering how few Vietnamese had the means to use the airport, I marveled at the number of people there. A crowd jammed one small area waiting for friends or relatives to arrive. Those allowed to leave and reenter the country were people of position in the new society or Vietnamese with known relatives in the United States or France. For many Vietnamese, the arrival and departure of international flights was the only entertainment they could find. Most of the spectators were young, in their teens or early twenties. Vietnam was a young country because many men and women who would have been middle-aged had lost their lives in the war. I found everyone friendly. A number of the young people were eager to practice the English they were learning in school. Some had learned English when they were much younger, before Saigon fell. From the difficulty they had speaking it, English apparently was no longer one of life's priorities. Most of them said very little to me but they giggled a great deal, talked to each other, jabbed each other in the ribs, and laughed among themselves.

When I put my bags down, a horde of excited kids immediately surrounded me. They wore patched but clean shirts and shorts. On the edges of the crowd were women, wearing just enough makeup so they would not feel drab despite their lack of stylish clothing. Wearing makeup was a measure of defiance. Hanoi was still having problems winning the hearts and minds of its southern brothers and sisters. Half of the country would always be North Vietnam to the southerners, just as Ho Chi Minh City would always be Saigon.

I had last been in Vietnam in 1972, and the thirteen years I'd been away had made an enormous difference. For Saigon and its inhabitants, there were deep changes. These become clearer the closer I approached what was now Ho Chi Minh City. Porters loaded my baggage into a waiting Japanese van. With the other members of NBC News, I began the drive into the city. There were no private cabs or buses anywhere. The state now owned all public transportation. The streets were clean, unlike the darkest days of the war, when overcrowding saw refugees sleeping in the narrow alleys they thought were safe from bombs, bullets, and the landscape of war. But the Cong Ly Canal on the route from the airport was as polluted as ever. An odor rose from its murky depths, filling the air with a stink so heavy I thought I could see it dancing before my eyes.

Buildings were falling apart and in worse shape than before. Paint was peeling off the walls. Most trees had no green leaves. Nothing was flowering. Enormous potholes filled the streets, and the sidewalks—what was left of them—had cracks and large fissures. It did not surprise me. Priorities had their place in Vietnam and the repair and care of city streets was not an immediate need.

The city was quiet. The pervasive pall before the start of the rainy season hung over Ho Chi Minh City. The streets were free of most traffic except bicycles and the occasional truck; there were almost no automobiles. But there were enough motorbikes, scooters, and buses to make the air heavily polluted. The poor-quality gas and the growing number of ersatz fuels, mixed with the heat and dust, did little to make the air much cleaner than it had been in the sixties and seventies.

The guide in charge of the van was from Hanoi. It was not as unusual to see North Vietnamese in the South during the war as is sometimes assumed, but they were mostly Catholic refugees who had fled below the demilitarized zone for what they thought would be religious freedom. This young man was not a refugee. He was there to work, but he was helpless at getting us to the Cuu Long Hotel overlooking the Saigon River. He knew almost nothing about the city. Our driver, also a northerner, was similarly lost. They had driven the route before but always with difficulty, using old maps drawn when South Vietnam was a separate country. Street names had changed. Tu Do Street, or Liberty Street, was now Dong Khoi or Uprising Street, also known as Street of the Final Assault, a revolutionary title befitting the new regime. I took it upon myself to direct the driver to our hotel and kept surprising our guide with my knowledge of the city's landmarks. On the way through the center of the city, we passed my old office in the Eden Building on Nguyen Hue.

As I looked at the Eden Building, emotions cascaded over me. Images from the past flooded my mind, of the times when I rarely saw daylight or breathed what passed for fresh air. Lingering memories of that old French-built building, once filled with hopes, dreams, and battles fought, won, and lost. My thoughts were of the men and women who covered a war it seemed would never end. For many

Vietnamese and Americans, it still was not over. I vowed that I would revisit the bureau and the apartment I had lived in one floor above to see who was living there now. It would be a test. How would I handle the memories?

The guide was tall and thin with a pinched but pleasant face. Although his teeth were rotten and his breath bad, he was only twenty-three years old. He would have been thirteen when the war ended. When I first came to Vietnam in 1966, he was four years old. When high-flying B-52s and Navy jets regularly bombed Hanoi, he was among the chosen moved from the capital to the coast. The government considered him and other children of officials to be the future of the new Vietnam and deliberately moved them out of the line of fire. Later, he received a university education to prepare him for a career in the foreign service. As the son of a Communist official with sufficient rank, he had been sent south by the foreign ministry for training. The tenth-anniversary celebration of Hanoi's victory over Saigon was his first taste of diplomacy.

A member of the elite in the blossoming new society before he knew anything about life, he was perfectly and completely indoctrinated into the Communist faith. He spoke with unquestioning rhetoric, replete with arrogant references to puppet regimes, running dogs, and the like. During the war, not even the most dedicated and long-standing government functionaries in the South—my primary source for official information—had peppered their speech with such nonsense. This young man was useless as a guide; he was more of an obstruction with his standard answer to every request: "No." I knew he was just doing his job. He was young and had not yet developed a capacity for subtlety. It was as if he were always looking over his shoulder to see who was monitoring him, marking his report card, making notes for his superiors and his father at home. When everyone was a free agent during the war, the selling of ideas and information had been a different game. People could choose their own brand of poisoned propaganda. It was a buyer's market for ideas and we continuously searched in the hope we would find the truth.

We reached our destination and I checked into a bedroom and sitting room on the top floor of the Cuu Long, once the proud Majestic Hotel. Rooming there was a new experience for me. In the past, workers and reporters from foreign countries other than America lived at the Majestic. Americans usually stayed at the Continental or the Caravelle, where I briefly had a room when I first came to Vietnam. The Caravelle was where many American reporters, cameramen, and soundmen lived, and in the early days of the war all three networks had their bureaus there. Once owned by nuns and Jewish businessmen from France, the

Caravelle carried memories of capitalism, so it was no longer the hotel of choice for the Communists. The mayor of Ho Chi Minh City did not want us living there during his country's anniversary celebration.

My rooms were clean, and most of the time the plumbing worked. Ho Chi Minh City's weak power supply kept the lights in my rooms, in restaurants, and all public places dim. We were in a state of permanent brownouts, and life in semidarkness was not what visitors were used to. It was a strain to read, to work, and to write, let alone to shave. Nevertheless, despite the twenty-five- and forty-watt bulbs, my room was liveable and very quiet. The hotel faced the Saigon River, where infrequent foreign freighters unloaded. My bedroom, however, was on the opposite side from the port. When I looked out, I could see only alleys, uncovered windows, terraces, and roofs badly in need of repair.

As was the custom, I gave my laundry to the hotel. A week went by, and I wondered if I would ever see my laundry again. Everything I needed was in that wash. One morning I chanced to look out the window and there was my wash drying in the sun. It was hanging on a series of lines on a terrace some thirty yards away. I counted my pairs of socks with relief. My clothing arrived in my room later that day. After that, if I had concerns I knew where to look: out my back window. I felt secure when I saw my shirts hanging on the line, rain or shine.

So there I was in 1985, back in Saigon. As did the local people, I had difficulty calling it Ho Chi Minh City but still I marveled at its faded beauty. Walking the streets, I enjoyed looking at the old French villas, with their high walls and nineteenth-century Mediterranean architecture. I reflected on how foolish the Chinese, the French, the Japanese, and the Americans had been in trying to dominate the Vietnamese and how they all had failed. Vietnam was finally free of all the outsiders who had ruled her, but its people had a long way to go before they could enjoy true freedom.

2

My Arrival
1966

MY NEW LIFE that was set into motion in Amsterdam in November 1965 finally became real in early 1966. Before I knew it, I had my necessary immunization shots for everything from cholera to the plague. I had a bottle of salt tablets to help me get through the heat and quinine pills in the event I caught malaria. I packed my two leather suitcases with lightweight clothing, my portable Remington typewriter, and a few books. The war had been steadily escalating for the last six months. American troop strength had reached new heights, and there were rumors that it would go even higher. And I, a part of the war—of it, but not in it—departed New York for the adventure of my life. Television news, no longer an infant, was off and running and would accomplish things beyond what anyone thought was possible. We in the Saigon bureau—a diverse crew like none ever before put together by NBC News—would, by fits and starts, help catapult our profession into the future. But I had none of these thoughts as I looked forward to covering a story that then seemed to have no end.

The flight from New York was long, tedious, and forgettable until we flew into South Vietnam airspace. Then everything changed. The unforgettable part of the trip took place when our sleek Pan American jet started its descent over Saigon. We flew high over the countryside. The landscape below us was barely visible to the naked eye. I saw only a blur of green and brown, some black, and occasional puffs of gray smoke from cooking fires or weapons discharged in battle. When the pilot received the all-clear to land, he turned the plane higher into the sky. When he reached his designated height, he started down at what must have been a ninety-degree angle. The steep downward turn caused him to plow almost straight toward the ground before he pulled up parallel to the earth below. It was the nastiest approach and the fastest landing of my life but, as I understood later, it was the only way to land in Saigon. Safety first: straight down, then pull up short, and don't give the Viet Cong gunners who patrolled the perimeter of Tan Son Nhut Airport an easy target. Over the years I lived through many such landings in Saigon and I never felt secure. Nothing matched a Saigon landing during the war. It took my breath away. And thinking of it today, it still does.

Once we landed, we taxied over runways that were always under repair but still filled with potholes. The plane moved slowly past rows of American jet fighters, combat-ready, armed and fueled for flight. There were C-130 transport planes, C-119s, and the strange-looking but effective Caribou, painted in olive-and-brown camouflage designs. Single-engine, propeller-driven spotter planes, big enough for only one man, stood off to the side. Each airplane had sandbags piled around it on three sides, protection against Viet Cong "sappers," enemy combat engineers with an uncanny knack of penetrating anywhere they decided might be worth attacking. Everywhere I looked, I saw strategic machine-gun emplacements on the runways. Troops with medium-range weapons guarded every corner. Heavier guns were hidden in the thick underbrush beyond the airstrip. Piles of earth-brown sandbags were everywhere, like defenses thrown up to protect a town against a rising river. Slender Vietnamese troops in skin-tight uniforms were on guard everywhere. They carried their weapons well and looked like real soldiers, but not always. Some young men stared at the sandbags instead of paying attention to their duty, watching the airplanes. Others sat around smoking. Some were asleep. A few soldiers looked frightened or bored. I found it difficult to understand their lack of urgency in guarding their air base and airport. I had assumed the South Vietnamese army would be more active. Over the years I learned the truth resided somewhere in the middle; there were some troops who did a good job. As with much in Vietnam, nothing was what it seemed.

As we taxied to the terminal, our pilot announced in a laid-back voice that he did not intend to stay on the ground very long. He would leave in a hurry, probably less than twenty minutes, depending on how long it took to off-load baggage and cargo. The aircraft arrived at the gate and we passengers, tired from the long flight and dazed by the harsh landing, stumbled out of the plane and down the steps. Trucks were waiting to pump jet fuel into the tanks. I watched a Western supervisor goad his Vietnamese baggage handlers to get the plane unloaded. I stood with the other passengers on the edge of the tarmac and waited for instructions from the Vietnamese customs officials. The pilot kept his word. In less than twenty minutes, the big jet flew away. I hoped for the sake of the passengers still on board that the next approach and landing would be gentler and smoother than the one we had just gone through.

The sweat began to pour out of me when I emerged from the plane, where the noisy air-conditioning had made the voyage somewhat comfortable. I walked into the humid Southeast Asian heat of Saigon and over the softening tarmac, past heavily armed Vietnamese troops and military police. Unlike the soldiers I had seen as we rolled across the runway, these men were alert. With the other passengers, I entered passport control, where our visas were checked. We filled out forms telling how much money we carried, including the denominations of the bills. Admonished to read the fine print that said if we violated the law we would face prison and certain banishment from the country, we moved gingerly through the process.

During the never-ending paper shuffling, the heat and strange orderliness kept everyone standing quietly. The line moved slowly. Ostentatiously patient, the old-timers had nothing but disdain for those of us who were newcomers. They studiously avoided looking at all the soldiers in the huge, cluttered building. When a gunslinging Vietnamese trooper in his fitted uniform crossed their line of vision, they sneered in disgust. These hardened men shut out the babel of languages assaulting their ears. In time I learned to do the same. But on that first day, I heard a terrible jumble of sounds reverberating through the enormous terminal: the singsong unfamiliarity of Vietnamese, a mixture of cultured and tortured French, the guttural roar of German and Dutch, harsh Korean, slurred Japanese, the polish of British English, flat Midwestern American, and the soft syrup of the southern United States. All the sounds came together as everyone tried to speak English, the common language of the war. I sweated in that hot, dirty, crowded building filled with unfamiliar odors that hung heavily over everything. It reminded me of a packed warehouse in the Kansas City stockyards.

When I reached the check-in booth, I managed to express to the official behind the barrier that I would be in Vietnam for a long time. I promised I would abide by the rules, regulations, and all the laws of South Vietnam—in his words, "your host country." I filled out my forms correctly, writing the appropriate yeses and nos. The inspector stamped my passport for entry into the Republic of South Vietnam. Officials in starched white shirts passed me through to the next barrier. Finally I arrived in Customs Control. Officers thoroughly searched my bags. By now I was exhausted by my sudden immersion in Saigon and my shirt and cotton trousers were sticking to my back and legs. I was sweating heavily but I had nothing to drink. Thirsty or not, I understood I should not drink anything until I knew if it was safe. After this last step, someone from the NBC News staff would meet me and drive me to my office and new home. Knowing this relieved my tension.

I felt out of place, in the minority for the first time in my life. The Vietnamese called us "round-eyes" and "tall noses" for obvious reasons. Their eyes were almond-shaped and large, their noses flat and wide. In less than forty-five minutes, all my boyhood movie images of the teeming Far East had become real. Like me, other recent arrivals flooded the center hall of the airport. I saw construction workers, salesmen, entertainers, many looking to profit from a war that had yet to reach its peak.

Most of the Vietnamese men at the airport were in uniform: khaki, blue, white, gray, or a mixture of these colors, their trousers always dark. Some were in the military. Many, like a hundred thousand others across the country, were in the police. These men milled about and shouted and blew their whistles, perhaps from fear, perhaps to show their power. Nothing appeared to make sense, yet people moved dutifully from one line to another. Flights were announced, baggage moved. In the cloudless sky, the sun relentlessly baked the building's metal roof. Oppressive heat steamed upward through the concrete floor. Thick, acrid smoke stung my eyes and irritated my throat. It clogged the air and seemed to form clouds under the high ceiling of the terminal. Almost everyone, including myself, had a cigarette dangling from the corner of his mouth. Most of the Vietnamese men smoked French Gitanes or Gauloise Blues. These produced strong, unattractive odors at best, a terrible stink at worst.

My eyes grew accustomed to the dim light and my nose, barely, to the foul smells. I tried to see and hear my way through the crowd and the din. The sounds—heavy, exotic—did not allow me to focus the way I wanted. Tired and unable to concentrate, on the edge of confusion about what to do next, I hoped my wait would soon end. Then Mr. Long, NBC's driver and fixer extraordinaire, appeared—my first personal contact with a Vietnamese. Mr. Long had come to meet me and guide me out of the West and into the East. It would be a long journey.

Mr. Long was a mythical figure in news circles during the war. He had a willingness to please unmatched by almost anyone I met or worked with in Vietnam. He shipped our film out of the country and had a knack for clearing anything through customs. He could obtain just about anything for anyone anywhere in Saigon and beyond. Shortly after I arrived and started to settle into my office, I told Mr. Long I wanted a glass top for my huge desk, which was left behind by the

German attaché who formerly occupied the space. (The office originally housed the German Economic Mission.) Several mornings later when I arrived at work, I found my desk covered with a sheet of polished, perfectly beveled glass almost a half-inch thick. I knew how difficult it must have been to find a piece of glass of that size and quality with a war on. I asked Mr. Long where it came from. At first he refused to divulge its origin. Then, with a big grin, he explained. On the way to work he had passed a barbershop and seen its double glass doors. After some coaxing, bargaining, and parting with a bit of money—but not too much, he assured me—he walked off with half the door, but not the part with the shop's name. "What are they going to do with half a door?" I asked. He looked at me and said, "They could sell it, too, couldn't they?"

He spoke unintelligible English but always made himself understood, even if barely. His words fell somewhere between his teeth and tongue. In all the years I knew him, his ability with the language never improved; in fact, it became more difficult to interpret as he got older, but I always managed. He always called me Boss. I never called him anything other than Mr. Long. (His actual name was Dang Khac Hoang; I've never been able to learn why he was called Mr. Long.) I did not find him that day. He found me. I wondered for years what made him head directly for me. I asked him once and he told me he just knew. "I knew who you were when I saw you," he said. It was what he did.

Mr. Long had someone with him when he picked me out of the crowd that day. Standing next to him was a beautiful young Vietnamese woman wearing an *ao dai*, the traditional Vietnamese costume: a long dress, black silk trousers, and long-sleeved bodice cinched in at the waist. A high, stiff collar gave the ensemble a pristine appearance. The brightly colored silk dress divided into two flowing panels, one in front, the other in the back. Both panels ended at the top of the shoes, where the pants narrowed, almost pegged and scalloped, around the ankles. Hand-embroidered designs of flowers and mythological figures covered the front of the dress. I soon learned the *ao dai* formed an aura around every Vietnamese woman, creating a rhythm as she walked, sat, moved, or rode a bicycle or motor scooter. I came to recognize the themes of flowing movement repeated in paintings, sculptures, and photographs everywhere in the country. The young woman who greeted me was the embodiment of this theme. Her eyes were semi-almond, large and dark brown: a mixture of laughter and sadness, as with many Vietnamese. Her hair, long and straight, fell down her back almost to her waist. Black as pitch and shiny from constant brushing, it lay partly over her right shoulder and fell in bangs over half her forehead. The total effect was a picture of warmth and innocence. She greeted me with a shy, sweet smile and a cautious hello. Her English was good, but more important, her sense of dignity and pride was supreme. She had a perfectly charming demeanor.

Her name was Tu Ngoc Suong but she told me to call her Josephine, the name her Parisian teachers gave her when she attended the Lycée Marie Curie for twelve years; run by the French, it was the best school for girls in Saigon. Josephine took my papers and completed my clearance into the country. I had no idea that one day she would become my wife.

Mr. Long, meanwhile, wandered through the crowd saying hello, making his presence known, charming everyone with his smile and the cigarettes he handed out. Above average height for a Vietnamese, he had gone to fat, with a potbellied stomach that hung well over his belt. He had round, sloping shoulders, lank black hair, and a mouth filled with deteriorating teeth amply sprinkled with gold caps. They made his smile look like a glittering checkerboard. An ever present cigarette was held between his nicotine-stained fingers. When Saigon fell he emigrated to the United States and years later died of stomach cancer, caused, I am sure, by all the cigarettes he smoked. His hectic life, driving correspondents and camera crews into danger all around Saigon and the nearby provinces, gave him a good excuse for habitual, heavy smoking. Cigarettes were cheap, especially from the PX or on the black market at ten or eleven cents a pack. With people dying every day from the war, how could anyone deny himself the simple pleasure of a cigarette?

Mr. Long cleared me through customs without either of my bags opened for inspection. The customs officer theatrically chalked them for clearance without a murmur. Mr. Long found an ancient porter who could barely carry my heavy bags. I wanted to help, but Mr. Long said, no, that's his job. Then he and Josephine led me from the building and into the blazing sun.

They gently guided me through the chaotic parking lot. The wizened, wiry porter, who looked to be seventy-five years old, struggled along behind us. When we reached his car, Mr. Long refused to let me sit next to him because the boss had to sit in the back. So I sat in the back of his old, battered Chevrolet, where he wanted me to sit and where I would always sit. Made in Detroit, the big sedan had little left of its original dusty blue paint. I put a Camel in my mouth and settled back for the ride into town. Josephine sat next to me, looking out the window. She carefully avoided saying anything to me but she kept up a steady flow of chatter with Mr. Long. I recall saying very little, if anything, to either one of my new care-takers. The car barked, coughed, and revved up enough to move like a wounded leviathan. The heavily armed Vietnamese military guards at the main gate of the airport cleared us through with a grunt and a wave, and we plunged onto the road leading into Saigon.

I had finally entered the teeming Far East, with the best still to come. Chugging along, the old car somehow made its way through the streets. We were heading for the Eden Building in the center of downtown, where NBC News had its bureau. I sat on the worn seat with its highly polished, cracked leather and stared thoughtfully out the window at my new home. It was like nothing I had ever seen: Bicycles and motorized rickshaws—the latter spewing the fumes of cheap gasoline into the air—were everywhere, clogging the streets. There were many cyclos, three-wheeled pedicabs with baskets in front for passengers or cargo, powered by men with strong legs who appeared to pump the pedals effortlessly. They competed for space with motorbikes and scooters made in Japan, France, or Italy. I saw American-made automobiles like Mr. Long's and older French Citroëns and Italian minicars that moved through the traffic with surprising agility. Men and women, girls and boys of all ages were carrying baskets, bundles, and packages. Some balanced containers precariously on their heads and walked with hip-swiveling grace. Others carried their wares in two bamboo baskets, one at each end of a long pole balanced over thin, bony shoulders. The women porters looked like the oldest of the old.

The unpaved streets were remarkably busy. No still photograph or painting could ever show their curious richness. There were so many people going about their business on the streets that I wondered naively how they found time to fight the war I had come such a long way to cover. I had landed in a third world country where too many people, with too little room, struggled to survive.

Even here, in the midst of a terrible and debilitating war that would worsen as the years progressed, advertising assaulted my eyes everywhere I turned. Huge freestanding billboards hovered over the roadways. The sides of buildings bore massive hand-painted signs. Thousands of smaller signs in shopwindows and on walls hawked Japanese TV sets and radios, American-made dishwashers and cigarettes, French toothpaste, beer from Hong Kong and the Philippines, fine woolens from England, rich silks from Thailand. Street vendors filled every available space on dirt paths and concrete sidewalks and in doorways. They sold soup, rice, cold drinks, hot tea, loaves of French bread, Vietnamese pâté, and other foods I could not then identify and wondered if I could ever eat. People squatted on their heels eating quick meals that were prepared in front of them. Portable charcoal burners heated soup, noodles, bean sprouts, shrimp, and pork. I did learn to eat much of this food during my years in Vietnam and to enjoy the many varieties of soup. I also discovered a fruit with the wonderfully funny name of chom-chom that tasted like a plum. Street food was tasty, cheap, and easy to appreciate once I stopped worrying about the lack of hygiene. Often I preferred a fast sidewalk meal over a conservative, dull restaurant.

Everyone in the hectic streets moved steadily and with purpose, with little wasted effort or excess motion. Both men and women had a regular gait from which they never deviated. At first I stared at everything and everyone. In turn, everyone studiously ignored me. When I arrived in Vietnam, there were already several hundred thousand Americans in the country. Most of them were GIs. Some were construction workers, government officials, and businessmen out to profit from the war. I was just one more American to the Vietnamese, no different from any other in uniform or out, no better and no worse than all those who came before me. The Vietnamese were leading difficult lives that they hoped would bring them to a decent future, and I was nothing but a speck passing among them, a glitch in their thousands of years of history. I felt that they hoped I would soon be gone so they could get on with their lives. Learning to live with being ignored, at least on the surface, is part of a Westerner's way in a foreign country, especially in the Far East, and it became one way I survived in Vietnam.

The odors seeping into the poorly sealed automobile were strong and strange to me. They were a mixture of overripe sweetness and pungency dominated by chile and garlic. Though air-conditioned, Mr. Long's car was still hot and uncomfortable. Dust from the streets filtered through rusted holes in the chassis. Both of us smoked, and we choked and coughed our way through Saigon's streets. Sweat continued to pour from my body as we drove slowly through the crowds. Despite all this, I had a pleasant introduction to the city that would be my home for more than two years.

Few buildings in Saigon were higher than two stories. The outskirts of the city looked jerry-built, unplanned, ugly. Builders had slapped together the newer buildings with cinder block and hastily applied concrete, then whitewashed them to hide the blemishes. Occasionally we passed vestiges of French glory and I could see a villa, magnificent and formerly fashionable, around a corner or past a bend in the road. A villa sometimes emerged from behind lush, towering trees, hidden down a quiet side street. Most of the villas displayed once-proud faces with their faded pastel-colored paint peeling, their facades crumbling from neglect. Parts of broken machines cluttered their spacious front yards. Concertina wire with razor-sharp attachments, stolen from the U.S. military, encircled many walled villas. All that remained of the French imperial past were these buildings, falling apart but still standing in spite of the war.

Some villas had become homes and offices for foreign workers. Americans and other foreigners in Vietnam enjoyed a level of comfort and privacy in the spacious villas—formerly the homes of rich Vietnamese—that they could not find in a hotel. These men were here for adventure, for a rite of passage through the military and life, and for profit. Some were in Vietnam because their governments or companies told them to be there. The men in uniform had no choice. There were always those who took their assignment, public or private, without argument. But that did not mean they had to live poorly, especially if they were officers on special assignment, in the CIA or other special branches.

In the mid-1960s, many wide streets that had been beautiful in the French colonial past lay sheared of plane trees and year-round flowering bushes. Trees that remained on a boulevard such as Le Loi were rare luxuries but they served no useful purpose. People were safer in the streets when ugly stumps were all that remained. Thick tree trunks might serve as a screen for a Viet Cong ambush. On many major avenues, the sidewalks had become rubble and the well-manicured lawns small dust bowls. Natural shelter from sun and rain no longer existed. My nose, mouth, and lungs filled with gasoline fumes and other foul debris that floated invisibly through the air. Saigon, through no fault of its own, had become a terribly polluted city.

Wherever I looked as we made our way, I had the gnawing feeling that life in Saigon would never be the same as it had been. Saigon, once a bud about to flower, might never find its way out of the rubble, its proud delicacy crushed. I hoped this was a passing phase, but I knew better. The war was becoming bigger and more dangerous. The American buildup to more than 550,000 soldiers had begun. Refugees, fleeing the war in the countryside, already jammed the cramped city. They were seeking security in what they instinctively assumed was safety in numbers. Squatters were everywhere. Shacks and tin-and-wood lean-tos abutted garden walls, buildings, even trees. Shantytowns had sprung up wherever there was any available space. I sometimes felt like one of those refugees. Aside from my clothing, typewriter, and books, I had not brought much else. However, I had not run from a destroyed village to this place. I had come because I wanted to be here. My two leather suitcases, used infrequently since my student days, still had Lafayette College stickers on them. The rest of my limited possessions were in storage in New York. What I carried would be more than enough for Saigon and the way I would live. I soon learned that I could buy anything I wanted in Vietnam and in then-booming Asia from Japan to Singapore. Had I known that, I would have moved with even less.

During our ride in from the airport, the sun remained hot, the sky cloudless. Heavy smog hung over the city in varying layers of thickness. My hour in the car seemed to last forever. We did not stop, not even for a drink. I was thirsty, my throat strangely raw, and I had the first hint of the cough that would bother me every day during my tour. The air conditioner in Mr. Long's car pumped more mist than cold air. I decided then that I would not allow the war to get in the way of American comfort, my comfort. Over the years, when air conditioners broke down, I made it a priority to get them repaired, no matter the difficulty of getting it done. After all, if American troops could have hot apple pie at the front, we journalists in the rear could have air-conditioning.

We arrived at our destination and the car chugged to a halt. I snapped out of my tourist's trance. All the staring I had done had dulled my already travel-weary brain. Mr. Long turned to me and said, "This is where you will live and work." We were in the heart of Saigon: 104-106 Nguyen Hue, the Eden Building. From the backseat of the car, I peered at its five stories of nondescript ugliness. Built by the French as an apartment and office complex, the building lacked any aesthetics. It took up three-quarters of a block, sitting stocky and compressed, each side looking alike. An indoor shopping arcade on the street level housed jewelry stores and custom clothing and dress shops. Inside the enclosed mall, a large movie theater screened Chinese and Indian films. Crowded inside and out both before and during the showing of a film, the theater allowed young Vietnamese, who lived in cramped quarters, to meet in public away from the glare of their families. Other shops and restaurants, including a bookstore, a barbershop, and a gourmet food store, faced onto Nguyen Hue, Tu Do Street, and Le Loi.

My arrival at the Eden Building marked the first time I stepped onto a Saigon street, an important moment for me. The street was packed. For an hour I had looked intently from behind a car window, safe, protected, and shielded from reality. When I opened the door and stepped out onto the sidewalk, the people and the city came to life. I smelled them, sensed them, felt their vitality. I could reach out and touch them if I wanted. They moved, stood, sold, bought, ate, talked, watched, and paused as if they were waiting for something to happen. They hawked, traded, argued, spit, and slept in doorways and sidewalks despite the constant noise. They seemed impassive and unimpressed with the quiet arrival of the newest American on their turf. From that moment, I became a full-time tenant in the Eden

Building, someone many Vietnamese would see every day for years but whom they would hardly acknowledge. I thought they might be every bit as afraid of me as I of them. When I became better acquainted with Vietnamese life and customs, I realized the accuracy of some of my first impressions. After letting me look around, Josephine escorted me into the building and up the elevator to my new office.

3

The Bureau

THE OFFICE. The bureau. Memories resonate in my mind, bell-like, from those years. The people in my bureau—the cameramen, soundmen, technicians, drivers, and office staff—were a remarkable lot. I learned something new about them every day and they revealed themselves to me, but slowly. They were Vietnamese, Korean, Japanese, English, French, German, Dutch, Israeli, and Australian. I often became frustrated with my inability to understand their languages. Their cultures sometimes seemed unfathomable and they often tested my patience. But I knew all of it would continue to fascinate me as I ran the bureau. When dealing with the Vietnamese office staff, I had to shift my Western mind into another gear and learn to think Eastern, if possible. It wasn't easy. Fortunately, those working for me had a delightful sense of humor. When a Vietnamese or other Asian smiled, it did not mean the same as when I smiled. I had to watch their eyes for the real meaning. However, the tipoff to what they really thought might be somewhere else and I had difficulty believing I would ever really understand my new world without learning all the languages in it.

I learned quickly that reporting war for television had its own problems and restrictions. Camera crews had to get pictures or we stood little chance of getting the story on the air. Television could cover the war only in its small moments. Our reporters saw part of an event, no more than what the cameraman recorded through the eye of his camera, which was not necessarily reality and rarely a rendering of an entire action. Some correspondents became fixed in their judgments and fanciful in their writing. It took extra effort on my part to keep them from going overboard and leaping into the land of hyperbole. I had to convince them to describe what they filmed, nothing more, nothing less, or we would confuse the audience. When we were accurate, the effort paid off. It meant continuous hard work at every level, with few rewards. When those rewards came, they were great for our spirits and eventually, as an added perk, for our reputations.

You cannot cover war without a touch of romanticism. The good war correspondent combines war-weary romanticism with a heavy sprinkling of war-weary cynicism. Often these different motivations move speedily down parallel tracks without ever becoming entwined. On my staff were risk takers who came away with a substantial payoff because they went where few others were willing to tread. Correspondents in war learn to take the considered risks necessary to survive. It sounds like a cliché, but there are no dead heroes in war, especially among journalists. The job of the correspondent is to stay alive and report the story to those among us who can only watch from the comfort of their living room or kitchen. Stay alive. Report the story. Tell the truth as you see it and know it. Sometimes the risk taker wonders why the conclusion, the applause for a job well done, matters less in the end than the rendering. He never assumes his story is weak or does not pan out. Perhaps he oversells his piece, overestimating its value. When that happens, he puts his future stories in jeopardy, because they, too, will be seen as oversold. I learned there has to be absolute trust between those in the field and those at home who ultimately decide how, where, and when a story will play on the air.

Soon after I arrived, I found myself enmeshed in the tentacles of JUSPAO, the Joint United States Public Affairs Office. This was the propaganda arm for the United States in Vietnam and was where the planning of the propaganda war took place. Housed in a building next to the Rex BOQ (Bachelor Officer Quarters), it held the military and civilian briefings, "the five o'clock follies," every day. Toward the end of the war, the briefings started at 4:45 to accommodate the wire-service and radio reporters' deadline, but we still called them "the five o'clock follies."

The public briefings were presented by American military officers and embassy personnel. At each briefing, enlisted information specialists handed us carefully worded information packets. These were the "official" word on the day's events. Anyone in Saigon, including cabdrivers and street sweepers, could end up with one of these packets in his hands. Some sold the information to the Viet Cong and their sympathizers as quickly as they received it.

Other briefings, however, were different. Often, either before or after the open session, American officials held a shorter, less crowded meeting by invitation only. Bureau chiefs usually attended these sessions, which were held behind closed doors. The briefing officer, CIA station chief, or someone from the American embassy would give us background or off-the-record information. We learned about upcoming military operations and Vietnamese political events the United States decided would be worth covering. It did not take us long to learn that the government's interpretation of events did not coincide with what we learned on our own. We listened anyway, willing to learn, hoping to discover a kernel of truth in a fog of lies.

As the war continued, everything we covered started to look and feel the same—even firefights where reporters faced great danger. Combat dominated our coverage, and rightly so. My New York producers and their news editors had an insatiable appetite for "bang-bang"—hard-hitting action with bullets flying and bombs landing. If the film we shipped did not show soldiers firing at the enemy, helicopters dusting off (evacuating) wounded troops, or jets bombing jungles and pounding rice fields, it was considered weak and lacking in action by deskbound newswriters and film editors. These so-called lesser stories did not warrant space on the evening news. They went to off-hour programs.

By early 1967, the people responsible for television news had little interest in stories about the Vietnamese people and their struggles. Editors in the States were steeped in their own prejudices and it made no difference if they were left, right, or center. They covered anything that involved Americans: antiwar marches, draft card burnings, and funerals for soldiers in small American towns. In Vietnam, it did not take long for most of us to be against the war, its futility, its stupidity. This was before it became fashionable to oppose the war, but I believe we were tired of seeing people suffer. And along with the rising death toll for American troops, the Vietnamese also suffered terribly.

As bureau chief, I decided daily what we should cover. And, daily, producers rejected almost every story about life in Vietnam. They had little interest in the Vietnamese government and how it worked, or didn't. Unless President Thieu or Vice President Ky did something foolish, editors in New York ignored them. The editors had no interest in the religious structure of the country unless a Buddhist monk burned himself to death. They had little curiosity about how the average Vietnamese lived his life and how a Vietnamese family coped when it lost a son in battle. I cajoled, pleaded, and sometimes managed to ram that kind of story down a producer's throat. He had to be in a weakened condition or desperate to fill two minutes of empty air time, but it occasionally happened.

On the surface, stories about the Vietnamese were unglamorous. The cities, villages, jungles, rice paddies, beaches, farms, and mountains looked no different from day to day. Stories about American troops had a local, hometown connection that did not exist for stories about Vietnamese in Danang, Can Tho, and Nha Trang. Few Vietnamese spoke any English, although many had a smattering of French, and the network thought they rarely made a good story unless attached to a horrible event. Our correspondents spoke no Vietnamese and hardly any French. We could do just so much to get pieces about the Vietnamese on the air if we were to keep our brains and souls functioning and, honestly, keep our jobs. We understood that with more than half a million American troops in and around South Vietnam, our stories had to center on their lives. We had to tell about their often supreme efforts to survive a difficult, bitter war, a war that everyone in uniform understood was growing increasingly unpopular at home.

Successful reporters in any medium must have strong egos. You cannot be self-effacing and make a mark in broadcast journalism. We were developing a new breed of reporter, men who were frequently on the air covering exciting combat stories. They often developed egos that limited their ability to express anything other than heated excitement. Some correspondents injected themselves too deeply into the story. Instead of playing the traditional role of the observer, looking on from the outside, they became a part of the story, skewing it from the inside. Self-importance clouded the tales they were there to tell, and nuance and subtlety died on the battlefield. The terror and fright induced by crackling M-16s and napalm explosions were all that mattered. Some of our correspondents felt that covering combat was the only way they could prove they were at a war. But to cover only combat can isolate a reporter. It sets him dangerously apart from the real world.

The audience's appetite for the thrill of the firefight also became a big problem. The excitement of seeing close bombing strikes by streaking jets or helicopters attacking enemy positions with their guns blazing can cloud good judgment in understanding a story. Sometimes the presumed smell and feel of battle dominates the meaning of a story—I say "presumed" because people watching the story can only imagine the smell and emotion. Film can do only so much; after all, it is two-dimensional. I believe some editors and producers started pandering to their own desire to give the audience what it thought was real. In truth, acts of war are transitory. Their result—craters and rubble, death and destruction, the fragmentation and disruption of life—is the reality of war.

Part of combat coverage is that often nothing happens. Our reporters did not ride every wave into action like movie heroes. Often they returned from the field believing the operation had been a bust. The platoon they covered had tramped through the jungle, did not find the enemy, and had come up empty. But even when no shots were fired, young American men were learning to kill to defend themselves. I wondered what adjustment these men, many of whom were teenagers, would make when they returned home. Very few of our reports caught those kids in the tragedy of war. We did capture the agony of the wounded on the battlefield. In war, the wounded were common, with some maimed for life. Death, the ultimate tragedy, never took a backseat to any story. Many were killed, and it happened every day. Sometimes we photographed the dead stacked like firewood in black body bags. Other times, we filmed the dead one at a time in lonely jungle landing zones. Sadly, we became immune to the violence and too accepting of the deaths of our fellow men, most of whom were only boys. The adage about being too close to the story never held more truth.

Soon after my arrival I thought of buying a new desk and redesigning the office space to fit more people and equipment. It became a project that took my mind off the war and my problems in keeping the bureau on an even keel. I had a number of problems, some of which were mundane. I needed a hot-water tank in my apartment because I had become tired of taking cold showers, even in that warm climate. My drivers annoyed me by saying "yes" to everything because they wanted to please. My tough, hard-nosed Korean cameramen and soundmen were suddenly homesick. I could not understand how the maid kept losing my socks. I needed a new air conditioner in my living room. I had to find time to make a PX run for recently arrived wine from Algiers, serviceable and wet, and tins of Ritz crackers, jars of Skippy peanut butter, and boxes of Tide. And, of course, cigarettes. Life would go on despite these small irritants.

Beginning to understand that I had much to learn about Vietnam and about myself, I lived in a world of soft subtleties and brazen shocks. People were passive and violent at unexpected turns. I thought the constant heat must have something to do with the way the Vietnamese, and Westerners, acted. I witnessed an interesting parallel during a street riot, a clash between Buddhist extremists and the police. The monsoon season had started. Heavy rains arrived late in the afternoon. Just as some civil rights demonstrators in the United States did not march in the rain, neither did the Buddhists. As if by tacit agreement, both sides put away their signs and batons and ran for shelter when the downpour started. These are fascinating people, I thought. This had become a wondrous place to spend a year or two.

I had moments of desperation and despair. I also knew great exhilaration and excitement. When I played my people, ideas, and stories right and everything worked perfectly, there was nothing better in life. There were very few periods of quiet. Sometimes, however, we found ourselves in the midst of a mild lull, and they all had the same cause: there were no major battles. At these times, I believed we were not doing enough to earn our keep, a strange feeling. Nothing would be happening on the battlefront or in politics. I wondered if everyone had taken a rest, getting ready for the next round. As these lulls continued, the correspondents and crews were forced to be inventive and come up with different kinds of stories: Pacification's successes and failures. Homeless kids. We became sadly immune to the sight of young children curled up asleep in doorways at midnight. I knew a major military operation would soon start and that when it did I would feel relieved. As much as I hated the war, it is why I went to Vietnam and never tired. In the bureau, war is what we covered to fulfill our mandate.

Each day brought something different. One day I sat in my office alone after emptying it of everyone—correspondent Dean Brelis, cameraman Vo Huynh, soundman Yoshiro Waku, and a driver named Tam Coi. They had been trying to console me in my anger and anguish over the unimaginable difficulties of my job and the hidden traps set by the powers in New York. In my first weeks, I had crises on top of crises. It did not help to receive a cable from New York questioning my use of camera crews. At that time I had an additional crew, a fifth team, to provide coverage for *Vietnam Weekly Review*. As the former chief writer, I had a special feeling for that show. But it was my understanding that I could use the fifth crew as I saw fit. I had a breaking story and had assigned the extra crew to general coverage (as opposed to specially assigned feature stories). When New York saw my daily lineup listing the fifth crew where it was not available to *Vietnam Weekly Review*, there was an explosion. I had known something like this would eventually happen. In my usual strong language, I told New York I had the right of assignment in my bureau. There were no battles to cover and our daily shows would be on my back if I did not provide them with stories. Without that fifth crew, we could not compete. The whole question was irrelevant, anyway. John Travieso, the new field producer for *Vietnam Weekly Review*, had become ill, which was not uncommon for recent arrivals. He was in his hotel nursing a bad stomach and was unavailable. New York did not respond to my explanation. I went to bed.

Entering my office at seven the next morning, I went to my desk and looked around to see that everything was in place. The office boy had picked up the overnight cables at the post office. One of them had my name on it. A real cable! New York only sent cables when the message was meant for my eyes only and it did not want the information made public; the telex served for all other messages. I opened the envelope slowly and read the message from Reuven Frank, execu-

tive vice president of the news division, quickly. He replied in words as strong
as those in my earlier message. His exact words were, "Steinman ExReuven nuts
your problems." ("Ex" attached to a name was old cable shorthand for "from.")
Plainly, my problems did not matter and the fifth crew had to be for special assignment only. Dazed, then angry, and feeling helpless, I wanted to lash out at
something, anything. Realizing the futility of such behavior, I calmed down. What
could Reuven have been thinking when he wrote that message? Did he want me
to drop coverage of the war? Should I cease covering politics and human interest
stories? When I showed the message to a recovering Travieso, he became upset.
He and I had an understanding and he knew of my close relationship with George
Murray, his show's executive producer. I decided not to keep this quiet from my
staff. I needed them on my side. New York's sometimes negative attitude was often a rallying point for us and created a bond between everyone that might not
normally have existed. Reuven's cable was no exception. The staff was puzzled.
In the next few hours, the streets of Saigon erupted with riots and terror. Every
available man in the bureau worked nonstop with no outward sign of fear. They
were trying to prove to me and to New York that they were capable and loyal and
that they respected how I ran the bureau. It was a classic confrontation between a
foreign bureau and the home office. I knew there would be more of the same the
longer I stayed in Saigon and I relished the thought of future battles.

Sometimes I got the best of New York. In case any of our teams were hurt in
the field, I wanted them to have a simple first-aid kit. A New York senior executive said they would cost too much and would not approve the purchase. I went
against his wishes and bought two dozen kits anyway. They appeared on my expense reports over many months and were overlooked by the auditors. Our doctor in Hong Kong, Henry Lee, assembled the kits to help with the most basic of
emergencies until a doctor or medic could arrive. They contained aspirin, malaria
pills, salt tablets, bandages and dressings, gauze, antiseptic, iodine, cotton swabs,
antidiarrhea pills, adhesive tape, water purification tablets, and a few other necessary items. Lee packed each kit in a small, heavy canvas case. The men took their
kits along on every trip they made. Were they used? I do not know, but they did
serve as a security blanket for the crews, more than I could ask for in this slowly
crumbling country.

My purchase of a new bed deserves special notice. For nine months I had been
sleeping on a prison-style cot that was falling apart at my touch. My back ached
from the sagging canvas and tired springs. As the crowning touch, a spring popped
in the middle of the night. I deserved a decent mattress. New York in its kind-

ness and everlasting wisdom would not allow me the money to buy a bed or for any single item over one hundred dollars. I realized it would be easier for me to get my money back by itemizing the individual parts. The bed, custom-made to fit through the narrow doors of the building and into my apartment, arrived in pieces. I assembled it in the bedroom and presented New York with a receipt for each piece. The mattress cost $33.81. The bedspring cost $21.18. The wooden frame was expensive at $72.03. I could not let New York forget I was in Southeast Asia, so I had the carpenter make a frame for mosquito netting for $12.71. I used the mosquito netting from the cot I discarded, so I saved NBC a few dollars. If they had allowed me to buy the bed, I would have listed simply the total price. Listing it on my biweekly expense report in pieces was the silliest thing I had ever had to do when it came to business affairs. It did get me a comfortable bed, though, and it taught me a lesson about using company money to my advantage.

The housekeeping chores in the office were endless. We needed new typewriters and I purchased several large, heavy-duty typewriters in Hong Kong and had them shipped to Saigon. One afternoon I became furious with Mr. Long for missing a flight with a competitive film story that had to get on the air. In front of everyone, I slammed my fist into the frame of one of the new typewriters. It bent in half like a V. I came away with a bruised hand for my fury. Mr. Long fled from the office and went into hiding. I went into my office, slammed the door shut, and sulked. Each time someone failed, it became the bureau's failure, and thus my own. I found it intolerable and my actions foolish. The machine? When I was last in the bureau in 1972, I saw and used the typewriter, still working, still bent out of shape, a monument to my stress.

4

It's a Wonder Anything Works

AFTER BEING on the job just a few weeks, I already had many complaints and requests for New York. I sent frequent cables and telexes and mailed sporadic letters laying out my feelings and describing Vietnam, the bureau, our work. I wanted equipment that worked and I wanted it yesterday. The more equipment we had, the better off we would be. We urgently needed a walkie-talkie system. I believed we had to have them to make the bureau better and faster than CBS and ABC. Just because we were in a third world country did not mean we should have a third-rate bureau.

I did not think my request unreasonable. Our bureau phones worked sporadically, if at all. In Saigon, there were few public phones available. In the field, there were none. Those that could be found in Saigon were not dependable, even those at the PTT, the phone company's main office. We couldn't run into someone's home and ask to use their phone, because most private residences did not have phones. In any case, it was difficult to get around town with streets blocked and traffic stalled. We could not escape the frequent strife in the streets and the many antigovernment demonstrations. Monks and nuns were setting themselves on fire, Buddhist sympathizers were battling police, and Viet Cong terrorists struck without notice. I could not expect a team to give me a call during a riot. But with a two-way system that worked, I could position my forces the way I wanted and my staff could keep in touch with me.

I understood the technical difficulties involved. The American military had promised they would clear a special frequency with the understanding they would cancel it if their needs were greater. I did not intend to carry on lengthy conversations. We were in need of instant communication, akin to semaphore. We could work out simple and brief code names.

Digby Jones, my wonderfully inventive Welsh maintenance engineer, and I exchanged letters and cables with the New York technical staff discussing how we would use walkie-talkies. New York did not believe that what worked in the States would work in Saigon. Digby believed he could make anything work. Then New York said it would cost too much to ship the equipment. I knew then we would not get walkie-talkies. In the end, New York denied my request, and in a telex message I accused them of being unrealistic. Someone wrote back, "I may sound like a crepe-hanger, but I have been in the game long enough to be realistic." Unfortunately, his realism did not give us walkie-talkies. This sort of thing was a constant frustration. Without giving us equipment to test in Saigon and beyond, how could New York's technical staff make judgments about what would work on the ground? Often the technical staff would promise equipment but would not deliver. I knew they had problems. Well, so did I; so did everyone in our third world backwater. When we asked for something, it meant we needed it badly. Do not promise if you cannot deliver, I told them. Sometimes I feared my temper would get the better of me. I knew that tack would not get me anywhere and would only inspire spite. We did need equipment, though. The climate in Southeast Asia eventually rotted everything it touched. Rubber gaskets crumbled in our fingers. The rubber molding on the cameras dissolved at a touch. Aluminum coffeepots suddenly had holes in them. Fortunately, we could buy all the coffeepots we wanted from the tinsmith on the corner.

My housekeeping chores never ended. They were part of running the bureau. The cabinets in my office were already filled with equipment when I arrived. I had more cabinets built to provide storage space for new supplies. Extra benches were brought in to help the cameramen and soundmen maintain their gear. Digby complained that he could not get any work done when more than three people were in the shop. People tended to talk too much and laugh too much, relaxing in the friendly atmosphere.

Some New York managers and producers visited the bureau, but I never thought they understood the problems we faced working there. It is important to understand the size of each room. Digby had a work space of eleven feet by eight feet filled with cameras, film magazines, batteries, and assorted machinery and tools. The narrow outer office was twenty-one feet long and nine feet wide. It was really just an interior hallway with wooden double doors opening into it, and it seemed forever filled with people. Assistant bureau chief Lem Tucker sat outside Digby's space. My office, at sixteen feet by eight and a half feet, was bigger than most, but the space included my huge desk (I never did buy a new desk) and the telex machines. In addition, Josephine worked in my office. She was the office manager and prepared the official papers we needed for everything we did in Vietnam. She also secured our exit and entry visas, a time-consuming activity, and translated and negotiated for us when necessary. At any moment, Josephine, Lem, one of the correspondents, and a New York producer and unit manager on special assignment might be talking at once. These conversations must have been important, but the mingled voices interfered with my ability to think. The noise of my ancient air conditioner added to the din. Some days I had no place to hide.

The Eden Building, with its high ceilings and thick walls, had terrible acoustics. You had to speak loudly and clearly, so the person next to you could hear. Whisper, as many Vietnamese did, and your coworkers had to strain to hear you. Too many people in one room made for a high and unpleasant noise level.

Building and installing the new cabinets allowed me to get rid of the rickety lounge chairs in the outer office. When there was little news and the bureau quieted down, the crews and drivers crammed into the small space like they were in a crowded bus. They played cards, noisily, but they had precious little space in which to move. I would have preferred to send them out of the office but if I needed them and they had wandered too far, we might miss a story.

By the fall of 1966, I had added four new staffers. Over the next few months, additional crews and correspondents arrived for special coverage. There were too many people in too small a space. My office, more crowded than ever, now doubled as the sitting room, making it impossible to think, get work done, or use the telephone. To the left of my desk were two teletype machines. Clipboards with incoming and selected outgoing messages hung on hooks over the machines, there for everyone on the staff to read. The constant stream of people distracted me, even if most of them belonged there. I tried to keep out the stragglers, of whom there were always a few. Behind my desk were two large windows crisscrossed with masking tape to prevent their shattering if an explosion occurred in the neighborhood. Daylight, whether sunny or cloudy, entering the room through the tape created strange patterns on my desk. I knew that if a rocket or bullet hit, there would be little chance to escape injury despite the tape. Fortunately, this never happened, and no matter how many sonic booms or explosions occurred nearby, the windows remained intact.

The correspondents' room, or newsroom, as we called it, looked different from the rest of the bureau. It had five desks to accommodate the usual number of reporters. It had a film projector, a radio booth with poor soundproofing, seven chairs, and five typewriter tables. It had a table for cups, powdered coffee, powdered milk, sugar, a coffeepot made of some strange local aluminum alloy, and bitter-tasting Nescafé imported from France. All this was squeezed into six feet by eight and a half feet of floor space, hardly enough to move around in. When three people were in that room simultaneously, I feared they might suffocate. In those circumstances, the reporters had difficulty writing, but somehow they managed. We could not even screen film stories sent by New York because of the impossible clutter.

One morning, while we were getting a crew ready for a trip up-country, two Vietnamese men marched into the bureau. I could see in their eyes and in the set of their shoulders that these were serious men. They carried large burlap sacks and leather briefcases and had rolls of wire slung over their arms. They came straight to me and started speaking rapidly in Vietnamese, pointing to various parts of the office and my desk. Not easily fazed, I grinned at them and took a deep drag on my Camel. The Vietnamese members of my staff crowded into my office and all started to talk at once—in Vietnamese, of course. Finally, unable to take much more, I yelled for quiet. The noise and chatter ceased. Tell me what is going on, I said. When the answer came, it turned into a great day. The visitors were there to install the additional telephone line I had ordered six months ago.

For the next three hours, the two men crawled and climbed over everything in the office. They used a ladder to reach up high and they went on their knees to get into corners and under the desk, stringing wire everywhere. They certainly looked and acted efficient and professional. Then, the test. The new phone refused to work. The men opened it, looked inside, rearranged the wires, put it back together. Then, another test. It refused to ring. The men said the line was fine but something was wrong with the telephone. But they had an answer. Out came an ancient French telephone, looking like something from the 1920s. It was big, bulky, and black, with a handset that weighed at least three pounds. With great dignity the men placed it on my desk. They continued to string wires, attaching them to walls and moldings, then again tested the phone. There were smiles from everyone when it rang. Finally we had our badly needed additional telephone line. There was polite applause and more smiling. However, it seemed that the installers did not know how to hook the new line into our office system, imported from Tokyo. Soon we would find the man who had installed our Japanese system and have him add the new line. Then I would welcome the applause.

■ ■ ■

In quiet moments, over coffee, iced tea, or a beer, I reflected on the war and its patterns and how they affected our work. Many battles happened before dawn or at dusk. Some were at night. Helicopters with special equipment made bombing runs at these times by dropping flares to light the terrain like a Hollywood set or a football game at night. My cameramen, who would go anywhere and do anything, feared filming these nighttime actions. They worried, understandably, about using their portable lights and becoming targets. Their lives could be in danger. They were also concerned about the quality of their film. Would the film editors and producers understand what they had shot?

It would be years before tape replaced film. The networks used videotape for storage, not for coverage (unless it came from a fixed camera at a major event). We never processed our film in Saigon because we did not have the facilities or people to do the work. We shipped all film as exposed negative and NBC developed it in other cities around the world. In time we started getting color prints of our stories from NBC New York instead of the usual poor-quality black-and-white kinescope versions supplied by the Pentagon. The camera crews now could see their stories in color. It helped them understand the amount of light they needed in order to get good, or at least usable, exposures and thus usable images. I talked to them about night filming and how they might take advantage of any natural light and military flares, but I ordered them never to use their own lights in combat and become an unnecessary target. Their lives had more importance than getting a story. My cameramen decided to try to film at night by forcing as much natural light into the lens as they could. Film can do wonders when you least expect it. If it worked, we would see some gripping effects. But they rarely had the opportunity and when they did, the results were spotty and not worth the risk.

5

Women in War

NBC NEWS did not have a woman correspondent in the bureau when I arrived or anytime during my tenure. When I ran the bureau, I helped—with the agreement of New York management—to keep women correspondents out of Vietnam. The prohibition of women reporters became an unwritten rule throughout my stay. I had nothing against women who were reporters; in the 1960s they were a small minority in broadcasting and had a long way to go before gaining acceptance. But I believed that having a woman on my reporting staff would pose problems I did not want to face. A woman covering combat? No thanks. I worried about facilities in the field. Bathrooms? Showers? Where would she sleep? Would she have the strength to troop through the jungle? How would my staff react? Vietnamese, Korean, and Japanese men treated women differently than did American men. Would my Asian crews respect, work with, and take orders from a woman? I did not know and I did not want to test it. I had enough to do without worrying about these things. How would men in the army, the marines, the air force, and the navy react to a woman reporter? Yes, there were military nurses, but they had specific training and duties. There were the WACs, but they were restricted to the bases and the cities like Saigon. There were USO workers and Donut Dollies, but they never went into combat. Besides, no woman reporter at NBC that I knew of was clamoring to work in Vietnam. Though women had covered other wars, and had covered them with distinction, I did not believe a woman television reporter belonged in Vietnam covering this war.

I make no excuses for my attitude. I was a man of my time, not a pioneer. As mentioned, I was not alone in my thinking: The home office—all the executives, producers, and editors—agreed with me, often leading the way. Women were only beginning to assert themselves in the 1960s, and broadcasters lagged behind in accepting them as equals. We were all of our time and, perhaps, sexist in our reluctance to work with a woman correspondent in a war zone.

In my last months as bureau chief in 1968, the possibility of hiring a woman correspondent was reconsidered. Various names came up, and one, Liz Trotta, rose to the top of the list. Liz was an experienced journalist working for NBC in New York, and a good reporter. New York led the drive to get her to Vietnam and I finally relented. I changed my mind with the changing times. I saw more clearly the world around me and thought, why not? We made our decision before I departed Saigon, but it was not until I arrived in Hong Kong as Southeast Asia bureau chief that Liz became NBC News's first woman correspondent in Vietnam.

I welcomed Liz to Hong Kong and we spent several days together talking about Vietnam and the problems she might encounter. She wanted the bureau to treat her as a correspondent first and a woman second. I relayed her request to Frank Donghi, my successor as Saigon bureau chief, asking him to treat her like any other correspondent and to send her into combat quickly so she could discover how raw life could be for the average soldier or marine. At first, Donghi showed reluctance, but then, after pressure from me, from New York, and from Liz, he gave in and she did very well. Several months later when I returned to Saigon to fill in as bureau chief, I had the pleasure of assigning Liz many stories, all of which she successfully completed.

The few other female reporters covering the war were mostly freelancers or stringers. They made their way to Vietnam on their own. Some worked for small radio stations and newspapers that wanted stories about soldiers from their area. We called these stories "hometowners," and at the network we had no time or space for them. Usually provided by the wire services, these allowed small papers to tell stories about local boys in the service. Other women worked for foreign news organizations, but these were often photographers. Of course, they also filed for major magazines and newspapers and did break through with their share of good stories. Though few, these women were noticed because they were women. We did not think it unusual to see a woman covering daily life in Vietnam or going to military and political briefings. A woman on the battlefield, however, remained an unusual sight. From the mid- to late 1960s, there were very few women working in Vietnam for the networks aside from Liz.

All the bureaus, broadcast and print, debated the wisdom of sending married men to cover the war. The discussion heightened when correspondents, camera-men, and soundmen began to arrive at our bureau accompanied by their wives and sometimes their young children. I did not want wives and children in such a potentially dangerous situation. I was, however, willing to let men visit their families in Bangkok, Hong Kong, Singapore, Manila, or perhaps as far as Tokyo. Men who worked at the bureau a minimum of six months could get time off to see their families twice in that time. The New York office disagreed strongly with my position. In time I relented and allowed wives of staffers, but no children, to live in Vietnam. Eventually men working for all the news organizations and other businesses unrelated to news brought their wives to the country. Most men working for private companies faced fewer daily risks than those employed in news. But I did not believe there was any advantage to having married couples together under these conditions. We were in a war zone. In Saigon, shells flew overhead when least expected. Terrorists struck freely every day. Did the adventure outweigh the risks? I did not think so then and I do not think so now. Wives were not present in World War II and in the Korean War. That should have ended the argument, but it did not.

Some couples thought that living together in Vietnam would help their marriage. But chances were if their marriage was in trouble it did not matter where they were living. The same problems would exist. In fact, the war and life in Saigon or another post tended to exacerbate any existing problems. The Far East, with its mystery and unique culture, often defied the average Western mind. That and the oppressive weather brought out the worst in people faster than under normal conditions.

A specious theory floated around that if a reporter's wife was in trouble somewhere he would be better off not knowing of it when covering a story. If she were in another country or another city, he would be unlikely to know if she were in another man's bed, drinking too much, popping too many pills, or eating fudge laced with hashish. He would not know his wife was having problems if he could not see her having them. As cynical as it may sound, many reporters thought their work would benefit if they remained ignorant of any serious difficulties in their private life.

In spite of their loneliness and the fact that there were few organized activities to keep them occupied, Western women in Saigon seemed well adjusted. Some found clerical work with U.S. government agencies or the huge American construction firms that were in Vietnam to build roads, install elaborate communications systems, and build modern ports and airports. Some found work teaching English to adults and children. Others were not so fortunate.

Western women could be seen every day sitting on the open-air terrace of the Continental Palace Hotel, which we called "the Continental Shelf," drinking vodka and gin and pretending to sophistication. Later, they ate dinner alone as they waited for their husband or lover to return from covering a battle or a less dangerous story. Some of these women told me they lived in fear of the unknown and had nothing to do but wait. Many wives and girlfriends became frazzled hoping for something, anything, to bring some excitement to their lives. There were limited diversions. Uninvolved in the life of the country and with no measurable skills, they had nothing they could trade to satisfy their needs and mollify their egos. Day after day, they wandered the dirty streets alone on a schedule of emptiness. Boredom was typical, marijuana smoking normal. High-quality pot was cheap and available for sale on street corners. Some women learned, like American GIs, to smoke cigarettes dipped in heroin. These women became strangers, especially to themselves.

Some Western women played tennis or went swimming at the Cercle Sportif, once an exclusive private club and the bastion of French colonial prejudice. During the war it survived on those who could afford to pay dues, mainly Americans and other foreigners. A few Vietnamese army officers and government officials were also there most days to play tennis and drink gin with fresh lime juice. They reveled in the knowledge that when the French ruled the country, no Vietnamese could enter the club unless they worked there, and then only through the back door. The Western women became sunburned, their hair streaked and bleached. Many were jealous of Vietnamese women, with their straight, long, black hair and their small, outwardly delicate bodies that managed to hide the steel-like inner strength they possessed. They were also jealous of what, to their uneducated eyes, were the uniformly beautiful faces of Vietnamese women and of the long, flowing slit dress and trousers of the *ao dai*. From a distance or in a crowd, that costume made all Vietnamese women look svelte and sexy. The jealousy of Western women extended to their own husbands and boyfriends, causing them to wonder each day where their men really were. Could they be found in some up-country mountain brothel? Were they sharing the hard pallet of a willing village girl who could barely speak English? There were Western women who believed their men were looking for something exotic to pass the time. Occasionally, they were probably right, which would not be unusual during a war. They either had not enough to do or did too much and none of it well. I now feel I understand those wandering women in the Vietnam of the 1960s.

6

Steak and Contour Flying

SHORTLY AFTER I arrived, I received an invitation to have dinner at First Infantry Division headquarters, the famed Big Red One, in Lai Khe, more than an hour west of Saigon. I eagerly accepted the invitation. A new bureau chief had come to town, ripe for an education on the rules of war. During the drive out, a bright sun dominated the cloudless sky. After dropping me off, my driver returned home. At night, the Viet Cong owned the roads and travel was dangerous. After dinner, an armed military helicopter would deliver me to Tan Son Nhut Airport and I would continue on to Saigon by car, taxi, or military escort, depending on the lateness of the hour.

I went to the command tent, where an intelligence officer gave a traditional military briefing, using large-scale maps, slides, and a rubber-tipped pointer. Another intelligence officer who had recently penetrated enemy lines graced our presence. He added little, saying something we all knew: The United States owned the villages by day and the Viet Cong owned them by night. When the briefing was over, armed MPs escorted me across the base for dinner with General William E. DePuy, a brisk fighting man with a reputation as a strong, no-nonsense leader. The general was short but appeared tall because he stood so straight. His tent was big enough to be a living room on Manhattan's West Side. The evening was muggy and very hot, especially inside the heavy canvas. Not a drop of perspiration appeared on General DePuy, as if his sweat glands were on leave. The rest of us, though, including the general's staff, perspired freely. We sat, not very comfortably, on matched dining room chairs under the tent's cathedral ceiling. Tall vodka tonics in frosted glasses cooled us off somewhat and kept us mellow. On the table were bowls filled with crisp potato chips. I marveled at how the chips stayed fresh and dry despite the humidity.

We talked about many things, including the war, of course, and why we were there. We discussed how we might prevent misunderstandings between the press and the military. Together we moaned, I the neophyte as well, over Vietnamese politics, how none of us thought we would ever tunnel through its dense maze. While we drank and ate on that hazy, tropical night, the First Division's big guns, mostly 105mm howitzers, kept firing from the camp's perimeter. The general explained that he was using "H and I" to attack the enemy "out there, somewhere out there." H stood for harassment, I for interdiction. The purpose was to kill or at least scare the Viet Cong and keep them off balance. I thought it sounded like a method for blowing up everything in sight. The general's staff told me that by using H and I as a tactical weapon, "we create our own form of long-distance diversion." That the shells landed without anyone ever knowing precisely what they hit hardly seemed to matter. It did, of course, because our military was not supposed to engage in wanton destruction, but the next day's evidence could never be exact. Usually the Vietnamese messenger who carried the news of success or failure shaded it to his prejudices, and the American officer attached to him interpreted it with his own bias. In any case, there were many bomb craters and many more unhappy Vietnamese who disliked Americans. Who could blame them?

We ate dinner at a long table covered with a pure white, freshly pressed linen cloth with scalloped edges. Sterling silver utensils surrounded fine white bone china. Uniformed stewards stood at attention waiting to pour French burgundy into heavy crystal goblets. The meal began with Saigon River shrimp covered with red sauce and a crisp salad of tiny lettuce leaves grown in Dalat in the Central Highlands. We had an elaborate entrée of tasty New York sirloin steak served with baked potato, freshly baked bread, and sweet butter. The dessert was Peach Melba made with newly churned vanilla ice cream. We drank strong, black coffee from delicate china cups. Fresh, heavy cream sat on the table in small pitchers. The furious hammering of the heavy guns firing from the edge of camp punctuated every bite of food and each sip of fine wine.

We talked and ate by the light of white candles burning brightly, a centerpiece that cast bizarre shadows across the walls of the tent. Romance and the madness of war. The meal had a surreal quality to it, but I would be in Vietnam for a long time—possibly years—and I knew more of the same would come my way. Until Vietnam, I had never been to a full-scale war. In those first months, I wondered to what end the United States continued to fight a war in Southeast Asia. No matter what our politicians said, it seemed we were helping a third-rate power that had nothing to give in return. We Americans were fighting for people who did not seem to care for our presence in this, their markedly underdeveloped country. They did not want us anywhere near their already decimated society, their ruined way of life. Of course, if I had to sit under "H and I" fire night after night, I would have felt no differently than those peasants. After all, they lived always in sight of—and in the sights of—America's big guns.

After dinner and small talk, I said goodnight and flew back to Tan Son Nhut Airport, my first experience with contour flying. Wearing a flak jacket, I squeezed into a heavily armed and armored helicopter gunship. The floors had steel plates lined with extra flak jackets. The flight began calmly but then became like a roller coaster at Coney Island, with trick flying of high caliber done cleverly to protect us from being shot at and downed. The pilot flew close to the ground, skirting houses and the tops of trees. It was no place for the squeamish or anyone with a weak stomach. We flew fast, flowing with the geographic patterns of the land. We swooped, dipped, and dove, making us a difficult target for any Viet Cong gunner lurking below. The trip lasted twenty minutes and seemed to end quickly, leaving me no time to think while I was in the air.

After touching down at the helicopter pad, I walked shakily to the civilian side of the huge air base. No one stopped me, though American MPs watched me carefully as I walked to the exit. Once outside the gate and past Vietnamese Air Force guards, I hired a tiny, ten-year-old Renault Dauphine taxicab. The cab was missing its floorboards and was so stripped of its interior furnishings that all it had for seats were bare springs without cushions. Curfew would soon start, and the driver, in a hurry, took me on a bumpy ride through the dark, dangerous, foul-smelling streets that was not much safer than my flight over the dense jungle. Like many things in Vietnam, I realized, survival might be easier if you did not give it much thought.

7

Fighting Cocks and Politics

BREAKFAST OR TEA—I was never invited to lunch and rarely to dinner—became something that, as bureau chief, I looked forward to having with prominent Vietnamese officials, politicians, and intellectuals. Once I had breakfast with Nguyen Cao Ky, then the premier of South Vietnam, at his heavily guarded home inside the Tan Son Nhut air base. We sat in the dining room of his sprawling but modestly furnished one-story house. During the meal, he and I did not talk. We ate a filling, satisfying breakfast of fresh pineapple and papaya, scrambled eggs, canned New Zealand butter, and freshly baked French bread with a crisp crust and chewy center. The meal ended with strong, black coffee that tasted as if brewed in New Orleans.

Ky's beautiful wife, Mai, a former Air Vietnam hostess, directed the two women who served the food. Her orders were crisp, understated, bordering on disinterest. She ate fruit and drank a light jasmine tea instead of the strong coffee her husband and I drank. During the meal, Ky and Mai started arguing quietly, yet with great anger and intensity. They talked rapidly in Vietnamese and enough French to make me wish I understood more of both languages. I did pick up the words "Hong Kong" and "Mandarin Hotel." Suddenly, Mai started tossing grapes at her husband, first playfully, then more forcefully. He became angry, standing up swiftly and leaning toward her, shouting. His face grew red. His mustache bristled. His arms stayed stiff at his sides. I had the feeling that if he moved his arms he would have struck her. After a parting outburst, Mai ran from the table like a whirlwind, tipping her chair backward and causing it to fall with a loud thud onto the polished wooden floor. After she left, the room fell silent.

Ky turned to me, mortified. The argument, he explained, was over his refusal to let Mai fly to Hong Kong to shop. She refused to understand, he said, that he was under fire for alleged corruption. The situation would be worse if she made such a trip at his expense.

Shortly before our meeting there had been published reports that Ky took bribes from Saigon's only horse racetrack, accusing him of fixing races. In some ways the charge was laughable. The poor horses plying the track were not worth the price of admission. They were small, seemingly undersized, and the track was like a backcountry road. No one with any sense bet on the horses and jockeys that had to run over that awful ground. Yet the track remained open until the very end of the war in 1975, when the North Vietnamese took it over and made it into a staging area and supply depot for their troops.

Ky told me he had received a call from the people in his embassy in Washington asking for information so they could report the truth to the State Department. He had also heard from the White House through the American ambassador in Saigon. He said he was furious with the reports and was contemplating booting the American journalists who had maligned his character out of Vietnam. He made an impassioned speech to me, claiming his honesty and denying his corruption. If he wanted to steal, he said, he knew many other easier ways. He said he could become a millionaire by snapping his fingers. He then loudly snapped his fingers to make his point. The worst result of what he called the irresponsible reporting was the emergency cabinet meeting he had been forced to call. He told me it was a tough session lasting many uncomfortable hours and that he was embarrassed by the hard interrogation from the other generals, who questioned his honesty and integrity.

Then he attacked me, as a representative of the press, for making his family life difficult. He lectured me on the need to report useful stories—war stories, stories about heroes and courage. For the good of us all, press and public, we should keep our collective noses out of his private life. We should have nothing to do with his personal finances. And we should never report anything about his wife even when she did good deeds, such as visiting an orphanage. I answered in as measured a tone as possible. I said that his requests could not be met. As premier, he had to be above reproach. If he were not clean, the people would eventually discover his misdeeds with or without the help of the press. He sighed and sat down in an ornately carved rosewood chair. As if he were serving penance, he leaned back in the hard, cushionless chair and muttered, "I know. I know." The bribery charges against Ky were eventually dropped because there was no proof he had broken the law. However, his reputation was forever tarnished in Vietnam and the United States.

Before settling into serious conversation, something Ky dearly loved, we toured his hard-packed dirt backyard and he showed me the fighting cocks he raised. He said that although everyone knew he kept the birds, he did not really like to talk about them. Concerned with his image, Ky refused to allow me to bring a camera crew to record his hobby. However, in his most professional tone, he assured me that cockfighting was a legitimate sport in Vietnam. He knew most Americans were against it, thinking it cruel to the birds. Ky told me the game was not as savage as people believed and explained it represented the victory of the strong over the weak. Cockfighting had one winner and one loser, the same as in battle. When one bird wounded another, the injured bird died swiftly and silently. That, too, he said, was the way it should be in war. The better trained, the motivated, always win. He told me he wished he could train and motivate his army as he did his birds, but he knew that birds and men were different, down to the lack of pain the cocks felt when slashed and incapacitated. If men could only be like birds, he mused . . . Then he closed the subject, turned his back to the cages, and walked into his home.

We talked for two hours. Though impressed, I found him to be more cunning than intelligent. As air marshal, Ky had taken control of South Vietnam in 1965 in a military coup. In spite of his theatrical and bold public persona, he struck me as a politician, a ward heeler who would have been at home on Chicago's South Side or in Jersey City. He knew street politics. Ky maneuvered between two constituencies, the Vietnamese and the Americans. I did not always believe he knew which one he was addressing, especially when he was out in the field with aggressive American reporters who encouraged him to make a fool of himself before the camera. He made outrageous comments designed to catch the attention of his American audience. Yet he managed to survive for a surprisingly long twelve months, more than expected for a Vietnamese war leader at the time. This was a major accomplishment, so in his eyes, he was doing very well.

Ky said the danger from his own ruling clique was his major concern. I found it hard to believe he did not fear the Viet Cong, who needed no pretext to kill him. It was surprising that the Viet Cong did not attempt to assassinate high Vietnamese and American leaders. After all, it had inside information and many opportunities. But village chiefs, teachers, and other provincial officials outside the major cities were easier targets. The provinces suffered most from terrorism and the civil war. The Viet Cong would fade away into the countryside after doing their damage. Of course, they had done the same after committing major terrorist acts in Saigon at the American embassy and the My Canh floating restaurant, and they hit scores of Vietnamese and American military billets and installations with impunity. But the Viet Cong rarely went after big, well-known names. Perhaps they found it easier to hit targets that were unable to fight back, which is, at heart, the essence of terror.

Contrary to street rumors and coffeehouse talk, Ky told me, he did not want to run for president. He insisted that eventually he wanted to return to flying and that his most fervent wish was to "bomb the hell out of North Vietnam with no interference from the United States." An admirable statement, if true. He put it out there for his country's far right wing, which made up most of his support, and for his sympathizers in the United States, and it sounded like a warmonger's plea. From a former air marshal fighting a desperate war, it was nothing less than I expected to hear. Still, I doubted he would have done it, if given the chance. I had the feeling he was unwilling to give up the good life of a national leader. He wouldn't risk his newfound prestige on a raid whose success he could not guarantee. He enjoyed his power too much—but you never knew what he might do on impulse. He insisted on discussing the strategy of bombing the North into oblivion. He felt that if he could lead a heavy air attack, the war would end that much sooner. And he understood that the symbolism of him, the premier, in a jet fighter-bomber over Hanoi would make him an unimpeachable national hero. At least until the next coup and the next ambitious leader took power.

Ky told me he admired Ho Chi Minh, or "my Uncle Ho," as he sarcastically referred to him. Ho was an inspiration to the North Vietnamese and the Viet Cong, and Ky insisted that as a South Vietnamese leader he had to accord Ho proper respect and had no choice but to refer to him by the affectionate nickname used in the North. But he still wanted to bomb the North to show that, in his way, he could be Ho's equal.

Ky also discussed the American people and how they still seemed to support the war effort. He noted, however, that there were more antiwar demonstrations in America, more people in the streets. He said: "We have Buddhists and you have hippies. We should not give either much thought or consideration." He never talked about Lyndon Johnson, not even when I asked him several pointed questions about his relationship with the president. Ky suggested he wanted to act independently of the United States and that he would do so whenever he had the chance. His off-the-record remarks confirmed the coffeehouse talk I had recently picked up in Saigon.

His comments were pure Ky. He was a man searching for answers, for a way to define his position in a war that was already foundering badly. He was sure of himself and he was tough, at least on the surface. These were rare qualities in the South, but Ky was a northerner, and the North Vietnamese had a different attitude toward life. They felt that life owed them for their sacrifices in a harsh land. In that, he understood Hanoi. I found it hard to accept Ky's glib bluster and bravado. But he pulled it off with aplomb and I could not help admiring his audacity in the face of so much adversity. Thankfully, despite his arrogance, he gave no lessons in humility.

He declined an on-the-record interview or film story showing how he spent his time when not fighting the war or directing the government. Originally, that had been the reason for my meeting. Despite his earlier tirade about the press, I asked him if a film crew could do a portrait of his personal life, but he said he considered the request inappropriate, that such a report would be of no value to an American audience. As he accompanied me to my waiting car, he relented and invited me back sometime in the future. However, he would soon be out of office and I never had the opportunity.

Nguyen Cao Ky had his own dedication to Vietnam, a peculiar, perhaps unique, idea of war, peace, and freedom. Unfortunately, he often expressed his ideas through his open, unyielding drive for power and glory. As the war changed in character, with a marked increase in death and destruction, Ky was weakened and had almost no role other than as a gadfly, without power. During the confused final days toward the end of the war, he became neutralized and ineffective in spite of his bluster. In the end, as at the beginning, he was never really in touch with the people. The people consequently never responded to him. With the war coming to a swift end in April 1975, Ky called for a thrust into the North but no one paid him any attention. As a private citizen and politician, he tried to rally the dismantled, disorganized army of President Nguyen Van Thieu as it fled from the onrushing North Vietnamese. When the end came, a surprised world shuddered to see South Vietnam fall so easily. Ky had no credibility. If the South had heeded him in the spring of 1975, the result would have been the same: failure. At most, the war might have dragged on longer, but it would have ended more bitterly. The path to peace would have been bloodier. The death rate would have been higher and the devastation to the land and spirit of the people would have been worse.

8

Routine and Then Some

SATURDAY NIGHT in Saigon, June 1966. Fifty monks and nuns were on yet another hunger strike seeking religious freedom. Ky was headed to Seoul for a major meeting away from the turmoil of Saigon. He seemed little concerned that his enemies would attempt to overthrow him in his absence. He must have believed he controlled his own destiny. A battle raged near Kontum in the Central Highlands, in hill country close to the Laotian border. I was rotating my teams to cover the action on another typical day, but no two days were ever really the same.

A general curfew had been in effect since 9:00 and the streets were empty. At 10:00, I was still sitting behind my desk, thinking about the many levels of war. Heavy guns boomed in the distance: my night music. A small helicopter flew overhead: the rhythm section. My air conditioner ran on, straining to cool my always stuffy office. Earlier, troops had lined the streets to protect the barriers and facades specially constructed for Sunday, which was Armed Forces Day. Buddhists were in their pagodas, snug on their pallets, dreaming of what mysteries the new day would bring. I still could not devise a way to cover their activities. I knew that the war would pick up again by Tuesday or Wednesday as the marines tried to enforce pacification, but marines and pacification are an aberrant combination, and they would be out for blood. Only time would tell if the plan would work. The 101st Division had spent days in the jungle looking for the North Vietnamese Army. The First Cavalry was chasing Viet Cong over mountain passes. I had one team with the First Division (the Big Red One), which was trying to prevent a repeat of the previous week's tragic ambush of American troops near Lai Khe.

I woke the next morning at dawn after a few hours of my usual fitful sleep. The city had become quiet, the stillness broken only by the occasional sound of a motorbike or a jet breaking the sound barrier. Our part of the city was having another planned power failure, a blackout this time and not just a partial brownout.

I worked by the meager daylight. It should have been brighter, but the cloudy sky hid the morning sun. Very little blue showed through and it looked like rain yet again.

I lived on the fifth floor of the Eden Building, one floor above the office. The need to be that near my desk had begun to wear on me. I felt like a firefighter but I lacked a fireman's pole to the floor below. Just as well. The bureau had been operating well and we had the edge over the other networks. We often beat the daily newspapers and frequently topped the weekly magazines. They would probably have disagreed, thinking they were winning a race that had become a long-distance affair, not a dash. But I thought NBC's advantage could continue if we maintained our drive and discipline.

That morning, Digby Jones was in my apartment taking inventory. One small room had shelves from floor to ceiling filled with raw stock and equipment. Digby and other staff were in and out of the place ten times a day. The only place I had to myself was the bedroom, and sometimes not even that if we were busy. There were times when I could not get into the apartment for personal needs or to process the bureau accounts in quiet. I had not bargained for this and I thought that management would agree it was no way for a bureau chief to live. I did not want to be stubborn but I had my limits.

That morning I wrote a strongly worded letter to New York, suggesting to director of news Bill Corrigan and the other managers that I be allowed to move. I would find a suitable place to live within a few blocks of the bureau and with telephone capability. I wanted to turn my current apartment into a combined meeting room, sitting room, screening room, storage area, and equipment room to test cameras and charge batteries. It could be a television studio for on-camera appearances by the correspondents, a place to enjoy coffee or tea, a bedroom when needed. It could be a card room, a bathroom, and a general workspace for anything and everything.

Several days later, Corrigan sent me a message turning down my proposal. The money men said it would cost too much to move me. The editorial department said I would be better off staying where I was because of my proximity to the office, the center of activity. Doomed to fail, I did not fail for lack of trying. To hell with proximity, I told them. But then I never brought it up again. I was covering a war, after all. In time, particularly with the Tet Offensive in 1968, New York proved right to insist that I remain in place. But I had started learning the difficulty of dealing with a foreign power: in this case, New York. Were those in the New York office the enemy? I wondered. I soon learned that I did not enjoy administration.

Despite all the worry and trouble, though, I think the best thing about the job is that I cured my ulcer. Maybe it was all that rice I was eating.

There was more than enough to do without my being unduly concerned about where I lived. From the military briefing officers we heard: "The long-awaited monsoon offensive seems to have started." I did not need a briefing to tell me. The buildup had been evident from the recent fighting. It brought me to my strategy for covering the war. Ideally, two correspondents would be with the military in the field. One reporter would be doing features, either in Saigon or elsewhere. Another would cover the Machiavellian machinations of politics and religion. A fifth correspondent would give me some badly needed breathing room which I could use to gamble with my coverage, rotating people to a better variety of stories. If one of these stories became hot, New York would not see special coverage. This system could give me an edge, the better odds I had been searching for to make the bureau successful. But I needed a fifth correspondent to implement it.

We had an election coming in November 1967 in a country that had never known democracy. Its people were mostly village dwellers who knew nothing of what happened three miles down the road and couldn't care less about it anyway. Despite where we were in staff, we were prepared to cover anything, but I thought it might take us until November to get ready for this story.

Meanwhile, my crews managed to stay in the middle of everything, and that was the way it should be. During a rare student demonstration in Saigon, a squad of National Police—called "white mice" because of their white shirts, gray trousers, and cowardly disposition—attacked the crew that was covering the story. One of my teams was roughed up and arrested during a Buddhist demonstration in Hue that turned into a riot when police charged the unarmed marchers. Another crew almost got killed by friendly machine-gun fire while on an operation outside Hue.

The political story became more complex every day. The North and South Vietnamese armies, the Americans, and the Viet Cong were on full alert. There were firefights everywhere and it would have been impossible to cover them all. I had little time to react, but I did, often without much apparent thought. I called it coverage by instinct, and my teams rolled with it beautifully. It was like working a city desk and covering an unstoppable fire, a fascinating set of conditions. My New York producers and editors, pious and knowing, sat in judgment on stories that none had experienced and few ever would. Throughout, we maintained our dignity and good editorial judgment and produced a constant flow of stories, most of which made it to the air.

Morale remained beautiful. The staff backed me because they knew I fought strongly for them. Never had they received so much new equipment. I respected their rights as people, including their right to express themselves. These were all proud men, and my association with them made me proud. I did not raise my voice too much, even during my frequent skirmishes with New York. Tension keys up life in the bureau. We were covering a war and that phrase bore repetition, even if silently.

The staff enjoyed immensely a cable exchange I had with New York over a three-day period. I received a telex ordering a detailed outline of who was covering what, the reason for the assignment, the R&R schedule, who was sick or injured. I was already sending that information to New York in shorthand every day. Now it seemed they wanted more. I wrote back that I didn't have time for their detail. I asked if this could be an attempt to direct our operation from New York. If so, those executives were making a mistake. Who was responsible? Bill Corrigan, Reuven Frank, others? What had been going on there over the last week? I demanded an explanation, though I thought I would probably never get one. My reply was carefully thought out, not written in heat but composed coolly and without passion. The staff understood that I meant every word I wrote.

Over those three days, I felt that New York did not trust me, my opinion, or my ability. I did what I wanted from my chair as I saw fit. The people in New York went to work, wielding their sharpened pencils like rocket launchers. Maybe they did not have enough to do. We were more than twelve thousand miles away. Day was night. Night was day. Unless there was a shift in time and attitude, the New York assignment desk would never understand where we were and what we were doing. Like everything else in Vietnam, it was a horse race, but I did not relish running against my own.

At the end of those three days, the New York desk started its less than subtle attack again. A copy of a cable to "All NBC News Correspondents" arrived on my desk. This time New York was requesting a detailed activity report every day for each correspondent. I thought we had cleared up that problem. Did New York really want that information? Our men ran and never stopped. They did it seven days a week. Everything was general coverage, meaning that no news program could keep a story exclusively for itself. I decided what to cover because I had the best vantage point. Then the crew in the field had to produce. The moment they failed to get a story would be the moment to reconsider our method of operation.

I often based my story selection on information I received from tipsters. Late one recent night, I had gotten a call saying we should go to Tuy Hoa where the

101st Division was engaged in heavy combat with a battalion of solidly dug-in Viet Cong. Then a call came from the First Cavalry saying they were taking over what would become a combined operation. They offered transportation and I could not refuse. I put Howard Tuckner and cameraman Lim Youn Choul on a supply flight at 7:30 the next morning. We beat everyone to the scene because the other networks' crews took the press flight in the evening, ten hours after we departed. The information officer did not understand why we did not want our seats on the press flight, but I said nothing. The next day he understood when he saw our team in the field returning from patrol. Graciously, he agreed to carry their story on the operation to Saigon. We had a clear beat because our team was ready to move when we received the information.

We ran a fire station in a burning slum, and our men rarely had the luxury of special assignments. But I knew that as a bureau we should be producing more features. I asked each correspondent for a list of stories they had an interest in. Of some fifty ideas from five reporters, only one was duplicated. At least half had excellent potential. David Burrington started to prepare for a feature but he never got to it. Another story interfered. A Vietnamese on my payroll who worked in the Saigon City Hall called to say that two monks planned to burn themselves in front of the Buddhist Institute, a good tip from a strong source. Burrington and a crew were on their way at six the next morning. That same morning, we received the best news of the day. New York was rescinding its request for details about our journalistic life, saying it had been sent to Saigon by mistake. No matter, I had no plans to reply anyway. And even better, my tip panned out. Burrington got the story.

9

Siestas and Demonstrations

AS WITH ALMOST all mornings, when I awoke, my favorite three-inch lizard was clinging to the bedroom wall. I never saw him move once in more than two years—if he was even the same lizard. Bats were sleeping under the eaves of the roof and mice were in the walls, sometimes scratching but not scurrying. Quiet pervaded everything.

I understood that according to legend, the Buddha had been born on this day and the Vietnamese would celebrate his birthday, but no one could verify the date or time. The exact date seemed to depend on who wanted to celebrate the Buddha's birthday and when they wanted to do it. I wondered if the Vietnamese really celebrated or did they only give lip-service to the Buddha?

The siesta began at noon. Despite the war, many people moved from the crowded, bustling streets, seeking shade, respite from the heat, and a chance for a deep, satisfying nap. During siesta, hardly anybody moved. The sun usually shone brightly. Wisps of white clouds dotted the blue skies. Depending on the time of year, it might rain. The rain came down in sheets and lasted only a few minutes. It would be followed by blue skies and then it would rain again, nature's take on repetitive action. By midafternoon, siesta ended and everyone returned to work.

Though other foreigners took siesta, I never did. There was too much work, and the war did not stop for siesta. There were occasions when I tried to take a siesta, but I always failed. Either I couldn't sleep, or the phone rang, or a crew had to get into my apartment to get stock or equipment.

The hottest time of day was between noon and three. Often during siesta time, so necessary in the tropics for survival, a common noise would shatter the tranquility of the day. The growl of a hot Honda motorcycle as it leapt and bucked over the city's patched roads always interrupted our moment of gentle peace. Saigon had a habit of seeming to resist quiet moments. Sounds of mortars landing and pistols firing, the thump of heavy cannon, jets breaking the sound barrier, and backfiring jeeps interrupted the fleeting blips of calm.

There were few moments of quiet, even during the occasional lull in the fighting. We never knew why there had been a pause in the action. We assumed the two sides were recovering from their wounds, catching their breath, and readying themselves for the next battle. That quiet always felt strange, unexpected, and eerie. Sometimes nothing moved on any of the many battlefronts. (Each engagement, no matter how small, between the North and the South comprised a "front." The classic definition, of troops massed in lines across trenches or beachheads, did not apply in Vietnam.) On the other hand, I often heard of so-called major military operations due to start in the Central Highlands, along the coastal plain, and in the Mekong Delta all on the same day. If they did, and I had the staff to cover them, we would be everywhere in battle. In those years, I did not realize how little many of these battles meant strategically—excluding, of course, the wounded and dead soldiers.

The Caravelle Hotel and the Continental Palace Hotel stood directly across Lam Son Square from each other. The Continental was charming, extravagant, exotic, filled with mystery. But the Caravelle was the most famous hotel in South Vietnam. Even at the height of the war, the Caravelle was liveable and surprisingly clean, though with mostly pedestrian rooms and dull furniture. The rates were high but within reach of most budgets. The elevators sometimes worked and the large staff helped the guests, if tips were good. The restaurant served bastardized French cuisine with decidedly American overtones. Most of the guests, after all, were American.

The Caravelle roof and its small eighth-floor bar were two of the more interesting and safe places in the city to unwind. Reporters and other working civilians freely exchanged stories of war and other adventures. Late at night after dinner— and, often, too much to drink—we would stand on the roof near the railing, watching the war from a distance as if through a telephoto lens. Often there were no lights anywhere except on the edges of the city. There, the sky was always alive with pure white phosphorus flares dropped by toylike helicopters. The flares, attached to miniature parachutes, would bob soundlessly in the distance, floating gently in the often windless night. They looked like fairies strung on invisible wires in a grade-school play. We could identify an action by the red tracers the helicopter gunships fired at real or imagined enemies. Anything moving on the ground after the nightly curfew was assumed to be the enemy. Bright flame in the sky over Saigon's outskirts was a nightly diversion.

Viewing the action from the rooftop was better than night baseball in summer. Occasionally, low-flying planes or helicopters dropped their flares over the city, sending a signal that there would be action. The flares would drift over the city blocks, lighting whole districts and making them shine more brightly than in sunlight. This allowed U.S. and Vietnamese troops to flush out the Viet Cong who freely roved those areas. Red flashing bursts from the gunships punctuated the crisp white light. We never learned if these forays were successful, but any success rarely lasted beyond the attack.

Sometimes a plane dropped a flare by mistake over the wrong neighborhood or an errant flare would drift until it landed far from its intended destination. Sparks from these flares would ignite houses, causing them to burn. People would scatter and more homeless would wander the streets of a city already swollen with refugees—the inevitable suffering that accompanied war and that always left an ugly taste in my mouth.

It is a cliché to say that war touches the innocent in ways too sad to enumerate, but it is worth repeating. Refugees fled from town to town, forever at the mercy of battles they never made or wanted. When curfew was in effect, the streets became a kindergarten. In the center of the city, dozens of children slept in doorways, protecting each other from further harm. The old adage "in numbers there is strength" helped street kids to survive. I saw children sleeping next to decaying garbage, oblivious to the rotten odors. I could never walk by the mounds of rot without being affected. My nostrils managed to slam shut, but never fast enough. The memory of those odors became implanted deep in my brain.

Late at night, when the bars had emptied and were closing, there was always a hungry whore or two hoping for some last-minute action to pay for her day and quiet her fears of the night, but these sad women had few takers. Walking the streets alone, I heard no sounds except the omnipresent chirping of crickets.

The Caravelle Hotel roof was Saigon's live theater, with the additional attractions of decent food, good companions, and excessive drinking. In time, however, after I had some experiences closer to the action, as most of us did, it lost its charm.

The Vietnamese have a wonderfully detailed history filled with epic heroes, battles won and lost, and poetry and stories to make one's heart pound. Their political life, however, lacked the logic and discipline that I knew in the United

States. Washington in its plodding manner was trying to guide the Vietnamese along that path, but with little success. Before November 1967, no one had been elected to office. "Government" was just another word for payoff. Appointments came through connections, often to once meaningful royalty and the mandarin class, as in China.

I soon decided that political theory was a scholar's game and not for me. In the war zone of Vietnam, the adventurer often replaced the gentleman, even in local politics. Life and death destroyed theory. The predominant attitude was: Get on with the war, get on with the killing. The reasons for both would come later when people paused for breath.

With the Catholics entrenched in power and running the government, the Buddhist extremists, less organized, were naturally concerned with their survival. They claimed the government was suppressing their religious freedom. Some Buddhists did not want their sons in the army, and some were willing to negotiate with the Viet Cong to end the war. Organized around powerful pagodas and charismatic leaders, the Buddhists were not a political party as we know it in America. They influenced the balance of power by calling foul when they felt persecuted. Sometimes they had justice on their side. But with a devastating war on, those in power decided that dissidents had to be kept under control. Passive resistance, something we generally associate with the East, did not work in Vietnam.

In May and June 1966, the Buddhists in Saigon and Hue mounted a drive for equality and power. They knew the two were inseparable if they were to succeed. The streets churned with saffron-robed monks fighting the National Police in their starched white shirts and gray trousers. The "white mice" used their wooden batons against anyone who stood in their way. They were famous for hit-and-run tactics and sneak attacks, and the demonstrators never knew when they would turn up or what could be done to avoid them. But the police treated everyone alike. Street vendors were not safe from their wrath. Storekeepers had to bribe them to stay in business. They took a cut of cyclo drivers' earnings. These unconscionable men held their hands out for bribes wherever they could.

The hot, often humid weather contributed to the intensity of the frequent antigovernment demonstrations. No two protests were ever the same. To complicate matters, ferocious monsoons, with their sudden winds and deluges of rain, swept across Saigon every afternoon when in season. The demonstrators and police would scatter for cover and wait out the weather until the skies calmed. Sometimes the demonstrations continued after the rain. The humidity would momentarily lift and a respite of cool air make its way over the city, giving the protesters new energy.

A few radicals, government and antigovernment, took charge on each side. They had the power to halt the demonstrations. The events in the streets gave the press and public something to think about other than the war: What effect would the marching monks, with their shaved heads glistening in the sun, have on government policy? But, though they made for good theater, the demonstrations did not reflect the concerns of everyday people in South Vietnam. Most Vietnamese ignored the extremists. I was used to people taking sides in America, and this "sidelines" approach was new to me. People stood around and patiently waited for the police to pin down their nonviolent opponents with tear gas and batons. When a march did not turn into a riot, the crowd would disperse quietly.

Survival came first and protest, for most, came close to last. When a riot took place on one street, people living and working a block away would go about their business as if nothing unusual was happening. I saw antigovernment demonstrations on one corner of a square while across the street it was quiet. Occasionally my best view of a peaceful demonstration was from a café. I would have a glass of iced tea heavily flavored with fresh lime juice and coarse brown sugar, a cigarette in my mouth, and Vietnamese folk songs of love, loss, and remorse playing on a radio behind me. Safely seated in a wire-backed chair, smoking and eating miniature pastries, the rally in front of me would unfold as if in a movie.

In downtown Saigon, sometimes my best vantage point was from the windows of my fourth-floor office. With its thick concrete walls, it felt almost like a fortress above the street. At times, tear gas fired by the police at rioters filled the room, entering by air conditioners that were pulling air in instead of sending it out. Our office boy never learned the difference between "in" and "exhaust." The tear gas on the narrow streets and broad boulevards of the city was never as bad as it was inside the bureau. Outside, I would drape a wet handkerchief over my nose and mouth to keep me from breathing the gas too deeply. Unless I was in the middle of the action where a tear gas canister happened to land, I rarely suffered. Often a light breeze helped disperse the fumes. (When the riot ended, I would throw away the handkerchief, which would be useless after being impregnated with CS gas.) But when the acrid vapors seeped into the office, they burned my eyes and nose and clung tenaciously to my throat, far worse than they did outside. The gas lingered in the corners and clung to the stucco walls and high ceilings of all the rooms, gripping everyone in the bureau.

By June 1966, Buddhist monks and their supporters were marching regularly in the streets and at least five monks had burned themselves to death that month. We could never be sure of the exact number. Sometimes we learned weeks later of a suicide in a distant, inaccessible pagoda. We knew that many monks had lined themselves up for immolation. The Buddhist leaders had more volunteers than they needed. I asked myself when it would ever stop. What did the American people think when they saw the aftermath of a burning on television? It did not take me long to become angry with the Buddhists. I had difficulty understanding how a person could kill himself for a cause, one I did not trust or understand. I believed it had more to do with power than with freedom to worship. But I was learning, to my dismay and frustration, that life in Vietnam defied explanation. In the Judeo-Christian tradition, we honor the sanctity of life, yet American soldiers were dying in increasing numbers. No one could calculate how many North and South Vietnamese soldiers and civilians died every day. The war did not tie itself up in a neat syllogism that I could uniformly apply to every situation. As I write this now, I know what I tried not to admit then, that Western logic had no place in Vietnam.

One evening that June while sitting in the bureau after a long, slow day, I received a phone call and learned that yet another monk had burned himself to death to protest the Thieu and Ky government's repressive religious policies. Another immolation. Another horror story. But one we had to cover. I sent a correspondent with a crew and followed in my car with additional portable lights and another cameraman. We headed for the An Quang Pagoda, where the burning had taken place. Also called the Buddhist Institute, it sprawled over several square blocks. I had heard but could never verify that the monks and their lay assistants, usually older women, managed to feed and care for a thousand children of all ages there every day. These were kids who no longer knew what it meant to have a family and had lost touch with real life. Kids who had no shoes, the soles of their sandals worn through, the bottoms of their feet hard as stone, encrusted with dirt. Sorrowful kids with absolutely no place to go. They were kids with no future, many with only the vaguest recollection of things past. They came to you in groups on the street, selling freshly roasted peanuts wrapped in small newspaper cones. If you did not buy, they might pick your pocket, rip the watch from your wrist, and disappear into the crowd. Anything you owned that was not tied down would run, not walk, from you once these kids had their small, hardened hands on it.

Inside, the pagoda looked like a garbage dump. There was a special smell, the ever-present odor of rot that still rises in my throat when I think of that sultry night. Black pools of water stood everywhere. The resultant mud was deep, up to my ankles in places. The long and spacious main hall looked to be the size of a football field. Thousands of people milled around aimlessly. The monks and nuns, thin and in saffron robes, all looked alike. Their heads were shaved and short bristles covered their shiny, sunburned skulls. I imagined they were trying to work their collective will, their black magic, on that odd moment in time.

The usual floaters, hangers-on, pickpockets, prostitutes, and money changers moved silently and purposefully through the crowd. Also there were the Buddhist Boy Scouts, wearing short khaki pants, woolen kneesocks, and wide-brimmed copies of World War I felt hats that made them look like Smokey the Bear, only smaller. These oddly happy boys did whatever the senior monks wanted of them. They acted as guardians and guides, but they were unlike any Boy Scouts I had ever known. They carried bamboo poles with rusty, twisted nails sticking out of the tips, held in a position ready to strike. Much as dogs guide sheep, they helped control the crowds and keep the press in line if we threatened to leave our assigned positions and move too freely through the mass of people.

Fortunately I had missed the immolation, but the results will live with me forever. I saw a body, burnt and swollen, its skin cracked and burst, its arms and legs frozen in a grotesque, crablike position. Smoke escaped from the charred fissures in the dead shell of the person that this once had been.

Most in the crowd viewed the horror impassively. I observed a chorus of crying women led by several heavy screamers, but these were paid mourners who had been called to the scene before the event. Unattended children ran everywhere. They tried desperately to get a look, crawling under legs, climbing on shoulders, searching for a way to catch a glimpse. They had heard the screaming and the bells chiming. They had seen the blaze and the smoke rising. They knew that one of their own had just ascended to Nirvana.

As foreign journalists, my crews and I could only observe and remain as unemotional as possible, but that did not mean we were indifferent. It was a difficult position to be in. What we saw defied understanding. Vietnam had a culture and religions far different from ours. It did not take long to realize how alien we were to that culture and, by extension, America to the war. In our own culture we would attempt to stop a person from taking his life, but in Vietnam we would have been interfering. If we had tried to stop an immolation, it might have started a riot. We could have been beaten and perhaps killed. Besides, in our role as journalists we had no right to interfere. So we filmed that immolation and any others we could, knowing the images would remain permanently in our memories and would shock our audience. To this day I question anyone's right to commit suicide. It is worth noting that the Vietnamese, Japanese, and Koreans on my staff frowned on the immolations. But they shrugged, said the monks were fools for wasting precious life, and went about their business.

I stood in the middle of the crowd watching my crew at work, a taste of ash on my tongue, defeated in my soul. How many Buddhist extremists could I see burned, I wondered, before I became jaded? How long would it take before I would become callous to self-inflicted death in public? Would the American people grow used to seeing so many dead bodies? Would they tune out the sound of shooting, the sight of blood? Or would television's first war cause Americans to view death and destruction differently, in ways I never suspected? My questions that night and in the years that followed were only the beginning of my concerns. As with all who covered the war, I had no idea where the constant living-room exposure to death would lead.

It would be years before the war came alive on the big screen. No significant films about Vietnam appeared until the war was long over. How could they compete with reality? But eventually, nightly television no longer provided the horror and titillation that went with innocent soldiers dying twelve thousand miles from home in jungles and swamps and on uninhabited hills that were finally worth nothing. Then Hollywood stepped in and created a larger-than-life fictional landscape to keep the thrill-seekers on the edge of their seats. But many of these movies were fantasies far from the reality of war's horror and boredom. For those of who were there, Vietnam will always be a land of mixed memories. A few remembrances are good, some bad, some skewed beyond recognition. So many are dreamlike yet seem to endure in a fierce, dominating reality.

When I returned to Vietnam in 1985, I did not see one orange robe or shaved head anywhere. Buddhist monks were missing from the streets of Ho Chi Minh City. The Communist regime kept them under control and relegated them to their pagodas, thus taking away their possible strength with the people. Silent streets had become the rule, broken only by the dissonance of chugging motors. Monks could no longer parade eight abreast as they once did, shouting slogans against the government until the police dispersed them with batons and water cannon. By 1985 the government in Hanoi had finally neutralized the Buddhists and everyone knew it.

10

Tipsters and Informants

SEEKING UNDERSTANDING and insight into the murky world of Saigon politics, I turned for guidance to the Vietnamese community. I needed help from those who knew the inner workings of Saigon's secret underground life. Internal Vietnamese politics was unfathomable, unpredictable, and almost impossible to cover. No American journalist, I believe, ever had a thorough understanding of the Vietnamese version of Tammany Hall. I knew a little, but that did not help me. Looking at local politicians, I wondered how they ever accomplished anything. I needed to know how they thought, what went on in their hearts. I needed assistance in interpreting their moods and actions in order to understand life in Vietnam's wards, particularly Saigon.

To help us find our way, NBC News put many Vietnamese on the payroll. I had many paid informants—civilian and military tipsters and Vietnamese reporters—who supplied me with information on everything. The reports I received were regular from some, irregular from others. I collected information solicited and unsolicited. I paid weekly or monthly and negotiated flat fees for gossip and fancy, rumor, and, often, wistful dreams.

Sometimes I paid in dollars, sometimes in Vietnamese piasters. Dollars, "American green," were most desired. Piasters, because of rampant inflation, a wildly fluctuating black market, and the instability of the regime in power, were least desired. A few Vietnamese had bank accounts in New York, Houston, or Los Angeles. For them, checks were the best form of payment. I even used U.S. military scrip, the official money of the American military in Vietnam. These bills were small, Monopoly-sized, in basic earth tones. They were illegal anywhere but on a U.S. military base. As a journalist covering the war, I had PX privileges. I could buy scrip at airport banks and on military reservations. I was not supposed to use it for anything except American food, drink, toothpaste, toilet paper, and the like—

the necessities of civilization rarely found in Vietnamese markets. But I also used it sometimes when it was the only way to pay for important information. I had no idea what the Vietnamese did with the scrip. I heard that Vietnamese military officers illegally exchanged it for dollars when they went out of the country.

Special problems arose when a tipster wanted payment for information before I had time to check its value. If the material seemed to be worth something—that is, if it was likely to result in coverage, a few lines in a story—I would bargain in the finely honed tradition of Vietnam to arrive at a mutually agreeable fee. The tipster game never ended. Like my friends and competitors, I bought my intelligence where I could find it.

The wedding cake–styled City Hall at one end of Nguyen Hue housed the mayor of Saigon, an official I hardly knew. He had been a minor local politician who would have fit into any American city, but during the war he became a figure-head dominated by the National Police. I employed a paid informant in his office. The informant mostly had no value, the same as his boss. But he occasionally gave me information I would not otherwise have known. He sometimes told me when draft roundups would take place, and I would send a crew to get pictures of young men being tossed roughly into the backs of trucks. Conscripted against their will, they would sometimes disappear forever from friends and family. I believed the government wanted the coverage to show that Vietnam, despite its corruption, seriously wanted to pursue the war.

My informant's tips resulted in several stories that pointed up the repression and dictatorial rule of war. When the police did not get their scheduled payoff from street vendors and black marketeers, they made swift, brutal raids in public. They displayed their anger, showing who was in control. Occasionally, an American congressman's outrage over the sale of stolen American goods on the streets prompted some of these raids. The government shuttered stores it did not like and closed semilegitimate places of business that did not bribe local officials. These places would reopen when the payoffs resumed or increased. The fast start we had on some of these stories was a tribute to my informant, though I often had to prod him to divulge his secrets.

For some time I had on my payroll a member of Nguyen Cao Ky's staff. He had been with Ky from the time Ky ran the air force through his days as premier and elected vice president. My informant told me of Ky's movements when I wanted to do a story on his boss. We often tried to get the loose-mouthed premier to say something outrageous, which usually required little prompting. We pointed the camera, put up the microphone, and Ky did the rest. My insider rarely provided anything valuable but he helped me appreciate the inner workings of the government: what the often fractious Vietnamese leadership thought of each other, their people, the war, and their uneasy partner, the United States. He gave me information that contrasted with the official pronouncements, little of it factual, that I regularly received from my unpaid public and private sources at the American embassy. I knew my informant took money from other news organizations but I did not care or complain. All I wanted and needed was equal time with Ky, and that I got. For all I knew, America's propaganda arm had my informant on its big payroll, but it probably put an entirely different interpretation on what he produced. He was a blustering man, decent at heart, caring for his family. Sad to say, I kept him around mostly for amusement.

A more interesting and dangerous place where NBC had a paid informant was in the office of General Nguyen Ngoc Loan, chief of the National Police. He ran a quasi-military force that supposedly helped the Vietnamese army control the streets of the cities, towns, and villages. Wherever one looked, there stood a policeman, his slow walk and stiff back broadcasting his inflated sense of self-worth. But these men were just window dressing, as useless as tissue paper. The National Police as an entity and its men as individuals never acquitted themselves well.

General Loan gained prominence and worldwide notoriety at the An Quang Pagoda in February 1968, during the Tet Offensive. In front of NBC News cameraman Vo Suu and Eddie Adams, a photographer with the Associated Press, he shot a Viet Cong prisoner in the head in cold blood. A year before, at the age of thirty-seven, he had been appointed chief of police by Ky. As head of national security—a combined FBI, CIA, and KGB—he ran his own fiefdom. He was the youngest and cruelest backer Ky had, and everyone in and out of power feared him because he used his authority for his own enjoyment.

Many Vietnamese I knew thought Loan was insane. They felt he epitomized corruption, evil, and toughness to the extreme and had the soul of a killer. They would never say that publicly and even when they said it privately they whispered. But Loan was a team player. He remained loyal first to Ky, then to President Thieu as he ran the country deeper into the ground. In an eruption of anger, it became his fate to immortalize himself with one well-placed bullet, probably a fitting expression of Vietnamese frustration during that terrible, uncertain, and disastrous time.

I met General Loan and learned something of his fury when he summoned me to his office for a private audience in the spring of 1967. I had recently sent a Korean crew to a police station in Cholon, the predominantly Chinese district of

Saigon, following a terrorist action. They took their pictures and stayed around to see if the police would drag anyone in for questioning. The police might have had such plans but they did not want anyone to see what action they would take. They shooed the crew away, telling them to leave immediately for Saigon proper. The crew lingered, only to have the police shove them, kick them, and threaten them with major harm. Several policemen drew their guns. The cameraman and sound-man were no fools. Their story was not important enough to risk being shot. They already had pictures of a partly destroyed police station and street vendors with minor injuries. They returned to Saigon with their fearful tale and a roll of film. Though their blood pressure had risen to new heights, they were no worse for the experience.

The Vietnamese hated Koreans. The ROK, the Republic of Korea Army, fought for the South Vietnamese but was as tough and uncompromising in the field as their enemies, the Viet Cong and the NVA, the North Vietnamese Army. The Korean army quickly, often inhumanely, pacified their assigned territory, the coastal plain of South Vietnam. My Korean crews faced raw prejudice when they were in the field. I felt that this event was no exception. I went to the police captain in charge, found him to be intractable, and lost my temper. We had a scream-ing match. I told him never to threaten my people again. The Vietnamese resent yelling, and trying to bully them is a waste of time. I knew better, but occasionally I felt I had to show the flag, even if it was not smart.

Soon after this, I got a call from General Loan's office, asking me to visit him at National Police Headquarters at eleven the next morning. I thought at first that he had approved my long-standing request to profile him, or else that my informant had been found out and I was in deep trouble. It was my informant who had advised me to send a crew to the police station in Cholon for the story.

I arrived on time with notebook in hand, but I sat in an empty outer office for forty-five minutes before a sergeant ushered me in with a perfunctory nod. For a man in his position, General Loan had a surprisingly small and bare office. The dank room held a battered metal desk and a gray metal filing cabinet. It had none of the trappings normally associated with authority. Loan asked to see my Vietnamese press card and American press credentials. He looked at the photos on each, which were identical, turned them over several times, checked my signature, and slapped them down hard on his desk, making a dull thud. There was nothing else on the desk except a beat-up black telephone.

He rose and started to pace, speaking to me in Vietnamese. I understood very little of the language and tried to tell him so. He held one hand up like a traffic cop and put a finger to his lips, suggesting that I should be quiet. His voice rose and fell as he walked back and forth in front of me, occasionally patting the holstered pistol at his side. He began to smoke and offered me a cigarette. I took one of his Salems, saving my Camels in case I really needed them. He then called for a pot of jasmine tea. It arrived in a stainless steel pot with one small cup on a lacquer tray. He poured the tea with care, sipped it noisily, and placed the half-full cup on the desk where I could see it. Periodically he took a drink, pointedly ignoring my obvious thirst.

He began to yell at me, but I did not know why or what he was saying. I thought, how unlike the Vietnamese I know. It went on for forty minutes. I sat and sweated, watching his attempts to control his anger and wondering what would come next. The only English I heard from him was "no, no, no," repeated at irregular intervals. I watched his nostrils flare. I heard his frequent intakes of breath. His eyes narrowed. His lips quivered, trembled, opened wide when his eyes opened wide, which was rare. Spittle formed on his lips. I guessed that his impassioned lecture had nothing to do with my informant. He was telling me, I thought, never to question his officers again, never to raise my voice to any policeman anywhere, any time. I did not know what he planned for me. I wanted to show my anger but that would have been foolish. Trapped, I had become Loan's prisoner, and uncertain of his next move.

Suddenly he stopped shouting. He motored down to normal speech, then stopped talking altogether and abruptly left the room. More puzzled than I was before I arrived at the station, I sat for another five minutes waiting and wondering. The door finally opened and Loan stuck his head in. He motioned to me twice with his hand—something Vietnamese never do, reserving that gesture only for dogs, lower creatures on the social scale. He said, "Di di"—go—and stepped aside. I left as fast as I could and returned to the bureau, much worse for the wear. That afternoon I did very little work; I had a few extra vodka tonics and marveled over my luck.

My informant at National Police Headquarters stayed on NBC's payroll. His method of giving information was usually to warn us to avoid a neighborhood or organization where students or Buddhists were preparing to meet or march. He thought it would be safer for us not to show up where the police were wielding batons and firing tear gas. These warnings made me move crews to the scene fast. Only toward the end of my tour did my informant begin to understand why I moved so quickly when he told me to stay away. Most of his tips had little value, but those that helped were well worth the few dollars a month I gave him. The best thing about him was his inability to keep his mouth shut. Every time something was about to happen, his greed led him to tell me and every other bureau chief everything he knew. It was never a problem when many reporters were present at the scene of a tip; safety in numbers was a source of comfort.

Another source I had was a Vietnamese reporter on my staff, Germaine Loc. Germaine, tough and direct, claimed she had been a paratrooper in the North Vietnamese Army. She took nonsense from no one, wanted her pay on time, and contributed more valuable information than I let her know. Her strength was reporting from the Saigon streets and from inside the coffeehouses frequented by intellectuals and poets. She was insightful about the few dissident students and underground leaders who somehow continued to flourish despite government repression. Germaine gave us a view of the Vietnamese that we would have had difficulty getting anywhere else, and she received more money from us than most. She served as our guide to the Buddhists and Catholics and I used her as a contact to open stories on orphanages, hospitals, everyday politics, and the politics of religion. She also worked as a translator for the correspondents and crews when needed.

For all her strengths, though, it was sometimes difficult to use what Germaine passed on to us. She tried to paint word pictures, but they did not translate into stories for television. We rarely did commentary pieces, stories with a correspondent speaking directly to the camera with no moving images to cover his voice. The producers in New York did not want to know what we thought, just what we saw. Much of Germaine's material found its way onto radio, where commentary and interpretation were more at home than on TV, or into the pages of *Time* magazine, one of her other clients.

Tips and information came by many routes. Although some came unsolicited, mostly we had to make the information come to us. Only a few providers wanted nothing in return. We therefore had to develop a variety of sources that I cultivated in different ways. The easiest, most pleasant method was over a drink and food. We would go to a good restaurant, one of many that had bloomed and prospered in Saigon despite the war. For American sources who worked for the embassy or a branch of the military, the best disguise was no disguise. Whomever they represented, military men were in proper uniform when off-base. To have dressed otherwise would have been a serious error of judgment, signaling that the meal and meeting were out of the ordinary. My sources had lunch or dinner in the open with me regularly. We ate good French food and, when it was available, drank poor

French wine at La Cave, Le Roi, La Miral, Guillaume Tell, and Aterbea. Ramuncho, downstairs from the NBC bureau, always served tasty buffalo steak, black-market sirloin, fresh salad, and excellent, sweet shrimp from the Saigon River. It became my cafeteria and lunchroom where, as at my favorite restaurant in Manhattan, I was always guaranteed a table. When in public with a government or military source, I never discussed my business, the news business. We talked instead about life and love, wine and food, where we came from and where we wanted to go. There were too many difficulties in discussing anything else in a crowded room.

The briefing officers for the army, marines, air force, and navy were excellent sources of detailed information that went beyond the open sessions. Behind closed doors, they filled me in on continuing battles, battles that were due to start, troop movements, and unreported squabbles between the South Vietnamese military and their American counterparts. They helped significantly in getting our crews around the country on military transportation. This was assumed to be our due, but was not always easy to arrange. A call from MACV, Military Assistance Command Vietnam, to Tan Son Nhut often would be enough to get our crew on a plane or helicopter to the battlefront. This was part of the open coverage we enjoyed during the war. American intelligence withheld almost nothing. They would arrange to have us ferried to the battlefront to cover the start of a sizeable action. When a battle went badly and American troops suffered a deadly ambush, the military was not reluctant to get us to the scene. Though at times the public affairs office desperately wanted us to cover only victories, mop-up operations, and other actions that put the United States in a favorable light, we usually had the freedom to go anywhere.

There were a few briefing officers who talked off the record to the press too much. When they were discovered, they were made to suffer for it. Their fate was to remain a briefer but with a muzzle, cut off from vital knowledge. They were put at the bottom of the promotion list, but this happened to many information officers anyway, because they rarely saw combat. Sometimes they were sent from Saigon to the Mekong Delta or the Central Highlands, more dangerous parts of the country. I knew one officer who was sent to a minor base in North Africa where he held his briefings in the desert. Another was sent to an island outpost in the Pacific, where he had nothing to talk about except volcanic ash and water. These men's careers were hurt for their supposed indiscretions, for revealing too much of a story before its time. Not everyone in the press knew how to use inside material or how to protect their sources. But the journalist seldom suffered. It was the man in the military who saw his career end.

Most military officers who were privy to intelligence, including briefing officers, did not want open relationships with the press. But they always had more information than they could reveal during their daily sessions with reporters. Over the years I developed friendships with many of these officers. We often ended an evening in their private quarters where we drank beer, wine, and liquor as we talked about the war. We openly exchanged what we knew about everything that was taking place in Vietnam. I talked mostly about local politics. They discussed battles won and lost, battles about to end, some about to begin. Much of what I learned proved invaluable. It helped me direct my daily coverage and to make long-range plans. I could not have survived without the help I received from those men.

They were not, however, uncritical of what we did and how we did it. Often they thought the press corps played a story incorrectly, had the angle skewed, the approach wrong. They accused us of emphasizing the localized, dramatic aspect of a story. They said we missed the big picture—for example, the goal of the military in a particular battle. At times they were right. When a correspondent, cameraman, and soundman were covering a unit action—a unit as small as a squad or as big as a company—nothing else mattered but the men and the story around them. I passed the complaints along to my staff and, when we could, we tried to make it clear in our stories that what the audience was seeing and hearing was a small part of a larger battle. From the troops, there would never be an argument: even a small action was the biggest event of their young lives. When a soldier, a long-suffering grunt, faced enemy guns and bullets in dense jungle, the big picture meant nothing to him. He had to keep from getting wounded, to stay alive. The best stories ever done by the networks and wire services were those that conveyed an individual trooper's feelings and those of his small unit, the men he depended on for survival.

Dealing with military sources was a two-way street. I craved information and I obtained it. I used it to get ahead of my competition, not only at the other networks but also at the newspapers and wires. The briefing and intelligence officers gave me data they thought I needed, but they also wanted to convert me to their way of thinking. They wanted to direct me to the battles they thought were significant. I used their information to cover stories I thought would be fresh and different from the opposition. But the other bureau chiefs and reporters also tapped these sources. Exclusivity was unusual in Vietnam. It did not surprise me to see my competition leaving an intelligence session as I arrived. In a restaurant having a meal or drink with a high-placed source, I often saw someone of equal rank dining with another reporter. As competitors, we never compared notes. Did our sources?

At times we shared a tip with a noncompeting news outfit, a wire service or magazine, because we used the information differently. We shared rides with still photographers from the Associated Press, our neighbor down the hall on the fourth floor of the Eden Building, or *Time* magazine. Neither could hurt us if they got to the story first. We even shared army and marine choppers to the front with our immediate competition when we were all headed in the same direction.

We rented many rooms at the Caravelle and Continental hotels, both a short walk across the square from the bureau. It was easier on the correspondents and non-Vietnamese camera crews to live in hotel rooms with full service, food and drink, telephone, and laundry. In apartments or villas they would not have had most of these amenities. At least half the hotel rooms rented by NBC were empty at any given time because our people were out of Saigon, and I put those rooms to good use. At base camps and at the front, my staff worked closely with PIOs— public information officers—and the intelligence officers in the units they covered. On occasion these men, many of whom were young, came to Saigon on business or on a well-deserved three-day pass. They knew that when they arrived in town we would welcome them to our rooms for a night or two. We treated them to a real bed with a mattress, a hot meal, and a cold drink. They could soak in a tub or revel in a hot shower while living in air-conditioned comfort. Though the rooms were noisy from the traffic below and jet fighters above, they were far from enemy bullets and mortars. These things meant much to men who had been living in terrible field conditions.

I never blatantly asked an information officer for anything in return. But when something big happened, or was about to, we were usually tipped early. We were free to tell the story of their unit, even if it had suffered badly in an ambush or suffered heavy losses on the battlefield. We gave precious little to our field contacts, but they repaid us well once we were in their backyard. When my crews returned to the bureau, I would ask about the young lieutenants and captains whom we had treated like civilians for a night. It was a highly mobile war and these soldiers came and went, some never to reappear. Most were reassigned. Some were wounded. A few died. The memory of their fresh faces and their quiet, "Thank you, sir," will always be with me.

11

Inside the Labyrinth

THE MOST INTERESTING reporter and the most complex person I worked with in Vietnam was Nguyen Hong Vuong, whom I hired as a favor to Robert Shaplen, the Far Eastern correspondent for *The New Yorker*. Bob wrote the best political stories on Vietnam. Among his other sources, he learned what went on by listening to Vuong, who was famous for his network of insiders and his intricate explanations of how politics worked in his country.

Bob called and asked me to lunch, so we met and had a fine meal. He offered to share one of his treasures, the services of Vuong. He knew I could use Vuong's expertise and knowledge and he thought NBC had the budget to help Vuong supplement his meager income. I said yes, agreeing that Vuong would be valuable to NBC News, thus assembling another piece of the puzzle. When Bob, who was based in Hong Kong, came to Saigon, Vuong's services would first belong to him.

Vuong was thin, emaciated, a warm man in his early forties who looked as if he were in his late sixties. When we ate together, he hardly had more than a bowl of soup and a single glass of wine. His stories resembled nothing I heard elsewhere. As wonderful as they were, they had little place on television or radio. I could not use most of what he told me. Yet there was no way I could stop myself from listening to him once he started talking.

Vuong would arrive at my desk late in the morning once a week, usually Thursday. He slithered into the office. If I did not know better, I would have thought he appeared out of nowhere. He would come up the rickety elevator and through the big double doors of the office as if he were a ghost. Once seated, he would wait patiently. I never noticed him until he moved in his chair. I would then acknowledge him with a nod and continue working. He would move his chair close to my side of the desk. Then he would start speaking in a whisper. I always leaned into him to hear what he had to say and in return, he bent toward me. Sometimes I took notes but most of the time I just listened, half mesmerized by the humming sound of his softly accented English.

Vuong would fill me in on the Vietnamese and U.S. political activity of the past week. Then he would tell me what he viewed in his crystal ball for the weeks and months ahead. Real time had no place in his life. His stories were labyrinthine and lovely, almost dreamlike, filled with convoluted patterns, deceit, and evil. Life was a conspiracy to Vuong. The machinations of survival in the streets made him happy to be alive. He told me about people, places, and events—even whole periods of history—not recorded in books, much of which I had difficulty understanding. I told him his references were arcane. Vuong replied that what mattered was the essence of his tales and the way he wove them. His stories were sometimes confusing, but strangely, after months of listening to him, their meaning became clear.

During Vuong's visits, I carried on with my usual routine. I would answer phone calls, read copy, and talk to drivers, shippers, reporters, cameramen, soundmen, and other journalists who happened by. I had to follow my routine to keep the bureau humming. When other business distracted me, Vuong would pause, wait tolerantly for my attention, and then continue his monologue. He never missed a beat as he spun his web of wondrous intrigue. Over the years he proved a valuable friend willing to take me on fascinating excursions inside the Vietnamese heart and mind.

After each session Vuong insisted we have lunch. "For my strength," he would say. As his whisper receded, I would agree and we would leave the office. I, too, thought he needed to build up his strength. He looked so frail, I thought he might disappear in front of me. We usually went downstairs to Ramuncho. I tried to vary my menu but Vuong always ordered cream of tomato soup with croutons fried in garlic and a glass of red wine. He never finished any meal we shared. I once asked him why. Was it me, the food, the restaurant? Did he want to eat elsewhere, or eat something different? He said no, he had no problem with the restaurant. He had simply had enough to eat. We were good friends, he said, so I should not worry about something that was unimportant to our friendship and working relationship. He gently and politely put the subject aside, his voice quiet, sedate. I could do little but respect his wish not to bring it up again.

Many American journalists I knew preferred not to eat Vietnamese food, though I did. Occasionally I would go with a Vietnamese source or reporter to a small family restaurant. These were everywhere in the city; some were right in the yard of the proprietor's home. They were very small, often with fewer than four tables. The family would buy whatever ingredients were available; a talent for improvisation and a love of blended flavors did the rest. The menu might offer a choice of roasted sparrow, baked pigeon, braised snake, broiled frogs' legs, eel in curry, or scrambled eggs and shrimp. The family restaurants were a step above the street stalls where old men and women cooked while squatting on their haunches. These people were Far Eastern versions of short-order cooks, stooped behind their pots and pans, slowly preparing boiling noodle soups and seafood stews on portable charcoal braziers. You stood and waited, salivating with others in the crowd until you had a steaming bowl of fresh food in your hands.

Occasionally Vuong and I walked to a restaurant outside our normal orbit. I will never forget one meal Vuong ordered for me in a home-style cafe behind the Caravelle Hotel. It was a huge bowl of clear, rich beef broth with slices of meat that tasted like spiced sausage. Pencil-thin bits of green scallion floated on top.

"Is the soup good?" Vuong asked.

"Yes," I said.

"It's a very special soup for a very special friend," he said.

Yes, we were special friends, I remember thinking. Vuong was intelligent, informed, fascinating, and caring. I could not figure out, though, what was so special about the soup. I finished the bowl, drinking all the broth and eating all the sliced beef and clear noodles. I drank my Algerian red wine and followed it with a pot of jasmine tea. Vuong looked at me with a satisfied grin on his long, horsey face.

"You've been tired lately," he said.

I agreed.

"You've been working all those hours, staying up very late at night and into the morning," he said.

I wondered how he knew so much about my work habits when he visited only one day a week. My curiosity passed. The restaurant was quiet, pleasant. I relaxed.

He asked again, "Did you enjoy the soup?"

I told him I did, especially the hot mixture of red and black peppers and the tender, yet crunchy, meat. Another large grin crossed his face and he told me I had just eaten something that would increase my vigor and add energy to my body and soul.

He had my attention. In the Far East, talk always turned to what to eat and how to eat to keep healthy. I could not imagine what he would say next.

"Please tell me what this is all about so we can continue with our lunch," I said.

He laughed like a child.

"I hope you won't be angry with me," he said. "You have just had a wonderful drink."

"Yes," I said, helpless in the grip of this puzzle. "But what drink?"

"The soup," he said.

"The soup? So?" I said.

Vuong smiled. "They make the soup from the penis of a freshly killed water buffalo. It will give you strength and increase your power for years to come."

I stared at him across the table in the now empty restaurant. We were alone, but I more than he. I felt the blood drain from my face and the beginning of a gag reflex in my throat.

"It's a joke, right?" I said.

"No," he said, still smiling.

I would not have eaten the soup if I had known its contents. But the gagging subsided as quickly as it had started. I felt fine. I had been in Southeast Asia for only a year. Who was I to doubt what Vuong said and whether his magic would work or not?

I consider myself fortunate to have spent many hours learning from Vuong. He was a friend, not just someone who worked for me. Another Vietnamese who taught me much and opened his heart and mind to me was Vo Huynh, a genius among combat cameramen. He was the older brother of one of our other cameramen, Vo Suu. Huynh lived on the same floor in the Eden Building as I did, the fifth. As a Vietnamese, he was prohibited by the nightly curfew from being on the street after ten or eleven, often earlier, depending on the whim and fears of the government. When he was not in the field on assignment, Huynh spent his free time in the bureau on the fourth floor or in the disheveled Associated Press office down the hall.

We had a telex circuit open continuously, except in poor weather conditions when we could not transmit or receive. At approximately eleven each night, I would start receiving telex messages from New York over our RCA International leased line—a primitive, unreliable system that was the best we could manage in those years. It received at sixteen characters a minute, each word forming its lonely self so slowly that it was impossible to watch without going mad. When the messages were complete, not garbled or requiring repeating, I would decipher New York's thinking, complaints, and compliments. Then Huynh and I would talk. Sometimes we sat for hours in my office accompanied by the steady sixteen clicks a minute. During curfew, the noisy Hondas, Vespas, and other vehicles stayed quietly parked by their owners. The telex machine would click away, the tapping broken only by our voices. Occasionally the whistle of the police chasing down a straggler or the roar of a jeep on its rounds would punctuate the stillness.

I would sit behind my huge desk, smoking Camels and drinking coffee or Tab, one eye on the messages as they came through. The other part of me would concentrate on Huynh as he sat across from me in a dilapidated easy chair with no stuffing. When he moved in the chair, its broken springs would creak. By the time he wandered into the bureau, Huynh would have already eaten and napped. He would work on his equipment if needed or if I was busy with other matters. He was as good a repairman as any in Vietnam. What he did not know he learned quickly. Once I was free, he would come into my office, sit down, and tell me in detail about the most recent operation he had covered. He would fill me in on what he had learned from his sources in the police, the government, and the ARVN, the Army of the Republic of Vietnam. He would also let me know what he had learned from Vietnamese reporters working for the other American news agencies. The Vietnamese were curious and loved gossip, and they had an informal information exchange. They never divulged what stories they were covering. Those they kept secret. They played with rumor and sometimes even with facts. Vietnam was still an oral society, not yet overrun by mass communication. The Vietnamese loved to talk and to distribute what they knew, in what I pictured as a small wheel that never stopped turning.

The military interested Vo Huynh more than any other subject. On one wall in my office I had a huge map of Vietnam that showed every town, village, hamlet, and city, north and south. It displayed every lake, river, stream, mountain, and hill, every road, walkway, and footpath. The map came to me from the U.S. Air Force. They used it to develop bombing runs over enemy positions. So I used the same map that American artillery officers used to shell Communist positions. What it did not show, I added as I received information, especially about the Viet Cong and North Vietnamese troops. I had coded markings for American, Korean, and Australian troop positions, their formations and strengths. Much of it was guesswork, but informed and well thought out.

Huynh and I would stand in front of the map, sometimes for as long as an hour. He told me where to find the enemy—his enemy too, though he came from North Vietnam. He would point to where their troops were moving, explaining why and where they might strike next. Then we would talk about our coverage. Was it time to move a crew to the Coastal Plain? Should I get a cameraman to Can Tho in the Delta? Should I send a radio reporter to Dak To in the Central

Highlands? If I had a Vietnamese stringer available, should I put him on call for fifty bucks to hang around Pleiku and wait for the inevitable mortar attack on the air base? If the North Vietnamese or Viet Cong had breached the perimeter of a base, it could mean the start of an enemy buildup. Why was it so quiet in I Corps (pronounced "eye" corps), the marine bastion that stretched from the DMZ to Hue and from the China Sea to the border with Laos? Were the North Vietnamese regulars readying an assault? Were the troops of both armies tired and licking their wounds, or restocking to get ready for the next attack, the next big strike?

Huynh and I would talk quietly, exchanging information, mixing what we knew in a stew pot, guessing at what we did not know. Rarely was anyone else in the office, but we still talked quietly as if we were conspirators. Then he would leave me alone to decide where I would send my meager forces. The decisions I made were mine but there were many I could not have made without his wise help and incisive analysis. There were times when he was wrong, times when he was not accurate. And there were moments when he was reticent, for whatever reason. Yet he possessed a wealth of experience and was a font of information. He gave to me willingly and freely because I listened to him carefully. I always took that extra minute to pay attention to what he had to say and to the way he said it. He was an incredible resource.

Despite the evenhanded way I treated everyone, the bureau had a pecking order with Vo Huynh at the top. On the rare occasions when the situation demanded, Huynh became the unofficial representative for the Vietnamese staff. If he had gotten involved in bargaining for salary increases for drivers and shippers and renegotiating expense allowances for sound technicians and other office staff, he might have become the unofficial shop steward as well. But he also might have become seriously bogged down in administrative problems. His stature as a photographer of unusual skill and courage might have suffered. He must have known that he was walking a thin line, and wisely decided to avoid that part of bureau life. He thought he had to be careful so as not to lose his position as senior cameraman. Just as well. Huynh's friendship and expertise shaped a part of my soul and informed a part of my spirit in Vietnam. His role as my extra pair of eyes and ears on many stories was invaluable.

Without Huynh and Vuong, my knowledge of Vietnam and the Vietnamese would have been sorely lacking. They helped me understand the country and its people. Through their friendship and constant interaction, I developed an affinity for the Vietnamese and the subtle way they thought. But I had great difficulty learning their language. Huynh and Vuong, along with other Vietnamese friends and coworkers, helped by speaking to me in English. They tried to make themselves understood without sacrificing the nuances. We had our difficulties speaking to each other, but I think when we spoke slowly and chose our words with care it usually worked. There were thousands of years of difference in culture and customs between us, and I do not believe we ever approached a level of complete understanding. At times we came near to penetrating each other's minds. When we did, it was exciting, although it lasted little more than a moment. If I had understood Vietnamese, there is no telling what I might have learned.

12

Saigon City Desk

APRIL 1967. From Sunday to Sunday, no day in Saigon was ever the same as another. This day started peacefully. Then, as suddenly as if by magic, the first real monsoon rain of the season came whipping out of the sky. The heavy clouds sent down raindrops the size of half-dollars. Tons of water fell on the streets and buildings and flooded the already muddy back alleys.

I was crossing Tu Do Street, returning from lunch at the Blue Diamond, when the storm came. I ducked into the archway of a souvenir shop owned by an Indian who was a money changer on the black market. I was soaked to the skin. I wore handmade Vietnamese rubber-soled sandals, made from discarded tires and leather thongs held together by soldered brass tacks. I never wore socks because of the heat. My uniform of the day, the week, the month, was lightweight tan chinos and a short-sleeved cotton shirt. My Vietnamese amah, or maid, kept my clothing clean. With my PX privileges and my tailor in Hong Kong, I had more shirts than I needed or had time to wear. Some foreigners in the Far East had shirtmakers because it was cheaper to have shirts made to fit than to alter shirts from the store.

Sadly, the Camels in my shirt pocket were wet beyond salvation and fell apart at my touch. I refused to carry them in the bulky plastic waterproof case favored by GIs and other Americans. I would soon have to make a PX run for my monthly allotment. Smoking three packs a day was not easy, but I managed to mix Salems with the Camels to help take the edge off my raw throat. I also knew a fresh supply of American beer had recently arrived at the PX. I would make that trip soon to stock up on both essentials.

In five minutes the storm subsided and the rain stopped. The sky again became bright, the air still. The temperature cooled, but just for a moment, by a scant two or three points from the 98-degree mark. It would be hotter still before the day ended. Water steamed off my body and clothing as I walked. By the time I arrived at the Eden Building, I was almost dry. I went to my apartment, changed into fresh clothes, and went downstairs to my air-conditioned office. I planned to attack the problems I faced daily in the bureau and with my bosses in New York.

Because I often responded defensively in the face of criticism, Reuven Frank thought that I shot too fast from the hip. He believed I attacked before I knew all the facts, especially when New York came down on me for something it thought I had not handled properly. In his most recent note he had strongly chided me for what he called my "frequent bouts of temper." He told me to hold back and neutralize my caustic tongue, especially in cable and telex messages that might be read by anyone. I appreciated his advice. He was partly right. I did sometimes overreact, but part of it was an act for the hardworking Saigon staff. I also had to show the sacred news desk and producers that we were the ones who put it on the line every day. We were the ones who went without sleep, ate lousy food, sometimes drank too much, and played too hard when the chance came our way, and we knew the story best.

We fought impossible odds and won more times than we lost. Too much happened most of the time for us to cover everything. The staff was too small. We had unreliable equipment that did not work in jungle heat, in rain, in sand, while being carried through streams and taken on long walks in the sun. Digby Jones was a master of improvisation, innovative and often brilliant, and he and the staff managed to keep the equipment together with toothpicks, paper clips, and chewing gum. But covering any part of the war consistently took a miracle. I had difficulty conveying that reality to the producers in New York. I understood I would probably never make them understand. I felt as if we were in a plastic bubble, rolling and floating with the changing wind. However, the bubble never burst because the collective spirit in the bureau worked to keep us together until the next crisis appeared.

Despite Reuven's admonitions, I continued to send tough messages to the producers in New York whenever I received a tough message from them. I knew my messages would upset them. But at more than twelve thousand miles from home, I could scream and get away with it. I was chauvinistic and possessive about NBC News Saigon. It could not be any other way. I didn't care if my emotions ran too high for the New York newsroom. It was the only way to exist in this hothouse.

The Saigon newspapers published daily lists of planned power failures. American advisors to the Vietnamese government had a plan to conserve power on the city's weak grid. Planned brownouts were the solution, and that made sense, but publishing when and where they would take place was irresponsible. The Viet Cong were ever on the loose and they read the newspapers too. They knew when and where the city would be dark and could strike with impunity. An excellent terror tactic was to blow up district power stations and kill a few important officials when the lights were off. Vuong told me the VC believed that further cutting the available electricity would make more people upset with the government and in the mood for revolt. But that did not happen. Perhaps the populace had been at war too long and assaults on their already difficult lives were meaningless.

Each morning we checked *The Saigon Post,* an English-language newspaper, and the other Vietnamese newspapers to see if we were scheduled to lose electricity. When the electricity died without warning, as it often did, we would check with the Vietnamese police and the American MPs to see if the VC were at work. No, they would usually tell us in pleased voices, the power failure had been scheduled. If we were so smart and such good journalists, why couldn't we read the papers and not annoy them with trivial questions? Nonsense, we said. We did read the papers; we were not on the list. Hmm, was their only response. We learned never to trust the published information. It was naive to assume the lists were accurate, however much we wanted to indulge in a dream.

On days when there was no electricity, many NBC staffers arrived at work breathless after trudging the four long flights of stairs to the bureau. But they learned to survive without the elevator, something they had to do frequently. To make sure the New York teletype always worked, I bought and installed four giant wet-charged batteries as a backup to the electrical power system. They were very expensive on the black market and I did not want to buy them there, but it proved cheaper and faster than getting them from New York, Hong Kong, or Tokyo. When we didn't need the battery system for the leased circuit, we turned it on during blackouts and brownouts so we could charge batteries for our cameras and sound gear. The wet cells worked for the few hours we used them and helped us survive the sudden losses of electricity. The expense was worth it.

Reuven Frank and I discussed how long anyone should cover the war. He thought the current minimum of six months was about right. I said it was too short. It took six months just to adjust to the weather, the squalor, the smells, the water, the strange food, and the different culture. Meaningful experience and knowledge came only after those long months of learning and training. Then a reporter could do justice to the war. I thought that one year was essential for correspondents and camera crews. I wanted them to stay at least eighteen months. If a man could adjust, he could make it. Some never did. It was apparently not important enough to argue about, and Reuven mulled over our discussion. I held firm. Together we made no decision.

Every two months, NBC News granted the staff—except the Vietnamese—ten days of R and R (rest and recreation) outside Vietnam. This allowed them to restock their lives, restore their sense of self, sleep in clean sheets, and eat dinner without a barrage of overhead shelling. But something always intruded and the staff would have their vacations delayed. New York granted the privilege, then I suspended it when emergency after emergency occurred, because we were understaffed. It was happening too often and I worried that I could no longer afford to delay R and R. It was bad management to continue a practice of delay. Each man knew the dangers of Vietnam and the unease of living in Saigon. Their hearts and minds were often in another place. Everyone worked at an intense level not found in any other bureau in the world. They went into combat because it was what they were there to do. Some returned to combat for ego gratification, others—I liked to think—for NBC News.

The longer I contemplated the constant pressure I put the staff under, the more difficulty I had with it. Each correspondent, cameraman, and soundman had to understand that we could live without him for ten days every eight weeks. They had to refuel, slow themselves down, and get ready for the next set of battles, real and imagined. I, too, had to have my R and R. I had to learn to walk away from my desk and leave it behind. But I found that to be impossible the way the war was going. I didn't see myself being able to get into a healthy routine until the following year. Then I would be out of Vietnam on schedule, every two months. So I hoped.

I rarely said anything harsh to the correspondents about how they were doing. I had to keep their morale high, even though mine sometimes flagged. I tried to be honest with them about my feelings, but I never revealed all of New York's thoughts. Only on the rare occasions when New York pressed me did I say something unkind. I had to be discreet or I would have had a revolt. On the other hand, my staff often heard only what it wanted to hear, believed only what it wanted to believe. Nothing frightened me more than watching grown men sinking in a swamp of self-delusion. We all suffered it regularly in our business.

Sometimes production fell off because there was no large military operation in progress. To keep fresh, we busted our humps to produce stories even when there was little news. But the feedback we required came to us slowly. Sometimes the New York desk did not comment on the technical and editorial quality of our work for three days. Were they too busy to tell us how we were doing? I believed their lack of appreciation of our isolation from the rest of the world governed their inability to respond to our needs.

I asked headquarters for daily usage reports from each news show. The crews and I needed to know how the producers looked on the material we sent them. I suggested that a New York copyboy write a log of each program at the end of each shift and transmit it to me. But I rarely received usage reports. Having spent many years in New York, I knew better than most how long it took to get things done but that was a poor excuse for not doing something as simple as creating reports on how our pieces were used.

If New York decided a piece did not work, they would send a "rocket," a sparsely worded, mean and thoughtless attack cable, about what they considered our failure to produce. The purpose of a "rocket" was to goad us into action but it often backfired, causing us to become angry and resentful with the home office. And that made it more difficult for me to keep spirits high, morale up.

For example, CBS aired a story about air force personnel in Vietnam building a dam in their spare time. We were competitive on the story but *Today* decided against it. Bill Corrigan sent a "rocket" saying there had been a lack of "usable film." Who was he kidding? What he really meant was, Sorry, no shots fired, no one dead. I answered his cable and said we did not plan to do anything different. When a news editor with the nickname "Bang-bang" passes on a story because there's not enough action, New York is the one with the problem. I thought we were doing well. Did someone want changes? Let me know. Don't pull any punches, I said.

Once a week the Department of Defense sent to Saigon a kinescope recording of the three networks' news broadcasts. This was a film made directly from the television tube. Watching the kinescopes in a theater at JUSPAO suggested to me that we were doing very well. Our competition followed us on many stories. I thought they had a weak, dull approach. Now and then they scored and beat us, which was bound to happen. But I felt our well-rounded approach said more and gave the audience a better picture of the insanity that people in Vietnam faced twenty-four hours a day. In the space of a few weeks we produced stories on the black market, the university crisis, the cabinet crisis, and a debate in the Constituent Assembly. During the same time, we covered a variety of breaking stories, including the immediate aftermath of several terrorist attacks in our neighborhood. We had been to the major battle of the month and four minor military operations. Our highlight pieces were two stories about the excellent care that wounded American soldiers were getting in field hospitals. CBS and ABC had barely recognized the existence of some of these stories.

Once we filed a series of stories on troops doing what they usually do on patrol: nothing. We planned the stories to show what really takes place most days for most patrols. New York's play report complained, "Nothing happens." Well, they got the point of the stories. Or did they? Did they mean that nothing happens during the stories and that is why they were not interested? Or that nothing happens because of the way we presented the stories? I did reach a point where I became frustrated and exasperated. Being too close to the story is its own problem. That was why I needed to go on R and R.

It was often my good luck to not know why the producers had passed on a story. For that, I was usually better off. It was disturbing to read comments like "Dull," "Same old pictures," "Same old story," "Nothing new." These never helped. I did not understand them. Were they the words of a so-called "astute" editor? They told me the editor had no appreciation of the story. Or perhaps that the story, and maybe the war, had lost its appeal and glamour. Both points were probably true. We had spoiled everyone with the high quality of our earlier material. That I knew. The new stories often suffered by comparison. Reuven Frank wrote that I should do a better selling job. But how hard could I sell without overselling? How far could I go without making a fool of myself, the correspondent, and the crew by pitching a story beyond its worth? Because I had to sell, there would always be a tendency to oversell. I could not take the chance of becoming the Willy Loman of NBC News. I preferred to undersell what we covered. I always got a charge when one of our stories took New York by surprise.

Only when I had the script and field notes could I give New York a thorough rundown. But I did not always see the script for a story until after it was shipped. I asked the correspondents to provide a separate script and dope sheet—the cameraman's notes—for my viewing, but that was not always possible. Most stories did not conform to a template. The need to ship on tight schedules, often on MedEvac helicopters, sometimes did not allow me to edit field material closely. When a crew could, it called me from the field on military phones. The signal, though, was sometimes weak, the call often useless.

At times the cameramen talked about art, their art. They would start speaking of angles and close-ups and "camera truth" and the New Wave techniques of the French. When they did, I ruthlessly cut them off. I reminded them why they were covering the war and pulled them back down to earth. Their emotions had to be kept in check, their egos stilled for the moment. I told them they had to cover the war in pursuit of fact. Forget art. Concentrate on air strikes, snipers' bullets, terrorist grenades. Forget about pot and LSD. Their highs would come from competition. Forget about falling in love. Their spirits would soar when their eyes saw things through the lens that no one else had ever seen.

Most correspondents did not have time to generate stories outside of direct combat. The demand for combat stories was too great. There were other stories besides the firefights, but New York was mainly interested in *the* story, always the war, ever the war. To give the correspondents some variety, I tried to be selective with their assignments. I, like them, wanted quality rather than quantity. But I saw it as a simple equation: The more stories we produced, the more airplay we got. Then the minor stories received recognition out of proportion to their value. It surprised us to see these secondary pieces showered with praise.

When there was hard combat and Americans were wounded and died, everything we filmed got air time. Those pieces appeared on all the news shows throughout the day. Death generated excitement about the war. It also bred more coverage. Without heavy combat and filmable firefights, we averaged between ten and twelve stories a week. With combat, the number rose to sixteen or seventeen, including riots and terrorist attacks. It would have been ideal to ship three different stories a day that gave New York the variety it wanted during heavy usage. But we could not control the bunching of stories, or how and where the stories occurred.

Sometimes I developed an individual story and we covered it. The correspondents had the right and mandate to improvise in the field. Naturally I missed at times. Once a squad of Viet Cong sappers breached the perimeter of Tan Son Nhut Airport. There were wounded, some damage to the base, but no deaths. I could not move a crew fast enough to get a decent piece to New York. We were in another part of Saigon working on an exclusive report, a rare enterprise effort, and could not get there in time. It was always a dilemma. What should I do? Go for the immediate, flashier action and damn the better, more meaningful story? Knowing there would be other Tan Son Nhut stories, I thought I made the right decision. I knew there would not be many unusual enterprise efforts and I believed we had to cover them when we could. Generally, though, combat had to take precedence, especially when I had so small a staff and no team could be out of place for too long.

During lulls in the fighting, when New York turned down stories that we considered to be of more than passing interest, their decisions puzzled us. Yes, I questioned every producer's judgment. If I did not, I would not have been doing my job, protecting and supporting my territory. I lived by a simple rule: When New York did not use a story, the producers were questioning my judgment as an assignment editor. If we did not cover a battle or a military operation, I usually had a strong reason for staying away. I did not mind criticism—it was their network, their privilege—but too many editors and administrators leaped before they looked and sent us injudicious complaints. I rarely shouted back because it did not make sense to dwell on any single report. Each day that passed brought new problems. I had to look toward tomorrow, which was always a mystery, and leave today behind. It did not mean I had sheathed my fangs.

I sent correspondent Bill Wordham, cameraman Bob Welch, and soundman Vo Suu to the central coastal plain near Bong Son where the First Cavalry was based. I put them there for one story, telling them to get into combat. Firefights were everywhere. They shrugged and departed on schedule. When they arrived, they moved quickly. Usually the most dangerous mission a crew went on was a long-range reconnaissance patrol. These men went one better. They headed out with the "Blues," twenty-eight men of the Air Cavalry who flew in helicopters as an advance guard looking for trouble. These troopers often got hit and, as we said in Saigon, their "kill count" was high. They entered firing. They left firing. There was no middle ground. Bill and his crew were the first television crew to go with them. They flew at treetop level, ran into snipers, expended heavy ammunition in return, fired canisters of CS gas, killed the Viet Cong they could see, and allowed their medic to work on a badly wounded enemy soldier. The team filmed every bit of the story. General Norton, the First Cavalry commanding officer, had not expected his men to run into trouble of that nature, which usually meant an enemy buildup in the area. He was delighted that his men returned unscathed and that we had our story.

I shipped the story with Wordham's strong script and recommended that the piece be considered for major airplay. New York passed on the story and gave no reason for its decision. I had asked New York to critique a particular story only ten or fifteen times. I did it again with Wordham's Bong Son adventure. I received an answer that stated, "After screening the raw footage, the film editor thought it was routine patrol stuff, but otherwise a solid piece." How could it be both? Had anyone read Wordham's copy? Had they read my cable? Did they really look at the film?

Wordham, as usual, stayed low-key. He never oversold stories. A producer before he was a correspondent, he knew a good story, especially when he had been in the middle of it. Vo Suu was also a pro. He had seen his share of action, and he said this had been a very rough experience. I did not contend the piece had value because the crew had been in danger. That was not my style, the bureau's style, or NBC's style. I did not demand that all our pieces have a place on NBC News's limited airtime. But I thought there had to be a greater appreciation of what we did. Our people had to have the respect they deserved for doing their job. I told Reuven Frank that one frustration of my job was bad communication, the frustration of trying to reach a party who is deaf, dumb, blind, and unable to appreciate anything you've done. After my mild tantrum, Bill Corrigan sent me a note that said, "Stop letting the correspondents and crews push you around." Pure New York nonsense, I thought. Had I become cynical? Yes. But maybe smarter, because I never answered Corrigan's message.

Without warning, the war started changing. The Pentagon announced the completion of the troop buildup. Early in our coverage, combat had come to us. But now the larger force had put the enemy on the run and, three times in any given week, my crews would spend their day chasing ghosts. Cameraman Jim Eury had been out alone for three days watching Operation Junction City in Tay Ninh and he came back with nothing. Wordham returned from a patrol through the jungle with nothing more to show for it but nine hours in the heat with bugs, ants, and leeches. He turned the fruitless trek into a story about the hell a twenty-year-old trooper goes through most of his days in the field. Enterprising? Yes. Unique? Not really. Howard Tuckner and a Korean team spent all day chasing around Junction City looking for Viet Cong troops who had become phantoms. They came back without a story. David Burrington managed a rare phone call to me from the field. He and cameraman Jim Watt and soundman Vi Giac had spent two days roaming near the DMZ looking for the remnants of a major battle. We had had a tip that a thousand marines had killed fifty-eight North Vietnamese troops. So many men for so little in return. Burrington and his crew also had no story. They did, however, have a frightening experience. Their marine helicopter had mechanical trouble and had to turn back to the base camp at Dong Ha. Mechanics found it had a faulty piston, bad enough to make it crash. They were lucky to return safely. I told Burrington to pack it in and return to Saigon.

Weeks went by when we produced hardly any stories. I would run into people from CBS and ABC and we would look at each other, shrug, and walk away. When we met at the regular briefings, we talked about how we hoped our New York offices understood that we were not standing around waiting for the action to come our way. I knew my staff had been digging, but they had come up with almost nothing. I assumed the following week it probably would change.

To try to make something happen, I moved two crews to Danang for a few days. Sources told me the Delta could kick off in a few weeks with a major American operation. Pacification, the darling of the Johnson administration, was no longer being talked about, but New York had no interest anyway. Village elections across South Vietnam were in a month. Buddhist-led demonstrations against the government threatened to keep the streets busy in Saigon and Hue. We continued to cover everything we could. My sources in military intelligence had promised me war. When nothing happened, they slunk away, red-faced. The enemy picked his spots with care, where he would suffer the least casualties. We knew there would be intense battles, but where were they? Meanwhile, I made my old plea to the producers in New York that they should get used to what they called "the routine patrol" because that is what they were going to get. Routine? These kids marched through the jungle as bait, looking to engage the enemy. Who decides a patrol is routine? No one who has gone into the field will ever say anything was routine in Vietnam.

The men I had working for me went on these patrols for many reasons. Ego. Me. Pride in their job. Recognition from New York. Notice from their peers. Competition. One American cameraman understood appreciation only in terms of getting more money. Vo Huynh appreciated our strong relationship. I wished I could increase his pay. I recognized his ability and brilliance as a combat photographer. I teamed Huynh with every green reporter going on his first assignment for field training. That was recognition of a sort, though it added unnecessary tension and danger to Huynh's life. Howard Tuckner got his job satisfaction from appearing on camera and posing when he did. George Page got his from what he called accomplishment. David Burrington enjoyed doing what he did; he was mostly having a good time and loved the business. Bill Wordham was what he had wanted to be for years, a correspondent covering a terrific story.

Some colleagues we called "war lovers." These were correspondents, cameramen, even a bureau chief or two. They worked for all the different media, and each one was a problem. Look around, no matter what war, and you can easily spot them. They exist wherever you find troops and, strange as it appears, they seem to live for being close to the action where they might be under fire. They are always at the front or at least near it. Of course, in Vietnam the front was always moving and changing. On any given day, there could be hundreds of fronts seeing action simultaneously. But these men were usually there for themselves first and their audience a distant second, though the audience became the beneficiary of their experience through the back door of their perception. They sometimes wore army fatigues they bought on the black market. If not fitted, these covered their bodies like loose-fitting robes. Some took their new clothing, wrapped like fish and chips in yesterday's *Saigon Post,* to the nearest tailor's shop on Tu Do Street, where they had them fitted almost to their skin. These men could not afford to gain weight, but in Vietnam hardly anyone added pounds. Weight loss was more common, so they could always depend on their tiger-striped, camouflage uniforms or their plain khaki fatigues to fit perfectly when they went to the field to cover themselves with their perception of glory. Some even wore a sidearm, the worst violation of the concept of the reporter as noncombatant that you could find. The weapon was usually a .45 with a bullet "up the spout," meaning in the chamber ready to fire, making these war lovers even more hazardous to be near. Most reporters and crews I knew did not want to be with them, especially when riding into combat. Staying in the field with them was dangerous. Even walking Saigon's streets next to one of them was foolish. It never made good sense to put yourself in harm's way unnecessarily.

I came to South Vietnam for the story, the adventure, the action, the experience, my career, the future, my ego. For all the reasons we gave for why we were there, we really could not list every reason. None of us denied it was the unforgettable, major experience of our lives. There was not enough money to compensate for the danger and stress. Someone had to sit in my chair, though. I looked on nothing as permanent because my life until Vietnam had been impermanent. When the young American cameraman was offered a raise and asked for more money I told him there would be no bargaining. I said New York's offer was final. This is what we are giving you, I said. It is more than you made when you arrived. It is more than you can make at home. I knew he would not quit. If he really wanted to leave Vietnam, nobody would get in his way. He suddenly became a small boy. He backed down, realizing for the first time where he was and that he would never have the same experience again, anywhere. He said he could not leave. He said he would tone down his demands and keep his mouth shut in the future. He thanked me for the raise. Then he said, "Please send me out now because Saigon makes me nervous. I can't see my enemy." I held him back in Saigon for three days to calm him down before sending him to the field. He remained loyal and developed into a very reliable, creative cameraman.

These young men, many in their mid-twenties, were there because this was where they wanted to be. I wondered how to handle these volunteers. They were shot at and they became scared. They prayed that they would not get hurt or killed, though they would never admit it. I prayed the same, though I would not then admit it. We paid them almost nothing to face hidden enemy guns. American materialism and financial gain did not provide the answer. We all paid for the risk and the danger we faced. If the offer was not what we wanted, we could break the contract and return home. It was our life. That is not as cold as it seems. I knew you could never pay a man too much for risking his life. Until that life ends, we will never know its value. How do we judge a life's worth when it seems so bright and glowing? To whom is that life meaningful? The simple answer is that it has meaning to the individual and his loved ones. The men in the bureau put their lives on the line every day. Yes, a cliché. I have no other way to put it. Almost no soldier goes into battle enjoying war. Few enjoy killing. They fight because their government says they must. Most will feel the pain for years to come. But what makes journalists hunt the unknown, especially in combat, with the rewards so limited, so slight? How many journalists can remain unscarred after exposure to fear in battle and frequent danger to life?

As with the Buddhists—and we were in a predominantly Buddhist country—each man had to find his own path. In combat he always faced the unknown. There he might find an answer, but not necessarily. He had the right to refuse further risk. He alone had the power to renegotiate his life, his future, his money. NBC sometimes had to fire a man because he made too many demands. We could not judge an individual's return in dollars or ego satisfaction. At some point it became a question of diminishing returns. The product—that is, the coverage—suffered with the man. In the end, the product often counted more than the man. I say that without being cynical. It was always easier to get a different product than to salvage the man. If the story vanished, there would always be another story tomorrow. For the man, there might not be a tomorrow.

In one typical week, I sent a team back to Operation Junction City, an endless operation where the troops chased the ghosts of the Viet Cong hierarchy without success. After a long delay, we finally secured an inside view of a Vietnamese prison. A crew covered a big Catholic rally and demonstration Saturday at the main cathedral on Kennedy Square. On Sunday, George Page and his crew filmed a piece on the failure of land reform. New York should understand the meaning of that story even without a firefight, I thought.

I still needed R and R, sunshine in another country, a change of food, a drink and ice I could trust, and a long sleep. Our new correspondent, Charles Murphy, arrived and I sent him immediately to Danang for his in-country orientation. Then I departed for a much-needed rest.

I took my vacation in Taiwan and returned after ten days to life in Saigon and the bureau. All my rest meant nothing when the bureau suffered its first wounded correspondent. Ron Nessen (later press secretary to President Gerald Ford) and his crew were on patrol outside Pleiku in the Central Highlands where, during a brief skirmish, he got hit at 1:30 in the afternoon. His soundman, Curtis Mitchell, whom we called Tony, was the first to get to him. He held Ron while blood gushed from his chest. Grenade fragments had entered his body and he went into shock. Medics treated him in the field. Then Tony helped make a litter out of bamboo poles and field jackets to carry him to a medical helicopter that was sent to evacuate him. Ron was in a Pleiku field hospital twenty minutes later.

I did not hear about the incident until 6:40 that night. After learning that Ron's wound was serious but not critical, I informed New York and my staff. The next three days were nightmarish. The correspondents and crews hovered near my desk filled with fear. Reality had struck unexpectedly, and they probably wondered if they would be next. I also felt it. When I dispatched a crew, I always did it with apprehension. I did not lose sleep, but the thought of someone getting hurt was hidden deeply in my mind. Over those three days I had to show strength. I had to let everyone see their chief was everything he should be. And I did not enjoy it. I am not a good actor. I had to keep New York executives from flying in to hold my hand and massage the bureau. The staff needed assurances that all would be well. We were a family. None of us was alone. Yet, I had no one to talk to about my fear and anxiety. I could not let my guard down. I could not show weakness.

I did not sleep for three nights. On the fourth day, we learned that Ron would fully recover. Finally, a positive feeling set in. The pressure from New York lifted and their rare phone calls stopped coming. The telex slowed to its normal traffic. The staff relaxed as much as it could. I started sending crews to the field again and they seemed anxious to go, perhaps to allay their own anxiety. We had our fingers crossed that no one else would get hurt.

In the confusion of Ron being wounded, cameraman Peter Boultwood not only filmed the story, but he did a stand-up and a narration to cover his footage. He outdid himself. He had film of the troops and Ron on patrol, the immediate aftermath of Ron's wounding, Ron lying in the grass while a medic attended him. Peter had shots of the MedEvac arriving and Ron being loaded on, followed by the helicopter departing for the hospital. Peter's narration was clear. His crisp British accent helped cool the heat of the story.

Peter told me he would not appear again in front of the camera. That was fine with me. He was not a newsman like our reporters. Peter had enormous talent when he pointed his camera at the action and human suffering. When Peter concentrated behind the camera, there was almost no one better. He became articulate with the camera and used it the way someone else might use his voice. The camera became his outlet, his means of speech. However, he was far down my list in how he cared for his equipment and the people with whom he worked. He had poor relations with Digby Jones because Digby had high standards for the equipment he serviced and demanded a like response from the crews. Peter gave him little in return. There were days when I was wary of sending him on a difficult assignment, not sure his equipment could survive the bump and grind of hard coverage. I had assigned Nick, our new soundman, to him permanently because Nick showed a feel and respect for the gear. Peter was slow to prepare for a story and equally slow packing to cover one. I found him to be unusual and interesting. Sometimes I believed he would have been better off as an intellectual, perhaps an Oxford don. However, he chose life as a combat cameraman in a difficult war in a difficult country. His troublesome tour was due to end soon. I will never forget him for the honorable and professional manner in which he handled the story of Ron Nessen being wounded.

Most of my problems with the staff were not serious. They were minor, and usually easy to repair over a cigarette and a beer. Howard Tuckner, however, caused more anguish for me than he was worth. As much as I talked to him, it never did any good. During one heavy action along the DMZ lasting three days under terrible conditions, he needlessly exposed his crew to danger. I expected my correspondents to seek action in battle. But it was something else when a correspondent deliberately moved his crew to the wrong flank during a firefight to give himself a better angle for his on-camera appearance. The crew could not believe it when it found itself in front of the attacking marines instead of behind them, where it should have been. Safety in combat is relative. Journalists must work on the theory of considered risk. But what Howard did was foolish. Camera crews were fast becoming reluctant to go into the field with him. There was no reason for a reporter to put himself and his crew in jeopardy. If alone, you could take whatever risk you chose. But when you are responsible for two other men in battle, they and you come first, not the story.

Of all the correspondents, Howard really scared me with his personal drive for glory. I had the feeling, now that Nessen had suffered a wound, that Howard's sense of competition extended too far. I thought he might even be looking for a "million-dollar wound," a ticket to fame that one buys with one's own blood.

When New York was not crabby and thought we were doing exceptional work, they had a tendency to go overboard. Because of all the praise, certain correspondents mounted their own pedestals. This threw their perspective out of whack and they lost sight of their true ability and talent. Inflated egos resulted that I would have to live with for years to come. I asked the New York desk and the show producers to temper their superlatives when they sent their much-appreciated notes of praise for good stories and for the few stories that were exceptional. We loved praise. When those cables or telex messages arrived, I copied them, distributed them to everyone, and posted them on bulletin boards. They were very important to the life of the bureau. However, some correspondents believed they had done everything on their pieces to the exclusion of their teams. They conveniently forgot the collaboration that made the story. I had difficulty controlling these men. Unfortunately, once that attitude appeared in the open, it had the power to change the bureau. I told New York they had to understand I lived with these men. I had to make them act according to my needs, the shows' needs, and within the parameters of what we at NBC News were trying to accomplish.

Howard Tuckner fit this profile perfectly. I had to tell him specifically what I wanted on almost every story. The simple stories, such as combat, that direct and produce themselves were the exception. Howard put down too many words, striving for descriptions of events that fought with the pictures, a bad habit and one that led to weak writing. After almost a year he still did not realize that when the pictures and sound are strong, fewer words are necessary. He could not write a straight narrative line. When I could, I reviewed his material before it shipped. Even after it shipped, it was possible to do a fresh narration track over the radio circuit we filed each evening. I refused to think how much worse it would have been had I not been there to look at his copy. His courage had expanded along with an ego that had swelled beyond definition. His inferiority complex placed him constantly on the attack. He knew sports and frequently maintained that the best offense was a good defense. In the bureau, no one was more blatantly aggressive. He was the most insular character I have ever met.

On average, Howard produced less than any man in the bureau. He believed it beneath his dignity to cover anything other than hard combat. His story interests were men at war, in war, or on the edge of war. If there were no weapons fired in his piece, he felt the story was a failure and he had wasted his time. Behind his back, his colleagues called him a war lover, but I did not think he fit the definition. Howard did not love war, as some correspondents did. But he calculated that combat coverage got him more attention. Over the summer he covered stories everywhere in the country, many by default. He drew the big ones because of Ron Nessen's wounds, other correspondents being on R and R, and Dean Brelis's being on a reduced work schedule as he prepared to rotate back home. Incidentally, my policy was clear. When a correspondent or crew member was "short," meaning his time in country was almost up, he remained in Saigon, close to home. It lessened the danger he might have run into at the end of a tour. So Howard got the big ones. He received many notes from New York praising his courage and his close action pictures. He started to posture and to pose even when he was not on the air. He kept exposing his crew to unwarranted danger in heavy combat. I warned him, scolding him futilely. In response, he went on the attack against me, the crews, and New York, finding a fault with everything, everywhere. He rarely showed compassion for human error, particularly in the military, where nineteen-, thirty-, and fifty-year-old soldiers were under profound stress. Howard had no sense of history, of the time we were living in, and the men caught in the web of a world he refused to allow himself to understand.

I had to live with Howard and others like him every day. I served as their wet nurse and I teased them, egged them on, pushed them, prodded them. They might have ended up hating me, but that was something I did not care about. Some did not listen or if they did, they did not hear what I said. They would wonder why a story did not appear the way they envisioned it when they shipped. They wondered why an editor in New York, Chicago, or Burbank changed the pictorial sequence. Why, they asked, was the narrative different from what they sent in? Did the editor and producer have the right to change sequences? I told them that sometimes producers make changes to help the audience understand the story. Producers in New York stripped the narration, shortened the story, and switched sentences to have a piece make better sense. Complexity in a story had importance, but when a story became too dense, especially in a two-minute piece, the density crowded out the complexity and the audience lost the thread. I warned the correspondents to tell their stories without fat. Their limited time on the air, similar to space in a newspaper, meant there was little or no room for additional material. I wanted them to get to the heart of their stories quickly. Unfortunately, complexity became a casualty of war.

I kept thinking that the unsung heroes in our bureau were the cameramen, not the correspondents. They operated gear that was often falling apart as they used it. But with their skill and faith in their equipment, when they pointed and focused they had an uncanny ability to see and create. I wondered if the audience understood who did what when we covered a story.

Living with Howard and all he put me through every day became too time-consuming and even painful for me, particularly with everything else I had to do. I had to get him off the combat kick and see if he could do something that was not quite as easy and far less dangerous. After weeks of frustration during a busy time in the bureau, I finally had a long session with Howard that took place behind closed doors in my apartment. We drank a few beers. We sipped tea. And we talked about everything. Everything. I hoped to have some effect on our relationship and how he saw his future as a correspondent. But now that Ron Nessen and Dean Brelis had rotated home and were gone from the bureau, Howard believed he had become the king of Saigon. He told me he was the best there was, the best there will ever be. The man fascinated me because he had not heard one word I said. There would be no solution until he returned to New York or another post. We had to make do and learn to live with each other. I hoped we would survive in one piece.

I had become the most fortunate bureau chief in the world. My staff consistently produced strong stories. They deserved the highest praise possible. We were covering the most important foreign story and had equal call on its domestic side. The news shows used more stories from our bureau than from any other foreign bureau for NBC News. I made almost all the assignments. It was unheard of in the news business to have the freedom I had carved out for myself. But how much power did I really have? I constantly fought with New York to maintain my independence. I was in Saigon. They were thousands of miles from me and the war. I knew the story where it was happening, from the ground up. They did not. Those in the States knew only what we presented and they had to trust the bureau's judgment. They were influenced by the Congress, the White House, the demonstrations in the streets, editorials in *The New York Times* and *The Washington Post*. To them, the war appeared fantastic and had become an unpredictable annoyance. I would have liked to bring them to the real world, here, where we faced the unexpected daily.

104-106 Nguyen Hue. The bureau was on the fourth floor and my apartment on the fifth. *Photo by Gary Bel.*

A view of the outer office
through a fish-eye lens.
I'm sitting, chief engineer
Digby Jones is standing,
and two cameramen are
seated at the desk outside
the maintenance room.
The desk to my left was
used by the drivers. *From
the author's collection.*

At my desk in my office at
night, speaking to Wilson
Hall, who for some reason
is wearing a suit—not the
usual garb in Vietnam.
Under the huge map on
the right is Josephine's
desk and the two telex
machines, one with strips
of message paper hanging
over the front. *Photo by
Gary Bel.*

The correspondents' room,
cluttered, crowded, and
messy. The film projector
at the back was used for
showing kinescopes sent
by the New York office and
the Department of De-
fense. *Photo by Gary Bel.*

One wall of the workshop
where the engineers helped
keep the cameras and sound
gear in working condition.
Photo by Gary Bel.

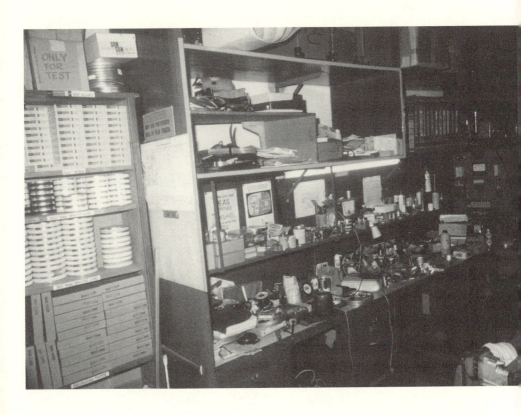

Cameraman Vo Huynh
and correspondent Howard
Tuckner. Huynh's Auricon
camera is hanging upside
down from a branch.
Courtesy of Vo Huynh.

Ron Nessen standing on
the tarmac at Tan Son
Nhut Airport. We rarely
wore ties, but Ron is
waiting for the arrival of
a VIP. *Photo by Gary Bel.*

Correspondent Liz
Trotta in the field.
Courtesy of Liz Trotta.

A team at a base camp: cameraman Bob Welch, soundman Vo Suu, and correspondent Bill Wordham. Vo Suu usually worked the camera but also doubled as a soundman. *From the author's collection.*

At my desk. *From the author's collection.*

Gary Bel, assistant bureau
chief, and Vo Huynh with
tripod, before the start of
a Bob Hope concert.
Courtesy of Gary Bel.

Clockwise, from left:
Cameramen Hoang Trong
Nghia, Phil Ross, and Peter
Boultwood, soundman Tony
Mitchell, correspondent
George Page, maintenance
engineer Lutz Gruebnau,
and Frank Donghi, assistant
bureau chief during the Tet
Offensive. *From the author's
collection, except photo of
George Page, courtesy of
Vo Huynh.*

Josephine Tu Ngoc Suong
in the bureau prior to her
wounding. *Courtesy of
Josephine Tu Steinman.*

Soundman and engineering assistant Phan Bach Dang and chief engineer Digby Jones in the maintenance room. *From the author's collection.*

Two of our drivers. Nguyen Dinh Coi, who we called Tam Coi, is holding the glass on the left, and the resourceful Mr. Long is on the right. *From the author's collection.*

Reuven Frank, executive
vice president of the news
division, on a visit to the
Saigon bureau prior to
the Tet Offensive. *Photo
by the author.*

Correspondent David
Burrington interviewing
an officer in the field.
Vo Huynh is on camera.
Courtesy of Vo Huynh.

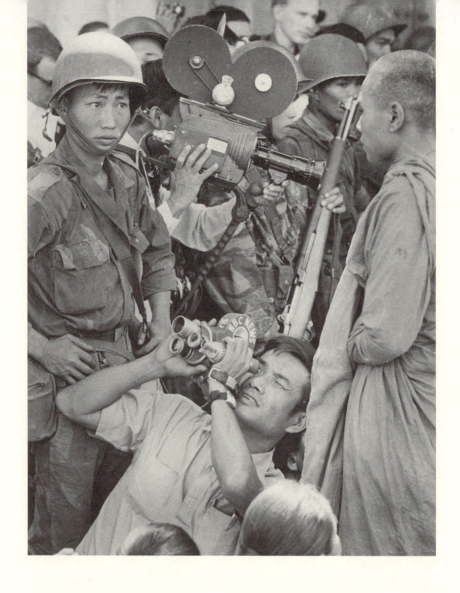

Vo Huynh, lower center,
with the Filmo 16mm
silent camera, filming a
confrontation between
the ARVN and Buddhist
monks. The Auricon sound
camera is being held by
Hoang Trong Nghia.
Courtesy of Vo Huynh.

Vo Huynh and, on sound,
Detlev Arndt covering a
speech by Premier Nguyen
Cao Ky, right. *Courtesy of
Vo Huynh.*

Vo Suu, with Auricon camera,
and Phan Bach Dang, carrying sound equipment, on a
Saigon street during the Tet
Offensive. Note the looming
American tank, which until
then was something that was
never seen in the streets of
Saigon. *Courtesy of Vo Suu.*

Woman vendor selling
peanuts, fruit, and fruit
drink. Vendors would often
walk miles before arriving
at their spot on the street.
Photo by Gary Bel.

The Continental Palace Hotel.
The terrace and open-air bar
that we called the Continental
Shelf is on the sidewalk at the
left side of the building. In the
foreground is the kind of
American car that was used
by our drivers. *Photo by the
author.*

Shot from inside a car or a
cyclo, this is a good example
of traffic on a Saigon street.
Photo by Gary Bel.

A view from my apartment
of the inner courtyard of
the Eden Building. *Photo
by the author.*

The statue of Vietnamese marines below my apartment, rebuilt after it fell apart. *Photo by the author.*

One of the press cards I used during the war. On my press cards for all my years in Vietnam, I used the same portrait from a Saigon photo shop. The years went by and I got older, but my picture stayed the same. *From the author's collection.*

UNITED STATES
MILITARY ASSISTANCE COMMAND, VIETNAM
OFFICE OF INFORMATION
APO SAN FRANCISCO 96243

PRESS CARD
NAME Ronald Steinman

AGENCY NBC News

IS ACCREDITED TO COVER THE OPERATIONAL, ADVISORY AND SUPPORT ACTIVITIES OF THE FREE WORLD MILITARY ASSISTANCE FORCES, VIETNAM

FOR THE CHIEF OF INFORMATION :

K. W. Moorhead
K. W. MOORHEAD
CDR   USN

EXPIRES 3 1 DEC 1966

VALID ONLY IN VIETNAM

Josephine, two weeks before her near-fatal accident, wearing an *ao dai* and standing in front of the Opera House that was then the home of the National Assembly. *Photo by the author.*

Josephine and me in Hong Kong in mid-1968, during her recovery from the shooting. *From the author's collection.*

Lt. Col. Nguyen Van Lan
and his wife, Hoan (Agnes),
before the fall of Saigon.
From the author's collection.

13

Breakdown

TENSION IS no stranger to anyone in a war zone. Stress on the job had a way of creating pressure on each member of my staff differently. Due to fierce competition, sympathy for the plight of one's peers, even those within the bureau, rarely existed. Seldom did any of us have time for tears for our brethren. Behind the closed doors of the bureau there were events that we at NBC News kept from the public. I wrote notes in the days immediately following some of these incidents. When I reviewed these pages, I thought at first that hindsight and a rewrite might better serve to explain the events and the reasons behind them. In the end, I decided, no. I would leave them much the way I first put them on paper, the way I recorded them originally, when these incidents happened.

Man breaking under pressure is common in combat. Reporters are really no different from anyone else, whatever we may think and want others to believe. The constant firefights, the prospect of being wounded, and the powerful threat of death can cause sleepless nights. The strain is enormous. The sword of danger is always present when a reporter is out on a military operation. In Saigon, fortunately, that direct threat was not as immediate as elsewhere in the country. But those of us who spent most of our time in Saigon had our own tensions as noncombatants. Our work had its own pressures because we were all that stood between our field operatives and the New York desk. Being in Vietnam perhaps helped tip some of us over the line faster and to a greater extreme than if we had been covering town hall politics in Wilton, Connecticut. This is the story of one man's collapse. His troubles did not start in Saigon. I believe they followed him there, though it is impossible to really know. Whatever their origin, they had a relentless hold over his emotions.

Lem Tucker was one of my two assistants in the bureau. Most of his duties were clerical, some were editorial. He sat in for me when I took a rest. Breaking in as a writer and reporter, he filed daily reports for the demanding NBC radio network. I knew him well because I took the time to talk with him over a drink, a meal, a cigarette. I became a sympathetic ear in a demanding world. My involvement with him rose steadily as he fell apart in a world he never made. He found himself in a land he never understood and hated, in a war he wished had never begun.

It started when Lem broke with his girlfriend, or she with him. It was unclear. I will call her Carrie. I do not know exactly what happened. Lem, as usual, was working hard. Carrie, however, was very demanding and at times, according to Lem, lacked understanding. Her job as a secretary for a construction company was not challenging, but life was not easy in Saigon, especially for a single woman. There were frequent street demonstrations. Terrorists moved through the city, tossing explosives with impunity. Early curfew made it difficult to move around at night. Lem thought he might leave NBC News, the country, the war, the story, earlier than he originally anticipated. I tried talking him out of it, but his decision became stronger each day. He was tired. He needed a rest. He planned to take Carrie to Hong Kong, hoping to repair their damaged relationship. As I put this on paper, the events seem more divorced from reality than when they occurred. The following is mostly verbatim from my notes, written as it happened.

Thursday night, April 13. Lem was in a restaurant on Tu Do Street, eating alone. Carrie walked in with a strange man and another couple. The restaurant serves as a press hangout. Carrie should have known better. Perhaps she wanted to goad Lem into action. She did. In a sudden fit of rage, Lem leaped at her with fists flying. He went wild. He broke up the place, knocking over chairs and tables, spilling bottles of wine, dumping plates of food. He kicked and flailed at everything in his path, his suppressed anger boiling over. No one got in his way. No one stopped him, certainly not the Vietnamese waiters and busboys. His energies spent, a few Americans forcibly escorted him from the restaurant. The management did not want to call the police because of the problems with paperwork and possible payoffs.

Lem wandered the streets for half an hour, still alone but sober. Then he returned to the restaurant because he still wanted to attack Carrie. He forced his way inside to discover she departed shortly after he did, afraid he might return and again lose his temper. He noticed the dining room had returned to normal, the damage hardly apparent.

Lem returned to the crowded, sultry streets of Saigon. He approached a few bar girls, who are normally desperate so late at night when curfew is almost on them. But they wanted nothing to do with him. Though many of these young women will do anything for a price, their hunger for money does not override their instinct for survival. Lem's rage was too obvious.

Lem knows my habits and called me at my office. I told him to come over. There was beer on ice, cigarettes, hot water for strong instant coffee, always time for talk. I spent three hours with him going over his life. I do not know enough about him to ask penetrating questions, but that was all right with him. He told me only what he believed I should know. We settled nothing. Tight from the few extra beers, but not seriously drunk, I gave him two sleeping pills and took him down to the street. I broke the curfew by walking with him to his small apartment a few blocks from the office. I have a curfew pass but it is no guarantee that I will be safe from the police if stopped.

Returning to my apartment was eerie. The streets were empty, but more than that, they were silent. A few beggars and a legless Vietnamese veteran were asleep in doorways. The one Vietnamese cop I saw recognized me from the neighborhood and asked me for a cigarette. I had a few remaining in my pack so I gave him those plus a light from my battered Zippo lighter. Our hands touched as he cupped the light to the Camel. We looked at each other in the sudden blaze of light, giving nothing away. He walked with me in silence the last hundred yards to the Tu Do Street entrance of the Eden Building. We rattled the steel gate to wake the Pakistani watchman, who grunted and grumbled as he opened the small door to let me in. The policeman slowly moved on, dragging deeply on his cigarette. I gave the night watchman ten piasters for a tip, the same amount I gave him when I woke him twenty minutes earlier to let me out. I entered the elevator and rode to my fourth-floor office. Checking the telex for any late messages, I saw the machine was clear. Then I went next door to the Associated Press office and found it also quiet. I walked to the fifth floor and into my apartment, hoping for a few hours' sleep. Did I talk sense to Lem, maybe help him out of his trouble? Was I successful? I knew he had revealed little to me of his inner life.

Friday. Entering my office at seven this morning, I found Lem asleep in the chair with the broken spring across from my desk. When I woke

him, he told that though I had left him at his building last night, he never
went to his apartment. When I disappeared from view, he moved from
the vestibule to the street and quietly followed me, staying clear of my
view in the still night. Minutes after I went upstairs, he also woke the Pakistani watchman but did not tip him. He took the elevator to the fourth
floor but could not get into the bureau because he forgot or lost his key.
He went to the AP down the hall and stayed up all night talking to the
overnight editor. Throughout the long night, he drank nothing stronger
than imported instant coffee. Black. No cream. No sugar. Lem told me
he got heartburn instead of a hangover. An early crew let him into the
bureau at four that morning as they were on their way out to make a helicopter flight at Tan Son Nhut. He probably had no more than an hour
of sleep when I woke him. I told him to go back to his apartment. He did
not protest. Perhaps he was too tired to fight, even with me.

Later that morning, Carrie called. She was in a panic. Her voice quivered with fear. Lem had been calling her office all morning. He said he
will beat her into submission if she didn't agree to see him. He threatened
to rape her, saying she would then never forget him. Lem's life is reeling
out of control. His threats and anger are parts of him that I have never
seen. Instead of informing the people she works for, Carrie wanted me
to help. She said I am responsible for Lem's actions. I am not, I told her,
but I will try to help. I called a mutual friend, who went to her office and
moved her to a safe place. He did this just in time. Ten minutes after Carrie left, Lem showed up at her office, shouting her name and demanding
to see her immediately. He rifled through her desk, looking for photos of
her new boyfriend. He scared people in the office with his wild eyes, his
profuse sweating, his unkempt clothing, his wild actions. He ran from
the office and from the building, still shouting her name.

I looked up from my desk and again he was in my office, standing in
front of me, head bowed, tears in his eyes, sobbing uncontrollably. He
stayed with me and one of the correspondents for more than two hours,
smoking, sipping coffee, saying little. We were watching Lem come apart
before our eyes, but we didn't say much either because we did not really
know what we were seeing. We decided that he should go and rest in
one of NBC's rooms in the Caravelle Hotel. The correspondent agreed to
stay with Lem and watch him for the remainder of the day. Then another

reporter will take a turn staying with him. We are all worried but we do not know what to do. I hope Lem's emotional spasm will pass.

Saturday. I went across the street to visit Lem. He said he wants to be admitted to a hospital because he is frightened of what will happen if he stays on the street. He is very tired, having had only a few hours of sleep in the last two days. He no longer feels in control of himself, he told me. He does not think he can be responsible for his actions. Ashen-faced, he repeated that like a mantra several times, then he fell into a deep sleep.

Sunday. Getting Lem into a hospital sounded like a good idea. I went to the American embassy for help because I will not put him in a Vietnamese hospital. Besides being sorely strained with normal wartime problems, the Vietnamese doctors can hardly handle a common cold. Asking them to help an American reporter with apparent psychological problems would be senseless. An American military hospital is the only answer.

I arrived at the American embassy at 2:30. During a roiling round of discussions, a high embassy official told me he cannot tell the military what to do. He cannot force them to make a decision against their will. "We are only guests in this country," he said. "Nobody"—meaning me, meaning the press—"has to be here. Any trouble you or your friend have is something you must solve by yourself. We, like you," he said, "are nothing more than guests in this country." Again, the guest theme raised its head, meaning we had no true status. I asked him if the military rules over civilians in the United States and in all those countries where you find an American in need of help. "Are you telling me that we live under a military dictatorship?" I said. "Are you telling me that here we have an American civilian in trouble and you will not lift a hand to help him?" I was harsh, direct, tough, and sick—sick and tired of his fumbling around, his refusal to do something worthwhile for an American in trouble. I also had a serious argument with the consul, who had the power to help. I had to threaten him. I shouted at him. He shouted back. We both sweated. I was exasperated. I asked how he could turn his back on a fellow American, although a noncombatant. The pressure I put on him ultimately beat him down.

After several hours, the embassy official also relented. He agreed to have Lem admitted to the 17th Field Hospital in Cholon, outside Saigon. We prevailed on the officer in charge at the hospital to have the resident psychiatrist examine Lem. I needed his help. I returned to the Caravelle, gathered up Lem, and Mr. Long and I drove him to the hospital. He signed himself in and a male nurse escorted him to his room, where, under clean white sheets, Lem swallowed a sedative and fell deeply asleep.

Naturally, I managed to get everything I wanted for Lem because I was relentless. I fear for other American citizens who might get into trouble in this troubled land despite a powerful American presence. Those I have been dealing with at the embassy are loathsome. I don't intend to name names because it is not worth it. There is no need to hang them. I have no hatred, only anger with them for their negative attitude. Their collective conscience, if it exists, should gnaw at their puny psyches in perpetuity. Maybe then they will get the message that it is not wrong to help one of your own when he is in trouble.

Monday. In the morning, Lem's doctor discharged him from the hospital. He appeared in my office, vibrant, filled with hope. He said he was back in circulation because the psychiatrist could find nothing wrong with him. A little rest and light recreation would help him relax and allow him time to get back in touch with himself. The doctor recommended he get out of Saigon, the best medicine he could suggest. Can I trust the doctor? Did he make the right decision? The doctor could be correct, but I think otherwise. Too much has happened too fast for me to think differently. But what do I know? I relaxed the vigil over Lem. No one stayed with him the whole day. We had jobs to do, work and play waiting. He appeared to be in good shape. Before going to sleep for the night he told me that he eagerly looked forward to his trip home at the end of his tour.

Sunday. I saw Lem briefly early this morning as I passed him on my way to Givral for coffee. I forgot him as I tried to catch up running the bureau and my own life. Then, early in the evening, the desk clerk of the Caravelle Hotel called, sounding very excited. In his broken English, he told me Lem had been drinking, had become drunk, and had wrecked the rooftop bar—the bleacher seats for viewing the war by visiting dignitaries. He said Lem was still in the bar, throwing glasses and bottles, pushing and shoving waiters, and using the bartender, a diminutive and very frightened man, for a punching bag.

I told the clerk to hold an elevator. I grabbed one of my correspondents, George Page, and we ran as fast as we could down the stairs to the street. We moved like acrobats, dodging the insane Sunday night traffic to the hotel across the square. We ran into the waiting elevator, punched the button for the eighth floor, jumped out, and ran to the bar. We confronted Lem, standing there waiting for us as if he expected us to appear precisely at that moment. It reminded me of a scene from a classic Western movie, everyone standing in a semicircle awaiting the gunfighter's next move. When Lem saw us, he made his move, a dash to a suite rented by an NBC correspondent who was then in the field. I will never know how Lem obtained that key. Probably he slipped the room clerk or floor boy a few piasters. After all, they did not care who lived where. We were all American and interchangeable, one the same as another. In that runaway, inflationary economy, every piaster helped, no matter where it came from or what had to be done to get it. Money truly talked.

We ran after Lem. He slammed the door of the suite and locked it. We heard him moving furniture around the room, piling it against the door. We asked him to open the door. Silence. We begged him to open the door. Silence. We *pleaded* with him to open the door. Silence. We tried turning the doorknob. Nothing. We tried forcing the doorknob open. Nothing. We ran into the door with the full force of our bodies. Nothing. The door did not budge. We rested. The growing crowd of Vietnamese onlookers and hotel officials stayed a safe distance from the room and did nothing to help us. They watched us worry over how to get inside and just snickered or smiled shyly when we failed.

Worried that Lem might seriously harm himself if we did not get inside to help him, I returned to the bar, found a telephone that worked, and called friends of mine in the U.S. Army information office. I needed advice. I needed help. The two officers I talked to said they did not know what to do. They would not touch that situation for all the booze in the Pacific. Anyway, they said, it is off-base and out of their domain.

With very few options left, I had to call the U.S. Military Police, the Army MPs. I knew they had no authority over civilians and they normally avoided anything involving the American press corps. One mistake with the press and they could find themselves on assignment in Green-land. A very polite captain listened patiently to my plea. He agreed that I had my hands full. We decided that we would figure out a reason for his involvement after we solved the immediate problem. He said he would quietly and quickly dispatch a couple of men. No sirens. No screaming vehicles. I did not want Lem in the hands of the Vietnamese police be-cause it could have meant jail. Worse, it would have meant a beating. The Vietnamese police are unsympathetic and offer no help to foreign-ers who hurt Vietnamese civilians or damage property. There have been serious, and sometimes fatal, unexplained shootings, especially when the foreigner was a Western construction worker or merchant marine. The Vietnamese National Police and the ultra-hard-nosed Vietnamese Army Military Police, both under military rule, are always quick to draw on Westerners who are drunk or on a rampage. So I had to keep Lem out of the hands of the Vietnamese.

Gasps came from the crowd. We saw fire coming from under the door of Lem's room. The flames started slowly but quickly licked their way up the door. Lem had set a fire in the room. The assembled onlookers took a collective intake of breath but no one moved or offered to help. I shouted for water. No response. Perhaps they were thinking he had set fire to himself, a religious act, one they knew well. Maybe he had. Far be it for them to get in the way of the Buddha's will. But why could they not understand that the hotel was in danger of burning down? I shouted again for water and this time George arrived with a bucket and threw it on the climbing flames. He left and returned with more water and we threw that on the door as well. Someone appeared with a bucket of sand. That, too, went against the door. The flames died out. Smoke filled the corridor. An ugly chemical smell spread everywhere. We could hear Lem cursing loud and clear from inside the room. Our audience moved back in the narrow hallway.

I had the feeling there were no capable people present except George and me. Everyone else stood and watched, gaped, swallowed, fretted, whispered, giggled. I needed no explanation for my involvement, why I stood there, my concern and anxiety. Lem worked for me as an employee of NBC News. I thought he was a friend in need. I had to get inside. In retrospect, I should have obtained a key but I did not have time. First, I again tried busting down the door with my shoulder. I bounced off the door and felt a searing pain down my arm. Then I started kicking the doorknob with my foot, the way I had seen it done in a hundred films by the heroes of my youth. I loved the movies. Time stopped. Someone in danger was behind the door and I had to get inside. After a dozen or so extra hard kicks with my right leg, the lock on the door weakened. George joined me and together we heaved our shoulders against the door until we forced it open. We pushed the furniture out of the way and entered the room carefully. We did not know what to expect. We tripped over the wet, stinking furniture. We did not see Lem in the main sitting room. My eyes went to the balcony. The double glass doors were closed. At least he had not jumped, though he still had that option. I moved quickly into the bedroom. I found him under the bedding, curled up like a baby trying to hide from a world that had become too much for him to handle.

Now the Vietnamese acted. They flowed into the room, crowding every inch of space. Lem untangled himself from the bed. He started throwing shoes and bottles and books at everyone in sight. He cursed blacks and whites and Chinese and Indians and the Vietnamese—especially the Vietnamese. He called them gooks and slants and slopes and yellow bastards, impugning their manhood and the honor of their women. He impeached them from the human race, calling them cowards and thieves and cheats. He yelled that they were so low they would go to bed with their mothers and sisters and enjoy it. The words flowed like acid from his mouth, his tongue thick, his normally carefully crafted speech slurred and disjointed. I kicked the Vietnamese out. They left reluctantly.

Despite the heavy air conditioning, Lem sweated profusely. I saw several empty bottles around the room. Knowing his actions over the last few days, I guessed he had drugged himself with downers mixed with sleeping pills and swallowed with cheap wine. I tried talking him down, to calm him, but he rushed me and threw a bottle at my head. I ducked under it and, swinging from the whole of my body, brought my right fist up and hit him with everything I had. His head snapped back and seemed to rotate on his neck, and his eyes rolled up under his lids. He appeared glassy-eyed and in a fog but he came back at me anyway, shocking me into a moment of despair. All my years of misspent street fighting and bar brawling were worthless. My hand and ankle were in pain. I had a swollen set of knuckles and a leg I could hardly stand on.

The two of us, warriors without reason, established a pattern of parry and thrust. He relaxed, charged, threw whatever he could get his hands on. George, in the middle of the fray, did his best to help. The crowd surged back into the room for a look. We cleared the room again. At one point we thought we had subdued Lem but he proved too strong, too determined, and it started again. A Westerner whom I have never seen before became involved. The four of us wrestled on the floor in a near orgy of anger and fear. I do not believe that any of us knew what the other was doing, even cared to know. I hardly saw the stranger's face and if I run into him in the future I will not recognize him. It doesn't matter. All I wanted was to get out of there, have a stiff drink and a hot shower, and go to sleep.

Perhaps ten minutes had passed since I called the military police. Then two MPs arrived, doing everything they had said they would not: Their siren screamed, their tires screeched, their lights flashed. Their noise out-did our noise. Both soldiers were big, young, and not sure why they were there or what they should do. When I ordered them to arrest Lem, they stiffened with resistance. Never before had they taken an order from a civilian. They had never received instructions to make a civilian arrest. This was obviously unlike anything they had in their book of regulations, and they were uncertain of their role. I invoked their captain's name and they made their move. Suddenly Lem had a knife. I do not know where it came from, but he had a very real, very long, gleaming and lethal-looking piece of steel in his hand. He continued cursing, stepped back, and then lunged at us. For some reason I was the quickest to get to him. I met him halfway and grabbed his wrist, twisted it with both my hands, kneed him in the groin, and shouted for him to drop the knife. He held on tightly and his steady stream of angry invective shocked even me.

Lem relaxed his grip on the handle, and George and I yanked the knife from his hand. The three of us fell to the floor and the worn, crumbling carpet. I had a slight cut on my hand from the knife. My side pained me from overexertion and all the shocks to my system. My ribs and chest heaved as I gasped for breath. Working the bureau has put me in worse shape than usual. I was beaten and bruised. The MPs, still trying to fig-ure things out, turned their back on Lem, allowing him to run into the bathroom and lock the door behind him. Once inside, he opened the small transom window and started throwing bottles and glassware onto the street by the main entrance of the hotel. The MPs, tired of the scene, smashed through the bathroom door with little effort. They easily subdued Lem in their best professional manner, forcing his hands behind his back and cuffing him in one movement. They dragged him into the elevator, out of the hotel, and tossed him in a heap into the backseat of their car.

On the street, I talked to the MP's captain over their radio and we worked out a plan for Lem. I arranged to have him held until I could figure out what to do with him. Perspiration was still pouring freely from Lem, but he said nothing. He was breathing heavily, occasionally gasping for air. One MP drove and the other rode in the back with Lem. I went along for the ride and saw that he was properly booked. The military arrested Lem on a charge of disorderly conduct and threw him into a cell alone.

My next move would be crucial. Back at my desk, I started calling those I knew who owed me favors. I had an explosive situation on my hands, a man out of control. He could hurt himself and others, probably without realizing it. Four hours later, with the continued support of the military police, I had Lem taken back to the 17th Field Hospital and readmitted for psychiatric observation. Even with orders from a staff general, the 17th Field Hospital in its best medical manner did not want to admit Lem. The admitting officer summoned the doctor in charge, a major, who contended that regulations did not cover civilians and he could not treat them in his hospital. Generals, he said, did not run hospitals. I suggested he call the general. He paled but did not budge. The military police captain, now part of my team, stood up, all six feet three inches of him, and looked down at the doctor sitting calmly behind his desk. He said, "Doctor, will you or anyone you know willingly certify that this fine American citizen can walk the streets of this wonderful, peaceful city without doing anyone, let alone himself, any harm?" The doctor sighed and agreed he could not do that. He shook his head sadly and capitulated, finally admitting Lem to the maximum security ward. Nurses heavily sedated Lem and placed him in a restraining jacket and he went instantly to sleep. The orderly double-locked Lem's room. The captain drove me back from Cholon in silence. We had nothing to say to each other in the sadness of the moment, so we parted quietly and returned to what passed for our homes. My watch registered two in the morning.

■   ■   ■

Monday. On my own, I had made the decision to involve the American embassy and the military police first to put Lem in jail, then to hospitalize him. On learning what I have done, many of my colleagues think I never should have contacted the embassy or the army. Some think I went too far with my decisions because I have either limited power or none. They think I crossed the line between the press and the government. They do not have a better answer for how to handle such a delicate situation, though. I had a sick man on my hands and I dared them to find a better solution. None could.

I took the unusual step of arranging to fly Lem out of the country on an air force medical flight. He had to be on a medical transport instead of a commercial airliner. It would have done none of us any good to have Lem bust out and break up a commercial jet. I visited Lem and told him my plan. I wanted to prepare him for his next step. When it came to a man's life and future, I did not believe in peppering him with surprises. The MedEvac solution scared him. Worse, nothing I said could quell his anger at me. Though still in restraints and under mild sedation, Lem tried to lunge at me but failed to move more than a few inches. He said he hated my guts. He cursed me out grandly. He refused to shake my hand when I told him I still considered him my friend. I said that no matter what he thought of me, I would always look on him favorably. He called me a traitor. He said I had railroaded him and committed him to get him off the streets and to keep him away from the woman he loved.

It was impossible to talk to him. I departed. I realize that many will not understand my actions, but I had hoped that Lem would. Later, he saw some newspaper reporters who were at the hospital to pick up their malaria pills, and he apologized to me through them. He told them he was recovering from the flu. They had no reason to doubt him. He asked them to tell me I was doing the right thing and that he wanted help. Once they learned parts of the story, they yearned for more but I divulged nothing and they moved on to other more interesting stories. Lem's hostile attitude toward me returned and never wavered until the end, when he finally flew home to the States.

When it was over and Lem finally left Saigon, I realized how tired I had become. I slept well again at night, although never long enough. I longed for an extra hour of sleep. The afternoon nap I usually resisted reared its lovely head and beckoned.

Over time, I caught up on my sleep and prepared myself for the next crisis to join all the other problems in progress. The swelling in my ankle, which looked as big as a baseball but felt as big as a soccer ball, eventually went down. I limped for days and became the butt of sweet jokes directed at me by my Vietnamese staff. They said they wished they could have seen me do my John Wayne routine. When I got angry with them for small infractions, they would lift their legs and kick at imaginary doors. They forced me to laugh and forget my anger. The cut on my hand healed. The puffiness around my knuckles disappeared. I did not want to experience anything like that episode with Lem again.

In less than a year, the damage to people in my bureau had been high. Besides Lem, I had one wounded correspondent. Under pressure from his new wife, one correspondent returned home two weeks after he arrived. Against all instructions by NBC News, his wife had come to Saigon with her husband and even tried going into the field with him. She made his life hell, and he had to leave before both became seriously hurt, physically and spiritually. One European cameraman combined sickness with evident fear and bugged out. An Australian cameraman developed severe stomach problems and returned home before his tour officially finished. Several Japanese and Korean cameramen and soundmen had minor wounds, frequent stomach problems, and occasional fear of combat. It had become depressing and I wondered sometimes if it was worth it. The people in our business worked very hard and were always active. The pressures were tremendous, the competition fierce. We fed an insatiable beast in New York and found it difficult to measure the return. Was it in dollars? Never enough. Was it in on-air appearances? Never enough. Was it in ego, or courage, or madness? Probably a bit of all three.

We did it, though, day after day. Life in Saigon sometimes became depressing, but I did not often get depressed. When I did, I found my own way out. Most important, the experience with Lem helped me discover how far I could push myself under stress. I knew I would never have to worry about myself again in certain situations. There were times during those eleven days when I did not think any of us would survive. We did. And if it happened again we would make it through again.

Sadly, Lem was not alone. Others would occasionally, unexpectedly, break.

In the bureau we had a young soundman who could not handle the pressure of war. No one knew this when they hired him. How could they? He was so young he made me feel old and I was only thirty-one. I'll call him Nick, and at twenty-two he was the youngest member of the staff. Nick worked hard, long, and well. He always pleased the difficult, demanding cameramen. He had courage and unusual strength. He might have had talent. We never found out if he did. But something was inside him that was not evident on the surface. Before joining NBC News, he had been on his own for almost six years. He told me he spent the year before he joined us wandering around the world and undergoing a variety of experiences. In his short time in the bureau, from his first operation to his last, he endured more than most men encounter in a lifetime.

When he returned to Saigon after a particularly bloody battle, we spent two hours sipping cold German beer at three in the morning. I thought I helped him wash the sight of blood from his eyes. After that, I spent more time with him, letting him talk, say anything he wanted, however he wanted. I thought his troubles were past him.

I was surprised when he came to me and asked for a raise. Granted, NBC paid him only one hundred fifty dollars a week plus expenses. Cheap labor. New York looked on him as young and inexperienced. His wage, less than many wire service reporters received, seemed good to him at first. But now that he had worked in the field, he did not think his pay high enough. He had seen the near death of a friend and coworker and too many soldiers wounded and dead, and he did not think life in South Vietnam was "so great." Once he looked clearly at what he had to do to earn his money, he thought it lousy pay for such high risk. He reminded me that he was twenty-two, going on twenty-three. He wanted to reach a decent old age. Nick could be hard and tough, but did not want to get himself killed. He would not keep facing possible death for one hundred fifty a week. No. He wanted more money. Nick would consider the risk of combat for two hundred a week. Yes. Two hundred a week. Girls were expensive in Saigon. Girls were important in his life. He looked on the extra money as recognition that he went willingly into real action. It would make a world of difference in his attitude, he said.

I told him I would try to get him the money. I knew he would not go on strike, that he would not quit. But New York turned down his request for a raise almost before I asked for it. New York said he had to spend more time in the country before it would consider paying him a higher rate. I had expected the managers at home would eventually deny his request. Being honest with my staff, I never promised what I could not deliver. Lives were at stake. I wanted to deliver for the staff, but broken promises had a way of backfiring. Morale suffered and staff response to lies had consequences that my sometime cheerleading could not repair.

About that time, Nick started having problems. I knew he needed someone to show him compassion. Without compassion, I would have been a useless person and a weak bureau chief. Despite his progress over the next few weeks, I had a strange feeling about Nick. Though combat became something he may not have wanted to face, he remained dependable. He showed up for assignments on time. He took care of his equipment. He did his sound work well. But he started having headaches and, with the constant pain behind his eyes, he also developed other problems. He missed an occasional flight from chopper pad number one at Tan Son Nhut, and then he would hold his head in his hands and apologize. He said he wanted action and I still sent him into the field whenever I could, not realizing there were hidden problems.

Combat ebbed and flowed in Vietnam. It depended on the season and the health and well-being of the Viet Cong and North Vietnamese and their long-range plans. Often after successive heavy battles, it became quiet. Nick's restlessness made me nervous. He had to keep going, he said. I wondered if he were trying to prove his value to us or to himself. One night he sat across from me and pleaded to go out on assignment. Vo Huynh had been ill with a fever and Nick wanted to take his place. He said he could handle the camera. I told him no. I would not have it. Nick had developed quickly but I would not send him out alone with the camera. I would not let him tread in uncertain water with unfamiliar equipment. Nick insisted that he did know the gear. On his last operations, Prairie and Deck House 4, he shot film and it turned out well. I told him he needed more time.

In Operation Deck House 4, Nick had had a harrowing time in the field when a landmine exploded near him, injuring several troops. Remarkably, he escaped injury. But it seemed he brought chaos wherever he went. Unluckily, there would be more. Nick was teamed with David Burrington for Operation Prairie. From the first, everyone knew it would be dangerous, "a hairy go," as GIs put it. Troops leaped from the choppers onto badly booby-trapped ground. Television crews and correspondents followed. Men were falling wounded everywhere. Nick jumped from the chopper when it arrived at the hot landing zone, and he accidentally fell on a landmine. For some reason, it did not explode. He did not know how he did it, but he managed to tear the explosive loose and separate it from its wires. Afterward, a GI came up to him and showed him the pieces. Looking at the disabled device shook him. Burrington said if it had happened to him, he would never stop looking for booby traps under his bed.

Later in the operation, Burrington, cameraman Hoang Trong Nghia, and Nick were in a shallow pit with bullets bouncing a foot in front of them. They later admitted they were terribly frightened, as they should have been. They told me they felt the blood drain from their faces. Nick thought the whole area had been booby-trapped. When the fighting let up, a demolition team checked and found nothing. But at one point during the operation, Nick helped a wounded soldier to safety. That is something most newspeople do when they can. In the chaotic field, reporters sometimes cross the line into acting like human beings. Despite the confusion and danger of the battle, Nick never faltered. He worked hard and did his usual good job on sound. He even took some film with the silent camera when Nghia changed magazines for the sound camera. Getting along with Nghia could be difficult, but he and Nick had become close friends.

Nghia was possibly the smallest combat cameraman in Vietnam. He had only just started using the heavier Auricon sound camera and he had not yet become confident with it. Before I switched him to the sound camera, a step up for combat cameramen, he had gone into combat alone with the small, hand-held Filmo, a half dozen 100-foot magazines, and a cassette recorder for sound. He shot good film and had a sense of how to photograph a story. But he wanted more for his pride and his pocketbook. Nghia stood at my desk every free moment asking to prove his ability with the sound camera. He wanted to work with correspondents on what he rightfully believed were more difficult assignments. He overcame the obstacle of his size by carrying the heavier gear in the office until his arms shook from fatigue. He spoke poor English with a heavy accent and seemed almost half Nick's size. Despite their differences, they got along wonderfully, and Nick asked for a permanent assignment with Nghia. I created a new team and for a time it worked.

Nick became an efficient sound technician. His skills sharpened each time he went into the field. He learned fast and my chief engineer, Digby Jones, became quite proud of him. In the killing zone of Vietnam, you learned fast or suffered the consequences. I could assign Nick to work with any cameraman. His sound did not approach studio quality, but that would have been too much to expect of any soundman under war conditions. Wherever he went he picked up the noise of the jungle and mountains. He captured the sound of weary soldiers on the move, guns firing, and boots trampling on overgrown trails. He recorded frightened refugees—their weeping, their coughing, their shuffling feet—honking horns, and hovering helicopters. Nick found the sound the story needed. He carried his share of heavy equipment and never complained. He cared about the product and contributed everything he had to the crew.

Back in Saigon after each military operation, Nick appeared relaxed, never showing signs of additional tension. After a normal assignment day in Saigon, he would demand that I return him to the field. He had to return to the action.

When I could, I got him back into combat. I had a theory that it was better to have someone willing out there than someone living in fear, one of those theories that I never proved.

Correspondent Ken Gale told me that Nick complained of bad dreams. Nothing specific, Gale said. He just reported that they existed. When I confronted Nick, he said the dreams came rarely and I had nothing to worry about because they did not worry him. I did not pursue it. There were, however, incidents that I could not ignore. I sent Nick with Dean Brelis and Peter Boultwood on a First Division helicopter medical evacuation, a story I named Alpha Charlie Company. After an ambush that ended in carnage, choppers came in to evacuate the seriously wounded and dead soldiers. While Nick worked, he cried. It did not alter his performance, but his tears ran freely. Dean told Nick he felt as badly as he did but advised that he save his tears for later, after they finished the story. On a story in the Mekong Delta about the Vietnamese small-boat navy, Ken, Peter, and Nick found themselves in a bunker undergoing a mortar attack. Peter told me Nick grabbed an M-16, ran out to the perimeter, and started firing. He spent the only clip he had and came back to the safety of the bunker exhausted, yet exhilarated. Ken and Peter said Nick told them the only way he could get rid of his fear was to get involved. He had crossed the thin line from being an objective reporter to a nonobjective combatant.

Then he went to Hong Kong on his well deserved ten-day rest. There, his life seemed to collapse. Some facts will probably never be clear. While in a hospital to check a minor problem, a skin ailment common in Vietnam, there apparently was a discussion of Nick's having an operation for an undisclosed illness. He became hysterical and engaged in a shouting match with the medical staff. They overpowered him, sedated him, and placed him in a bed under supervision. With all his problems in Saigon and in the field, he had never experienced sustained hysteria. He was never considered ineffective in covering combat, and later he told me his breakdown in the serenity of Hong Kong surprised him as much as anyone. Perhaps civilization had suddenly become too much for him.

Maybe Nick was too young to be in Vietnam. Perhaps, despite his experience with life, he did not have enough seasoning to get him to the high ground when needed. I make no excuses for him. He made none for himself. He folded, had a nervous breakdown, maybe because somewhere along the way he lost faith in himself to be able to keep leading the life of a combat journalist. Failing to cover a story is not a sin. There are those who cannot take combat. Perhaps Nick fit that profile. He might not have enjoyed being shot at, but who did? The most important sign my staff gave me about their inner selves was when they admitted they were afraid on a story. Many came out of combat excited and flushed. The next day, a letdown would set in and it usually took another day after that before they were ready for more work in the field. Nick never had those symptoms. He never admitted to me that he had any fears. I knew Nick had reacted violently to the mortar attack in the Delta. There were other members of the press corps who did the same and some who did even worse. Part of Nick's problem might have been his lack of maturity. For all he had done, he had far to go before becoming the adult he wanted to be.

After he was released from the hospital, I sent Nick home. He returned to New York an anxious, confused young man. His problems went with him. He had no idea what awaited him. NBC headquarters did not have any immediate plans for him. I thought NBC News should hold onto him, if possible. I believed he had a future in the business. That he was like a gypsy and might continue being like a gypsy for a long time was something he would have to recognize. The longer I stayed in the Far East, the more I realized the need for adventurous men like Nick. In time the adventure ends. When it does, it is a problem we all must confront. Nick's adventure ended too soon. As his link to the outside world, I had to show faith in him. He thought I did not, and was disappointed that I shipped him back to America. I explained it was not part of some devious plot to put him out to pasture before the end of his first race.

After Nick left, I wrote the following lines:

Now he is gone and strange, almost forgotten. We have to remove his name from his mailbox. We will delete his name from the list of American correspondents. He has had his last Vietnamese visa issued and stamped in his passport. He will become a nonperson in Saigon. The girls on Tu Do Street will miss him. Nick is a bare memory, a wisp in time. I hope New York does what it can for him but I pray they do not pamper him. He would resent that most of all. People should treat him as a man but they must understand he is still a boy. Nick needs leading, but gently, always gently. For his own well-being, I would rather see him eventually dumped hard from this business than to see him build to a more subtle fall. That would be terribly unfair to him as a man. Nick was a hell of a kid. We were all very fond of him and we all wish him well and a speedy recovery. Covering this war is not for the fragile. He should not let us forget it. In many ways, he is a reflection of our own vulnerability, of our tenuous hold on our own lives. It is a wonder that more of us do not, as he did, break under this awful daily strain.

These were not the only breakdowns, just the most serious. The other stories are not as dramatic and were not as emotionally threatening to the people involved. Some men refused to cover combat and others wanted to cut their stay short and go home early. At times correspondents and camera crews, alone or together, in combat or even on the street, found it difficult to cover their assigned story. Stress did not respect nationality, age, or position. Many foreign nationals on staff felt they were truly alien in an alien land. The Vietnamese staff, despite being well paid compared to Vietnamese who did not work for an American company, was not immune to the vicissitudes of daily life, the difficulty of getting their families safely through the day. Most doubts and fears did not last very long, though. People usually fought through their problem in a day or two and then went willingly back to work. Their spirit of competition and their own pride won out.

Through it all, I remained sympathetic and never doubted my staff's dedication to NBC or to their craft. Under the conditions we worked, I understood the burden each person carried every day and that they sometimes became too difficult to endure. The staff knew they could come to me with their problems and that I would give them a fair and sympathetic hearing. After their time off, whatever form it took, they returned to work refreshed, their attitude repaired, their performance improved, and their life, at least temporarily, normal—if anything could be considered normal in war.

14

Inevitable Changes
1985

IN 1985, WHEN I returned to Vietnam with NBC News to cover the tenth anniversary of the fall of Saigon, I wandered when I could through the parts of the city where I had lived, taking pictures of the places that were once so familiar to me. More often than I thought possible, I found myself free of my ever-present guide. The "minders" sometimes wanted a few moments away from me, from all of us, really, to pursue their private interests and needs. Often I felt as if I were in a spy novel, a hovering watcher on my tail wherever I went. But now and then I would look behind me or across the street and not see my assigned guard anywhere. The guides' disappearances, which were never official, signaled me that I had an hour or two of freedom.

We called them guides, minders, or wardens; the designations were interchangeable. Some British camera crews called them "keepers," echoing a term from Northern Ireland. These terms were upsetting to them because of the crass and cynical jailhouse connotations. Whatever we called them, they had a job to do, to watch us individually or in groups throughout our working day and beyond, if required. In truth, they did very little actual minding except at the most unexpected times. Most places were not off limits in police-controlled Ho Chi Minh City. I wandered all over the city and into the suburbs on unofficial business more frequently than allowed. I knew I had freedom from national security surveillance. Anyway, I could not understand the meaning and nature of security in that terribly poor nation, especially in the center of the crowded city. What did the new Communist government fear? Hundreds of miles away, war still raged in Cambodia between the Khmer Rouge and Hanoi's troops, a foolish war for power in a region that no one cared about and that meant little to anyone. But I had no desire to see that war.

Official Vietnamese watched and followed me whenever I entered an area until I left the neighborhood. There were times when local security people and Communist cell members tracked my path through their streets. They openly made note of the pictures I took and tried to guess what I wrote in my notebooks. Those who spied on me were obvious and I could easily detect them at their work. Either they wanted me to know they were watching or, because of their ineptness, they were making an unintentional mockery of their craft. At times I would wave to a man taking notes as he watched me walk or ride down the street. The scribbler would feign innocence and look away. It was like living in a grade B spy novel. Once I caught an older man watching me and he smiled at me and nodded sheepishly. But he continued taking notes, probably describing my innocent walk through an outdoor fruit market. I noticed he wrote nothing when I purchased a small banana and carefully peeled away its thick yellow skin. He watched as I ate the sweet, yellowish-white fruit with obvious joy. I guessed there were some things not worth recording, even for an imitation spy.

The guides were supposed to be on duty twenty-four hours a day but that was too much to expect. After all, we were in Saigon. Ten years of revolutionary zeal and strict Communist control tended to collapse under the mysterious weight of Saigon's aura and shady past life. At night our guides relaxed and we were usually alone. The men and women assigned to us did not work after six in the evening, unless absolutely necessary. We learned they had their own lives, and sometimes loves. Their own pursuits were often more important to them than watching us every minute.

During the day, when it became too hot to do any work, the ancient, civilized Saigonese custom of the siesta wisely prevailed. Everyone rested or slept through the hottest part of the afternoon. Work started early in the morning. After the noon meal and a nap at home, work restarted at three or so and continued into the early evening after sundown. This had to be the explanation for the disappearance of the staff of the Foreign Press Center each day between twelve and three. After three, they resurfaced. They often worked past midnight, calling us with the answers we had been seeking all day.

While the guides rested, I could look at the streets on my own. The geography remained the same. Many signs for shops and restaurants were gone, torn away or erased, eroded with time. Establishments I knew and frequented in the past were now inhabited by families who needed a place to live. Squatters preferred to use these former businesses for their homes than return to towns and villages wrecked or changed by the war. Small sidewalk businesses had set up in place of some of the shops. Repair shops, food stalls, tailors, and the occasional black market outlet selling radios and foreign beer filled empty storefronts.

I passed the old French Opera House, once the site of the South Vietnamese National Assembly, home of the first freely elected body in Vietnam. Ten years after the war, it had become a theater for folk song and dance presentations meant to prop up the Communist regime. Next to the whitewashed Opera House stood the Continental, the old French-style hotel. The Continental was undergoing extensive repair and was then closed to the public, but high-ranking Communists from Eastern Europe still stayed there, enjoying the large, old-fashioned rooms with their high ceilings and cooling wood-blade overhead fans. When the electricity shut down, though, the rooms were as hot as any other hotel's. During the war, the Continental was famed for its outdoor restaurant and bar, where you could see everyone and everyone could see you, and which we dubbed the "Continental Shelf." There, I remembered, people bought and sold drugs, bargained for sex, and would sell you a hot camera if you had the money and did not care whose hands had touched the goods first. Everyone, of every nationality, made it to the Continental at least once. Some people camped there permanently. Others were part-timers. Engineers, stockbrokers selling mutual funds, USAID clerks, auto dealers, construction workers, transvestites, and male and female prostitutes were all part of the floating crowd. Most Americans who were not in the press or the military but who had signed on to work in South Vietnam for six months whiled away their hours in that nineteenth-century atmosphere. Construction workers, the civilian high rollers of the war, had contracts for eighteen months. They made big money, drank, smoked dope, and slept with everything that walked. Some even put money away for their future.

The Caravelle, across the square from the Continental, had hardly changed on the outside. But inside, reporters, television crews, and curious civilians no longer slept, ate, drank, and watched the war from the tiny bar and larger rooftop garden. Figuring where an attack might come from next had been the reigning game in town as we sat nursing a beer or drinking awful Algerian red wine on the hotel roof. The Air France office on the corner of Tu Do Street below the Caravelle had been closed for years. In 1985, there were not many people traveling in or out of Vietnam. Those who traveled usually did so illegally by boat.

Ramuncho, the restaurant that was once owned by a former general who had become a senator, closed when Saigon fell in 1975. It had been occupied by squatters for many years, and the name above the entrance had fallen down. When I looked closely, I could see the outline of the letters. I saw children at play on the small balcony, the only vestige of the restaurant where I once frequently ate.

Aterbea, another of my favorite eating places, was owned during the war by an old man from Corsica and his wife, a very young, charming Vietnamese. She usually tended the cash register, and he ran the kitchen and greeted guests when he had time. They made the best cheese soufflé I ever ate in the Far East. Their loaves of bread were always fresh and chewy, the crust crisp and flaky. Their grilled seafood was excellent, their salads fresh. A family of squatters occupied the once-bustling storefront, having moved in when the owners moved out at war's end. The long wooden bar running the length of the dining room remained intact, but was covered with cardboard boxes. I had no idea of the fate of the chunky Corsican and his young wife, who always smiled and warmly greeted everyone.

Givral, on the corner of Nguyen Hue, was still a coffeeshop, but no longer a center for small talk and hearsay where Vietnamese journalists and politicians congregated daily to exchange information, not caring if it was true or false. During the war, Givral served strong, black coffee richly roasted as only the French could do it. They baked excellent pastry and not a day went by that I did not have a box of it on my desk. I often had coffee there and, early in the morning, iced tea heavily laced with fresh lime, the first of many glasses to help get me through the heat and the unavoidable, wearying depression of midday. Brodard, a coffeeshop similar to Givral, was also still open on Tu Do Street. Crowded like its cousin, it, too, no longer served as a political hangout. I recognized no one at either establishment. No surprise.

Ho Chi Minh City barely bustled. It was no longer the city it once had been, Saigon, the Pearl of the Orient. Now faded, its color gone, its brittle luster was lost beyond buffing. JUSPAO had become a state store selling cheap handicrafts. The Rex BOQ, next to JUSPAO, was now a refurbished hotel and office complex mostly catering to East European businessmen, with a dance hall, also run by the state, on its roof. Once an important American officers' billet, the Rex Hotel, with its dark tiles and dim lighting, now looked like a hotel one might see in Bulgaria. At street level, the Rex movie theater stayed busy. Different films were showing from early morning until the evening. People lined up in large numbers to see films from the Soviet Union and East Germany, most of which were dull and filled with propaganda. They offered some respite from the problems of everyday life and were popular despite their lack of artistic quality.

The city was still heavily populated, but the streets around the Eden Building, the most crowded and noisy during the war, were not busy. I walked freely without being jostled. I had no way of knowing, but I felt some people recognized me. After all, I had been in and out of the entrance to 104-106 Nguyen Hue continuously between 1966 and 1971. It would not have surprised me to discover that people I knew then had moved elsewhere, some possibly to the United States. Many might have remained, though. As a rule, Vietnamese did not move from their neighborhood. Each part of the city was like a small country village. People only moved in the late 1970s, because the government forced them. Then the new regime sent many city dwellers against their will to the countryside as farm laborers. Productivity fell and the experiment failed. Though the streets were clear, I felt many older residents were still somewhere nearby, watching silently.

Most people moved about on foot. Little public transportation existed and there were almost no privately owned cars. Older men and women, of which there were many more than the young, were always going somewhere. Often they would pause at the few remaining sidewalk bookstalls. They went in and out of the few bookstores, especially the huge government shop on Tu Do Street. The Vietnamese loved to read and had a tradition of great epic poetry. The book displays I saw were only shadows of those in the past, when the people had a taste of relative freedom. Many of the books were in Russian and German, two languages most Vietnamese did not know. I saw biographies of Karl Marx and Lenin and thick books on agriculture and iron foundries. These were books that people ignored. They still bought newspapers because they were the best source of local information once you cut through the propaganda. For a view of the world outside Vietnam, many tuned in to the BBC World Service—in secret and well after dark.

As people moved about, they bought the Vietnamese version of fast food from the sidewalk vendors. Elderly men and women still displayed their limited food selections as beautifully as they could. At least that had not changed. For that alone, it remained timeless Saigon, recalling my earliest memories. The vendors would probably always be a cheerful echo in a city working hard, but unsuccessfully, to hold on to its past.

15

My Apartment
1966–1985

APRIL 1985, Ho Chi Minh City. Sunday to Sunday still seemed the same, no matter the year. Sudden rain soaked through my clothing. I was again standing in front of the Eden Building. In a burst of enthusiasm, I had decided I would return to my apartment. I wanted to see if any ghosts remained, and to learn who now lived in my former home.

My fifth-floor apartment had had two bedrooms, one bath, a large living room, and a small kitchen. It overlooked the ugliest statue ever created, one giant concrete Vietnamese marine kneeling behind another giant concrete Vietnamese marine. Their bayonets fixed, their rifles at the ready, they had them pointed at the National Assembly a short distance away. Everyone suspected it was a thinly veiled threat by the dictatorial Thieu regime against the country's newly elected senators.

I recall watching the statue being built. It took several days and nights of full-time work to slap globs of wet concrete over the flimsy metal frame, which was supposed to support the weight of the statue much like the skeleton for a papier-mâché doll. One night at three in the morning, I heard a loud crash. It felt like an earthquake and sounded like a Viet Cong terrorist explosion, as if an ammunition magazine had been blown apart. In my apartment, the vibrations made the walls shake and my bed move. Rudely awakened from my deep sleep, I momentarily panicked. What had blown up? Did I have to scramble up a crew to cover the story? Who could I call to find out what had happened? I heard no sirens or overhead copters. Once I realized that my walls, the ceiling, and my own person were in one piece, I ran to the window and looked out across the city. Nothing. Then I looked down. I could not believe my eyes. Klieg lights were shining brightly on the scene below. The statue seemed to have collapsed under its own weight. Tons of olive-toned concrete had become an odd mixture of rising dust, gravel, and globs of still-wet cement. Vietnamese soldiers were shouting at each other, pointing their raised weapons. I heard gentle voices below and laughter rising from the rubble of the fallen masterpiece. I heard Vietnamese giggling in the hallway of my building. Then, the sound of pattering feet and doors softly closing as they returned to their apartments and bed.

A jeep roared up and a full colonel stepped out. No more laughter. His soldiers, who had been building this monument to the glory of the military, knew their commander's fury. I could not see the officer's face, but the sound of his screaming voice rose above the noise and confusion on the street. Someone with authority had finally taken charge. The situation quickly changed. Roadblocks sealed the area. The bright lights were turned off, and many soldiers departed. I returned to sleep. In the morning, the debris had disappeared.

A few days later, under calmer and quieter conditions, labor details finished the work. Everyone made jokes about the finished statue. Cartoons appeared in newspapers, on latrines, and in other unlikely places. Network news shows included the story in their broadcasts about the National Assembly. Young couples posed for snapshots at the statue's base. Then we forgot about it. We took it for granted. It became one of those mysteries of the war that everyone accepted and ultimately ignored. The statue disappeared when Hanoi occupied Saigon and had the monster brutally torn down, as it had long deserved. Getting rid of what had been a less than subtle threat against the assembly by President Thieu was a tasteful gift from the new regime and one of its only gracious acts.

I always walked the two small, zigzag sets of steps to the NBC News bureau on the fourth floor, down the hall and one flight below my apartment. I never used the elevator for one floor. I never trusted it, as it was often broken and we could never find technicians to fix it. Besides, the elevator never felt safe even after being "fixed" by a man we had never before seen. Coming in from the street, I usually walked up the stairs, and I always walked down because I found it faster. I knew during my first weeks in the job that, while it was convenient for my office and apartment to be close together, the two parts of my life were, in reality, *too* close. After headquarters strongly denied my request to move, I learned to live with my situation. I enjoyed the proximity of my home to the bureau, and the speed with which I could move between each, especially in an emergency. That short walk between floors, however, allowed me to put needed distance between the mirrored parts of my life in Saigon. At night, in the pitch black, when there were no lights, the distance seemed greater than it did during the day.

In 1985, I stood nervously in the arcade as the elevator seemed to beckon me to enter. It was daytime and hardly any lights were on. The few barely glowing bulbs gave off a soft yellow haze in the hallway, making it feel dim and sickly. At the elevator, I pushed the "up" button and heard nothing. No switch clicked through. No motor cranked or turned over. No elevator made its way down or up in its concrete sleeve. The Vietnamese who wandered in and out of the building were polite, probably more than ever puzzled with the foreigners here for the anniversary of the fall, especially those they suspected were American. They gave me furtive glances, but otherwise ignored me. Having lived with those looks for years, it did not disturb me. Understandably, I was feeling more at home than at any other time on the trip. I had walked the steps thousands of times in the past. Still not trusting the elevator, I decided to walk the steps again. My goal, the fifth floor. Yet I remained apprehensive and for some reason never felt more alone than at the foot of the stairs of 104-106 Nguyen Hue.

I remembered all the nights when bats flew chirping in the hallways. Small, friendly lizards climbed the walls, feasting on the hordes of tiny insects that lived in the tropics, helping keep nature in balance. Now sunlight filtered into the stairwells through the open, latticed windows and forced its way through cracks in the worn, battered shutters that barely kept out the dust, wind, and rain. Yellowing paint peeled from the wooden window frames. At my feet were cockroaches and water beetles, some as big as Brazil nuts and with shells just as difficult to crack. At least the bats stayed hidden until night, when darkness ruled. The insects slithered and scampered, seemingly without direction, over floors and steps strewn with refuse. In the past, dirt was everywhere because of the war. What could be the excuse for not keeping the building clean now, I wondered? I should not have cared, but I once lived here. I wanted it clean as if it were still my home.

I took the steps slowly, steadily, knowing that if I did not, the heat could get to me faster than my lungs might hold out. I reached the fourth floor and resisted taking a left turn at the corner to enter what had been the bureau. Although I had spent most of my days there, behind my desk, I first wanted to see the place where I had slept, relaxed, made love. The apartment had become my sanctuary where I had endless talks and arguments with my staff and friends. Where I sometimes drank too much and always smoked too much. The place where I read and thought and to which I ran to escape the rigors and daily horror of the Vietnam War.

I arrived at the top of the stairs. Pausing to catch my breath, I rested, trying not to move a muscle. I stood motionless on the fifth-floor landing and looked down the long, dark hallway. The hall felt empty, strangely still, except for the singsong, birdlike sound of Vietnamese voices that wafted their way up to sky above the indoor courtyard. There the gently ringing trills drifted freely toward the sky, disappearing into the blue, gone forever but replaced by new sounds, as if in perpetual motion.

I looked down at the courtyard five floors below. Raising my head, I saw the floors above laced with ribbons of wet, colorful clothing hanging out to dry. Clotheslines were hooked to the corner railings of each floor's balcony and encircled the deep, well-like interior of the building. The clothes seemed to hang on threads. When I looked down again, the courtyard appeared bottomless. This was where my maid, my amah, would hang my clothing so it could dry after she washed it each day. Thankfully that had not changed.

I stood on the balcony a few feet from the entrance to what had been my home. Normally I think of myself as brave, a daring man. Yet I had a great deal of difficulty finding the courage to knock on that wooden door that I had opened and closed thousands of times during my years in Vietnam. The door looked different. It seemed to have had a recent coat of paint, a flat, dull, characterless brown. I reached for my key and realized I did not have one. Then, as if by reflex, I knocked without thinking, and having done it, wondered why I stood there at all.

My heart pounded. Sweat popped unexpectedly from my forehead. Blood rushed to my head and I flushed with excitement. I felt giddy. What right did I have to be here? No sound came from inside the apartment. That did not surprise me. The Vietnamese were not very demonstrative, especially in their own homes and in the middle of the day. And the occupants could have been at work or visiting neighbors. I struggled with the decision to knock again or flee, when just then the door started to inch open. First I saw one black pupil, then a wide, pockmarked nose, then knobby knees and bare feet. Finally there emerged an average-sized, skinny, middle-aged Vietnamese with very black hair who stared at me with a puzzled, bewildered look. One thin, calloused hand firmly held the inside handle of the door. The other hand slowly stroked and rubbed the already worn edge of the door frame, adding to its finely polished, high luster.

He looked at me and through me simultaneously. I knew I was standing there, yet I did not think he believed I could be real. My Vietnamese had always been poor and my pronunciation worse, but I tried what I knew anyway.

"Chao ong," I said. "Chao ong," I repeated in case he did not understand me.

"Hello," I translated. "I lived here—for more than two years. I lived here."

He looked at me for another several seconds, seconds that seemed to last forever. His eyes locked onto my eyes. His head never moved. His expression stayed firm, unwavering, unyielding. I could understand his tension. I was a stranger and, more than that, clearly an American, at least a Westerner. Did he have anything to fear? I smiled to put him at ease. Then he released his concentrated gaze and in one swift, soft motion carefully closed the door in my face. The inside latch clicked into place and what followed was silence, feeling like the silence immediately after death. The man had dismissed me, though politely, without slamming the door the way an American might have done, the way I might have done. I did not know if he understood what I said in Vietnamese, let alone English. I had desperately wanted to step inside the apartment, to discover if anything remained from such an important part of my life. It was not going to happen. I could not knock again and further impose my strangeness on his privacy. My body felt liquid, formless. My head had become light and hot, much too big for my body. I felt embarrassed and oddly ashamed. I did not own that apartment. I had passed only a small part of my life in the war. I could imagine that much of this man's life and his family's, as with all Vietnamese, had been touched by the war's awful history. What right had I to intrude?

Before I knew it, I had run down the stairs and stumbled out of the building. I hit the stark brilliance of the midday sun as if it were a wall. My breath came in steady gasps. My lungs heaved to regain much-needed air. I had escaped and, for my own protection, hoped that at least I had become invisible. I sensed, however, that everyone in the building and around it was aware of my mission, knew I had tried, and realized I had failed.

When I was bureau chief, I listed NBC's long-standing and faithful maid—who was also my laundress and sometime cook—as part of my family, to protect her and her family from government harassment and the reprisals she might face working for an American company. When Thieu ran the country we did not always know what his various agencies were doing. Anything could happen if we were not careful. For some in the government, the fact that An Hoa worked for an American news company could be reason enough to subject her to retaliation. She might draw the sting of bitterness or jealousy for what others considered her good life and high wages.

I remember being awakened from a deep sleep once at two in the morning by heavy pounding at my door. Whoever it was seemed to be on the verge of taking the door off at the hinges if I did not respond. With some trepidation, I asked who was there and, incidentally, what the hell was going on. The Viet Cong roamed freely and there were always rumors they might start kidnapping Americans. I did not think they would knock if they wanted to enter. Why should they when they had the weapons? The knocking stopped, and a voice on the other side of the door claimed to be the special police, there for a legal reason. The speaker's English was good, but he had a thick, southern accent. At least I thought he sounded southern, but that was no guarantee he was telling the truth. I opened the door a crack, peered out, and saw three men in peaked hats, white shirts, and dark gray trousers, heavy guns in holsters at their hips. One man, the spokesman, brandished a flimsy, almost see-through, official-looking paper in his left hand. His right hand stayed firmly on the white bone handle of his U.S. Army issue .38 police special. He wanted to know where he could find An Hoa and, that aside, why she was living in the Eden Building. It took me a moment to clear my head and figure their purpose. I supposed they thought that, at two in the morning, they would discover something illegal or immoral. I asked to see the paper the leader wielded. By this time, every apartment door on the fifth floor had opened a fraction, revealing anxious, sleeping faces, probably wondering if they would be next.

Without allowing the paper out of his small, knobby hand, the leader showed it to me. Pointing to her name, he waved the handwritten form rapidly in front of my face like a crude, personal fan. With my door now wide open, we stood toe to toe, facing each other with only the worn doorsill separating us. He stood at least six inches shorter than I. His chin jutted upward and he lifted his face close to mine. He spoke excitedly, covering my face with a fine mist of spittle that showered upward, unhindered by the broken, rotten teeth that filled his mouth. I could smell the mixture of garlic, fish sauce, and hot red peppers on his breath. The strong odor made me shudder with disgust. In my mind, I saw myself bending over him with a large brush coated with toothpaste, scrubbing his teeth and gums to the nub. I needed a cigarette or a drink, probably both.

The two other officers stood well back from the apartment entrance. Their eyes flickered nervously in the dark hallway, where tiny shafts of light emerged from all the partly opened doors. When my interrogator shut his mouth for a break, I tried to explain that An Hoa had become part of my adopted, extended family. She lived down the hall with her child in a room that was part of my official lease. I paid her rent, her salary, her medical bills, and her Vietnamese social service costs, what little she had. The officer in charge nodded his head in understanding, but he still breathed heavily. I thought he might suddenly start salivating and drooling. Then he said everything would be fine for the rest of the night. He made it clear that someone would return in daylight to run a further, thorough check. If he was hoping for a bribe, I had no intention of satisfying him. For some reason, no official ever came back to see me. No one checked on An Hoa's room. From that time on, I assumed there were no illegalities.

After Saigon fell at the end of April 1975, no one thought of putting a sign that said "for rent" in front of the bureau chief's apartment or the office. The government immediately canceled all leases. Private ownership was converted to state control. The government resettled people, when it could, and moved many off the streets. During the war, Saigon's population swelled to three or four times its normal size. With little living space available, commercial property that once housed foreign companies became an obvious place to put the homeless.

The war had ended, and NBC News would soon no longer exist in Vietnam. An Hoa, the only remaining legally listed tenant of NBC News in the building, visited the newly formed People's Committee now in charge of the district. She claimed the apartment and office as hers. She had the good sense to take over both as quickly and quietly as possible. Never able to pass up a bargain, she recognized a good deal. She also realized that the People's Committee was not yet sure of its role and that she could take advantage of them, at least in the short term.

An Hoa prayed every day that NBC News would soon return and her life would again be normal. But in the meantime, she had to figure out how to earn money to live. Her cleaning days were over, but the apartment presented possibilities. Among them were the opportunity to make and sell ice. An Hoa decided to start a business using the small freezer in the kitchen refrigerator and the larger freezer where the bureau's cameramen had stored film away from the heat.

An Hoa became an ice maker in a city without ice. Although she did not become rich, she eked out enough money to live. Each month, a member of the People's Committee knocked on her door to collect the rent. She paid him with a pail of ice. Twice a week she put on a red armband and picked up a long, sharpened stick, her symbols of cooperation with the government. So armed, she patrolled a section of the building with another woman. They kept what the People's Committee called the "beggars and undesirables" from camping in the Eden Building's spacious arcade and once-exclusive shops. Twice a week for years, she feared for her life every time she took on the role of policewoman. But in order to survive, she learned to live with her unhappy task.

In time, she realized that informers were following her when she went to sell ice. She recorded all her transactions to the last detail, but the stool pigeons still reported her activities to the "people's cell" in the Eden Building. Because she worked and could pay for everything she bought, she sometimes sought a choice cut of pork from the butcher, requesting extra fat for added taste. This was in defiance of government regulations. The butcher reported An Hoa to the People's Committee for a subversive act. The record of accusations against her loyalty and character grew by the day.

The Eden Building used more than its share of power. The building committee regularly checked the amount of electricity used by An Hoa, assuming she had to be the culprit because of the freezers she used to make ice. Eventually, building inspectors checked every apartment for power theft. They found seven families who were tapping into an outside set of lines and paying nothing for the electricity they used. Years later, after coming to the United States, An Hoa recalled to me how afraid she had been when uniformed inspectors thoroughly searched her living quarters. They even emptied the dirt from her herb and flower pots onto her well-scrubbed floors. She never understood what they were seeking. She wondered if they thought she was hiding thin strips of twenty-four-carat gold, which the Vietnamese coveted and called taels. Did they think she was planning to escape? When they realized she had not been cheating on her electricity, the inspectors left her alone, but not in peace. Many people in the building, which was so similar to a small village, were jealous of An Hoa's enterprise. Large families wanted the apartment and the office, which she continued to keep perfectly clean. To help them survive, informing against their neighbors had become a way of life for some in that concrete, brick, and plaster hamlet.

In the years after her initial burst of productivity, An Hoa produced little ice, selling most of it to the food vendors on the street, many of them her friends. They exchanged some money, but mostly she survived on barter. Her ice makers were small and the power in her apartment weak. It took a long time to produce enough ice for her to make a decent wage.

In time, Vietnam allowed the Western press to visit and do selective, carefully scrutinized reporting. One day, a man from NBC News in Bangkok or Hong Kong—An Hoa was not certain where he was from—came for a visit to negotiate the return of the equipment left behind when NBC vacated the bureau. An Hoa had managed to keep everything and nothing in the office had gone missing. Valuable cameras, sound gear, and lighting equipment were all there. And the rooms were clean and neat, not at all like they were in the war years. Back then,

An Hoa started washing the floors at five in the morning each day, dusting where she could, and sweeping where she could not wash. But then the correspondents, camera crews, and other staff came to work. By late evening, the floors looked like the New York Port Authority terminal on a bad day. After the war, she still swept daily, making sure the rats, roaches, and carpenter ants did not get into the equipment. She dutifully paid the rent on time, checking every day that the locks on the front doors had not been broken.

Discussions between the American and his Vietnamese adversaries did not last long. NBC lost. The Vietnamese won. It should not have been a surprise to anyone. Recognizing that the battle was over and that he had no further business, the American left the country with nothing. Now that the office was no longer her responsibility, government officials ordered An Hoa to hand over the keys. The next day, representatives from three ministries went to the former fourth-floor offices of NBC News. They cleaned out every piece of equipment, including the furniture, the shelves that lined the walls, and the ancient air conditioners, and they removed the glass top from my desk. An Hoa did not understand it, but they even took a badly corroded aluminum coffeepot with holes eaten into its bottom. We boiled water in a series of those pots over the years to make dark, Nescafé instant coffee that we drank throughout the day. It was a strange treasure for the Vietnamese to confiscate.

Afterward, An Hoa peeked into the bureau and saw nothing there. She told me she felt strange because her ears reverberated with the ghostly clatter of tele-type machines, the ringing of telephones, the singsong lilt of Vietnamese, and flat American voices shouting, whispering, pleading, singing, begging, laughing, even crying. She closed the doors quietly on the phantom echoes in her head. The sounds in her mind ceased. She realized that the NBC News bureau had finally come to its end. She also knew, though, that the spirits of the past would always be with her.

Some years later, with the help of NBC News, An Hoa obtained an exit visa to emigrate to the United States. In the weeks before she left, a building inspector visited her regularly to make sure her papers were in order. She had been grow-ing longan in pots on the balcony outside her front door. The rent collector and inspector always took one sweet, rich fruit for their own enjoyment, eating it in front of her while waiting for the rent or her papers. They never asked permission. They never said thank you. Their presence made An Hoa nervous and apprehen-sive about her departure. She paid her now greatly reduced rent on time and did nothing to cast a negative shadow on her actions. Toward the end, the inspector said there would be trouble for her unless she somehow managed to contribute to his personal welfare fund. After all, he told her, the state provided almost nothing for his family. He demanded a bribe to ensure that she would have a safe and hassle-free departure. She had no choice and she gave him the three hundred dong he wanted—at the time, a fortune, almost a year's rent. No one harassed or pressured her for anything after she paid the bribe. But she did not feel free until her airplane was off the ground and over the Pacific Ocean and she was headed for a new life in the United States.

When An Hoa left Ho Chi Minh City, the office was still empty. NBC News' long era in Saigon had finally ended. An Hoa never knew who moved into the office or the apartment, her last home in Vietnam. And, as I discovered when I gingerly knocked on the door of my old apartment, I was not to know either.

16

To Eat Is to Live
1985

THE SOUTH VIETNAMESE honor food as an important part of their lives. After their victory, the spartan northerners were not fully able to eradicate the culinary sensitivity of the South. Not even revolution can change taste buds. On my return visit, to my gratification, I found the Saigonese still knew how to cook, though in 1985 the necessary ingredients for a good meal were not always available. The Vietnamese had learned to bake perfect loaves of bread from the French, an art they never lost during the war. Sadly, ten years after the war ended, it was difficult to find good bread in a city once proud of its many fine bakeries. There was not enough flour and yeast.

The Vietnamese are passionate about their food. Every Vietnamese I ever met greeted me by trying to feed me. It is an ancient and honored tradition to share a meal with guests in one's home. Vietnamese often greet you by asking when you last ate. "Have something to eat," they will say. "We know you have been traveling. You must be hungry. Welcome to our simple home." Then they will make a slight bow with their hands folded in front of them to show their humility and generosity. They let you know that as a guest you have to eat and drink when you pass through their door. Their humility makes it impossible to refuse their hospitality. Unless you share whatever they have to offer, they feel they have not made you welcome. A family would rather not eat themselves if there is a chance their guest might leave the table hungry. Not to offer food would insult their guests and probably ruin relationships forever. It could bring shame on the family.

In my first days back in Saigon, I ate in the restaurant on the top floor of my hotel, the old Majestic, overlooking the river and the port. For lunch, I sometimes started with tiny shrimp in a strong, hot, red sauce mixed with finely cut onions.

Then I had chicken soup with vermicelli noodles and fresh straw mushrooms. More finely cut onions, crisply fried, floated on the broth. Breakfast, however, usually disappointed. The scrambled eggs were small and rubbery. The fresh-squeezed orange juice tasted flat. To add flavor, you dumped in large-grained, gray, roughly refined sugar by the spoonful. Most of the sugar stayed at the bottom of the glass, being too coarse to mix in fully. When it came to fresh fruit, mangoes and small, almost hand-grenade-sized, pineapples led the way for taste.

It did not take more than a few meals to know that the food at the Majestic, now called the Cuu Long, did not satisfy. To get away from the unchanging daily menu, I went looking for a typical Vietnamese café and some North Vietnamese beef noodle soup, known as *pho*. The soup was said to be tastier and richer in the South, where the ingredients were less scarce.

In 1985, most restaurants operated from the living room, dining room, or patio of a family's house or apartment. The South Vietnamese loved to eat out and depended on small restaurants to meet their needs. During the war, there was a vast variety and huge supply of food in the South. The choices were fewer in 1985, the supply limited. The problems of running a restaurant ten years after the Communist victory were enormous. I stopped at several small storefront restaurants that had three or four beat-up bridge tables and wire-backed chairs. They were out of food. I eventually found what I wanted in a government-controlled restaurant on Le Loi Street, around the corner from the old Rex BOQ.

I stepped inside the restaurant at noon, in time for lunch. The basement room, with its low ceiling, already had too many young men crowded inside. During the 1960s and early 1970s they would have been eligible for the draft. If they were unlucky and could not escape conscription, they would have served in the ARVN. Their chances for survival would not have been good and they could have ended up dead teenagers. In those years, if they were discovered hanging out doing nothing, the police would have asked them questions. Why were they on the street and not in uniform? If their answers were insufficient, the police would arrest them and send them away for limited training. When finished with training, new conscripts received an ill-fitting uniform, a pair of boots and heavy socks, a loaded rifle, a knife, and a knapsack. Then the army would send them to units far from their homes where they would go into battle and perhaps be wounded or killed. If you looked old enough, conscription would be your fate. Without identification, conscription would be your fate. If you looked the wrong way at a Vietnamese policeman or MP, conscription would be your fate.

Because they hated the war and feared they would die for a lost cause, many southerners deserted after their first battle against the hardened, motivated Viet Cong and the often dangerous North Vietnamese army regulars. Some younger deserters worked the back alleys of Saigon near the airport, which the GIs called Scag Alley and Soul Alley. Here were drug dealers and prostitutes, their madams or mama-sans, all for the right price. The Vietnamese kids roamed the alleys bare-legged, wearing ragged shirts and torn short pants. They were lookouts, there to sound a warning in case of surprise raids, usually by disgruntled police not paid enough in bribes. Some became petty criminals while others became pick-pockets. They would ride two to a motorbike, motorcycle, or scooter. The kid in back would grab the watch off your wrist, the fountain pen from your pocket, the briefcase from your side. The press called them Saigon cowboys, but honest Vietnamese, of which there were many, called them bums, hustlers, and crooks.

Not every South Vietnamese deserter chose the path of crime. Older desert-ers often reenlisted in a unit closer to home. Then they could see their family, sometimes slipping away for a day or two at a time. These men were called flower soldiers or ghost soldiers because they remained on the payroll of their first unit, which allowed their original commanding officers to line their pockets by collect-ing the deserters' meager salaries.

Ten years after Saigon became Ho Chi Minh City, young men much like their long-gone brothers sat in that faintly lighted, very dirty, noisy restaurant. They hurriedly slurped their food and drank great quantities of Saigon Beer, the new name for the "33 Brand" produced in South Vietnam in the war years. The beer tasted awful, stale and repulsive, and had not had a large following among Ameri-can troops and civilians. There was always the chance of finding something float-ing in the bottle that had once been alive. Sanitary bottling was not a skill or art in Saigon. Ten years of government control over industry had done nothing to improve the quality of the local beer. I knew when the frothy liquid touched my tongue and hit the roof of my mouth that nothing had changed. Fortunately, a thriving black market existed for Heineken and various Japanese brands. The smuggled beer came off of foreign ships and could be found stacked on the streets near the port. The imports were not available in the restaurant, however, so I drank Saigon Beer.

I sat at a filthy table with dirty dishes piled high in front of me. The staff ignored me for ten minutes. As I expected, almost no one spoke English. My waiter, a skinny old man, finally arrived, cleaned off the table, and dropped a menu in front of me. Then he dumped the dishes in a bucket filled with cloudy water and disappeared. When he came back, it took me a few minutes to make myself clear.

With the help of my limited Vietnamese and the simple menu, I ordered lunch. Again, I had a long wait in the stuffy heat, which the Vietnamese did not seem to mind. The lukewarm beer came with ice in the glass. Refrigeration, a problem in the past, continued to be a problem in 1985. During the war I had learned to drink my beer with ice, a blasphemy in America and most of the world. It was necessary in South Vietnam if you wanted a cold drink. That afternoon, I sipped my beer carefully, convinced that the water that made the ice had gone directly from the brackish, polluted Saigon River into a freezer without being boiled first. It was unsafe to drink anything but boiled or medically sterilized water. I took a chance at lunch. Fortunately I did not suffer for my gamble.

My waiter plunked a bowl of *pho* on the table, then turned and ran from it as if it were repulsive. Perhaps some old fear of Americans prevented him from serving me properly. No matter. I had in front of me a big yellow plastic bowl faded from age. I saw only a few thin strips of beef boiling in the steaming broth, but there were many greens. I took my first spoonful of the watery broth slowly and tasted a strip of stringy, tough beef. Although I had often eaten *pho* outside Vietnam, this version tasted only fair, yet close enough not to be disappointing. The taste of ginger, garlic, lemon grass, cilantro, and pungent *ngoc mam*—a fermented fish sauce—came through.

While I ate, I watched the young people drinking heavily and having a good time. Their gaiety seemed forced, perhaps caused by all the beer they were consuming. It appeared unnatural, considering where the country had been and how the war had turned out. I was the only Westerner in the room. The Vietnamese stared politely. I drank my soup and sipped my beer. Though I felt no hostility, I saw puzzled looks from many in the crowd. Who was I? What did I want? Where did I come from? Why was I there in that restaurant, in Ho Chi Minh City, in Vietnam? I was clearly not Russian. My clothes said that I was an American. My mannerisms were not awkward like a Russian's. More important, Russians, a big presence in Vietnam in 1985, never frequented Vietnamese restaurants. Some people smiled and then turned away. Others looked at me through the corner of their eyes or from behind their ever-present sunglasses. The Saigonese still had something left of their sense of style.

I understood why the North still had problems with the South, particularly here, in a city infused with a Westernized state of mind that would not change. Energy churned beneath the surface, making it difficult for the Communists to change things. The young men wore their hair too long. Many seemed to have nothing to do, nowhere to go. Massive unemployment dominated the growing work force. Some young, however, dressed better than most people I observed walking through the city. Through no fault of their own, though, their trouser bottoms were too wide and their flowered shirts at least ten years behind current styles. Others wore only the clothing they could buy in Vietnam or make themselves, if they could afford the material. Some wore hand-me-downs. When the Communists took power, style fled. It had no place in a country trying to rebuild itself.

The young men and women I joined for lunch were children when the war ended in 1975. They had little, if any, personal recollection of those days. But even these teenagers trying to escape in beer and conversation knew about the war and its ravages. Their elders had told them stories at home over cups of hot tea, and Hanoi, whenever it could, preached its version of the long conflict. Living in Vietnam made it impossible for them not to be familiar with the war we called the Vietnam War and they called their war of liberation.

As hard as I tried, I could not detect the spiritual damage that had been done to these people. That, of course, stayed buried in their minds. However, the physical destruction, both to the people and their country, dominated everything. Everywhere I went, I saw men in their thirties and forties missing hands, arms, or legs. They walked with sticks or canes or one or two makeshift crutches. Some people's arms and legs and what I could see of their slender bodies were permanently scarred and disfigured. They were victims of hot, searing metal from exploded bombs, shells, and bullets fired from rifles and machine guns. They were the rule, not the exception, in every neighborhood, in every village, at every corner and crossroad.

When I left the restaurant, armies of roaches were crawling over the tables. Other insects stuffed themselves on the small mounds of discarded food the waiters swept to the floor. Nobody seemed to mind but me. Of the customers who were there when I came in, hardly any had left. The noise level remained high and the beer still flowed. I thought it must be a badge of honor to see how many empty bottles they could pile on their tables. I paid my bill and walked outside. The brilliant midday sun shone brightly on my face. Thousands of white-hot stars invaded my eyes. I turned quickly away from the sky, searching for shade, trying to refocus. For a moment I had forgotten the power of the sun in Southeast Asia. I had a headache from bad beer, strong sunlight, and too much noise. Yet it could have been worse.

■   ■   ■

The new cooperative restaurants were better off than the few private ones that tried to stay in business against great odds. The cooperative restaurants were usually able to obtain what they needed from the government and did not have to fend for themselves. They had more food because they were allowed to buy at lower prices. Though mainly supported by local residents, they snagged the occasional foreign tourist or businessman who could afford an expensive meal. The sale of one expensive meal a day could pay for a restaurant's upkeep.

Official Vietnam, because of its need to control the economy, wanted to kill off the privately owned eating places where people might choose to eat. Private restaurants and small cafés often had pretentious menus that were throwbacks to the war years. They insisted on listing dishes they assumed people wanted to eat, even when they didn't have the ingredients. "Boeuf Bourguignon" had hardly any beef. "Spaghetti Bolognese" at least had real spaghetti. "Sauce Americain" was something I never understood. There were a variety of other French and American dishes too exotic and outrageous to name.

When I ate at private restaurants that were trying to hold onto their past glory I often learned that the sophisticated Italian, French, and American foods they offered were not available. At times it was impossible to get even a simple Vietnamese dish. The Chi Lan restaurant, near the Central Market, had a menu of perhaps one hundred offerings, with vivid descriptions to match, but little more than a dozen choices were actually available. I had a poor meal there and bad, though cordial, service. The family running the place tried their best, but the results were disappointing and they knew it. An ample quantity of imported beer helped get me and my guests through the evening. The proprietors apologized profusely for their inadequacy. I accepted their apology and left a generous tip.

The owners of private restaurants always did their best to make me feel at ease in what they considered an extension of their home. They wanted to relax me with a drink—beer, wine, or tea—and make me feel welcome as a newly adopted member of their family. Quite often, I was fortunate to find a decent meal to go with the hospitality. Hot food would be prepared on a charcoal grill, in a charcoal pit on the floor, or in a large wood oven in an open kitchen. Even in the worst of times, some cold food was usually available.

Many restaurants and cafés were expensive, even for the few Vietnamese who had extra money and wanted a night out. Most restaurants could not survive on the infrequent tourists, official guests of the government, and the occasional journalist. There were not enough of us to support them. So the restaurants prepared simple (at least for them), everyday Vietnamese food for those who wanted it and for the rare foreigner who knew what and how to order, as if he were eating in the kitchen of a friendly stranger.

When a Vietnamese family went out to eat, it was either to celebrate a special occasion—a birthday, wedding, winning a bet, winning at cards, winning the lottery—or it meant they had saved their hard-earned money and pooled it with several other families or relatives for a rare, once-a-month splurge. Saigonese who loved eating out were embittered that their lives had become limited. They loved the thrill of sitting in restaurants and coffeehouses, talking and gossiping, and listening in on "Radio Catinat," their shorthand for the rumors that floated over Tu Do Street, which was once called Rue Catinat. They wanted a good time, life in all its moods and tempers. People did not want to watch their world, once full of pleasures, vanish before their eyes.

When I watched the Vietnamese having a good time, as I did while having lunch in the basement restaurant, their fun seemed forced to me. It lacked spontaneity. Their liveliness was too intense. They were people trying to be happy and not succeeding. They suffered from a dry existence, their high-flying southern spirit dampened. Every time I saw individual vitality squeezed in the name of some declared ideology, I wondered about the real nature of North Vietnam's victory over the South. When I discussed ideas with Vietnamese Communists, they avoided current issues: food, productivity, standard of living. Instead they preferred to recite their version of history, boring you with their endless discourse. It sent your mind on a flight elsewhere, which was probably their intent. They wanted to throw you off the scent, the reality of their daily problems. There were angry old men in Hanoi in 1985 indulging their will—and to a degree their revenge—on the South, exercising their power in the name of socialist destiny. Until that changed, the Vietnamese people had small chance of an improved life.

In 1966, most of us covering the war thought a lot about the future. We wanted to survive, to eat and drink as best we could in spite of the war. Excellent Chinese food was available everywhere. We often dined at the Diamond in Cholon, famous for its cracked hot pepper crab. We ate at the Golden Lotus, the Blue Diamond on Tu Do Street, even Cheap Charlie's behind the Caravelle. Arcenciel in Cholon featured Vietnamese girls singing American ballads as if they were laments, which is what they became when translated into Vietnamese. Sad songs went well with helicopters churning overhead, and wailing sirens complemented the orchestra's reedy, off-key melodies. For an expensive 1940s-style night on the town, we had Maxime or the Eden Roc. Prices were painfully high and the food worse than the entertainment. Poor Italian food and cheap, acidic, North African red wines could be found at La Dolce Vita and Caruso. These were restaurants managed by well-connected Italians, Corsicans, and other Frenchmen. They had to have connections in high places to keep their establishments open, protected, and safe. But they could not make a decent plate of spaghetti, though they tried. There were thousands of Korean troops in Vietnam and many other Koreans working for American news agencies and other foreign companies. We enjoyed hot, spicy food with a special Korean edge and homemade kimchi at the Eskimo, a restaurant that was exceedingly clean and antiseptic. Once you stepped inside the Eskimo, you experienced a truly frigid air-conditioning system unlike any other in the country. Thus, the name.

Civilians working for the military or for the huge construction companies that were building roads, ports, and airstrips under multimillion-dollar contracts crowded these restaurants and clubs. There were also merchant sailors and the usual mix of international hangers-on, making money off the war and spending it as fast as they earned it.

In the 1960s and 1970s, going to Maxime in downtown Saigon was like going to Studio 54 in New York. It had a similar aura, though not the chic. Later, its glory faded and it had to work hard to retain even a touch of its past, but by 1985, even with the scarcity of food, Maxime had become a showcase restaurant and a good place to eat in Ho Chi Minh City. It surprised me to have so many good meals in a restaurant that had never been known for the quality of its food. They served mostly Cantonese dishes with the distinct Vietnamese touch of lemongrass, diced ginger, garlic, and finely sliced tiny red peppers. The cracked pepper crab was almost as good as that I had had at other restaurants, particularly the Diamond in Cholon, where in 1966 I first struggled through an entire meal with chopsticks and a ceramic spoon, with no knife or fork to help me. Now at Maxime almost twenty years later, chopsticks were an extension of my right hand. At the same time, nostalgia had become an extension of my spirit.

Shrimp, usually available, were always fresh and clean. Green pepper, onions, and scallions, or spring onions, were firm, their color sharp and bright. Beef, rarely available and of uncertain origin, had a lively tang when mixed with mush-rooms and large chunks of white onion. Lemongrass, fresh or dry, helped make the beef dishes distinctive. The brown sauce surrounding the sparse chunks of meat was light, not too heavily laced with cornstarch. Tiny red peppers were hot and fiery, adding a touch of brightness to many otherwise drab dishes. The roasted pigeon, a Vietnamese specialty, failed the palate, though. They were gamy and stringy, and I blamed the taste and texture on the birds—perhaps they had been trapped on the streets, rather than raised for eating. Crab claws were small, probably too young when harvested from the sea, but the meat was still sweet, though sometimes soft and stringy.

Some nights there was less food than others, even with the restaurant a government showplace. There were times when we ordered a dish in advance only to have nothing arrive at our table. From meal to meal, we never knew what vegetable would be available. String beans appeared once, then they disappeared forever. Carrots had a good run for several days, then they were no longer in evidence. Onions were always plentiful, sweet and small and often the main ingredient of a dish. With onions and peppers, a good chef could salvage most meat, fish, and fowl. One restaurant served tough mutton. There were never many sheep in Vietnam, especially for meat. I wondered where the mutton came from. Maybe from a can left behind by the Aussie soldiers who battled bravely in the swamp south of Saigon near Vung Tao. Maybe it wasn't mutton at all, but a goat that became too expensive to feed, worth more in a kitchen pot than tethered in an alley next to someone's home.

In Maxime, to ensure getting the meal we wanted, we had to leave a large deposit days in advance. That way, we could order our food from the small, but quickly growing, free market. The government was against farmers growing for profit, but officials were quietly learning to tolerate it. The restaurant did not have to depend on its often inadequate ration to feed us because we gave the owner enough money to go outside the system.

During most meals we drank Heineken beer. We could buy it a few blocks from the Majestic Hotel at the burgeoning, open, black market. We paid the equivalent of a dollar a can. The beer came from Holland, and stamped across the top of each can were the words, "For Duty Free Sales Only." There were many ships in port, and one Scandinavian purser told me he loaded extra beer in his home port to sell in Saigon. He made a great deal of money smuggling. Other canned beers, Kirin and Asahi from Japan and San Miguel from Hong Kong and the Philippines, also came off the ships.

In the well-organized black market, neatly stacked cases of beer by brand and national origin were openly displayed. The stacks stretched as high as twenty feet. Vietnamese men scrambled to the top to lower down a case of whatever label you wanted. Uniformed police patrolled the area, sharing in the profit. Prices rarely varied. It struck me as another example of Hanoi allowing its almost wayward southern sister city a bit more freedom than any other city in the country. Interestingly, I never saw an empty beer or soda can anywhere on the street or in the too-common mounds of garbage found on the corners. People salvaged all malleable refuse and recycled it for walls and roofs, a practice that was little changed from the war years. In the 1960s I had looked in awe at the shacks and lean-tos with roofs and walls made of "tinnies," those heavier, lead-based beer cans of the day. I still marveled at the ingenuity of these resilient people.

In wartime, Maxime had been a center for glitz and corruption. It looked like a set from a 1930s gangster movie, but in color, dominated by flickering strobe lights: a Christmas tree without the pine needles. The huge nightclub had served as a playboy's haven. Taxi dancers and prostitutes, often one and the same, were everywhere, and drugs were openly sold and openly used. Free-spending, often drunken construction workers from everywhere in the world squired very young, slim, and once shy Vietnamese girls who had no pride in their heritage. It had become more important to feed themselves and their families than to honor the past. War and its uncertainties made it easier for these young women to forget their strict, conservative upbringing. Corrupt Vietnamese military officers, who never heard a shot fired, gulped Napoleon cognac well past the ever-changing nightly curfew. Get-rich-quick Vietnamese and Chinese profiting from the war completed this scene of grotesque, pre–World War II Berlin transported to Southeast Asia.

Big band music, heavy on guitars and violins, filled the room with that odd mixture found only in Saigon, Manila, and Hong Kong: Rolling Stones–style rock and roll; always the Beatles; sweet, bouncy bubblegum music; and folk songs like "Danny Boy" and "My Bonnie Lies Over the Ocean." Lithe Vietnamese women vocalists stood absolutely still on stage. They rarely moved behind the microphone. Many had surgically uplifted breasts and straightened noses to mimic what they assumed was the American look found in *Playboy*. They wore beautiful, formal, silk *ao dais* and sang their songs in lilting, birdlike voices. Their words floated in orderly lines over the dank, large room, high above the noise from the dance floor and restaurant. The noise in the room—loud talk, clanking dishes, continuous music—overwhelmed everyone. There were floor shows copied from old Hollywood movies. Dozens of female dancers entered and departed by large circular staircases to the right and left of the stage. Crowds waited outside in the night air. They were anxious to get in, but never forced their way past the flimsy barriers.

There were people who were willing to pay those in front of them for the right of passage, the right to enter first.

Vietnamese soldiers fresh from fighting in the field knew Maxime well. Carrying loaded weapons, they drank, ate, and played until drunk, high, or exhausted. Then they would try to leave without paying. They were soldiers, and they felt they deserved a free night on the town. After being ejected, they sometimes returned and shot up the gaudy nightclub. Often they caused a small riot and we would come running with a crew. Fortunately, there were never any fatalities. Miraculously, only a few patrons ever suffered even slight flesh wounds. After covering one of these incidents, I watched the Vietnamese military police beat a half dozen soldiers who were falling-down drunk from too much brandy and beer. The young soldiers wore tiger-striped jungle fatigues made in tailor shops throughout the city. They were so drunk, they hardly seemed to feel the blows to their thin bodies. I could tell, though, from the taut muscles on their strained faces that they had recently had more than their fill of combat. A few hours in the stockade would give them some peace before they returned to the war. Then it would start all over as they again faced death in the jungles and swamps of their faltering country. I doubted they would ever return to Saigon, unless in a plain box or an earthenware jar holding their ashes. Incidents like these gave Maxime its mystique, one forever fixed in the city's soul.

No one ate the poor food at Maxime. Food was just part of the table setting, or an aftermath to a night of heavy drinking. The prices were outrageously high. You didn't go to Maxime to eat, but they always had a big supply of imported beer and whiskey, including scotch, sour mash from Tennessee, and American rye. You could buy cheap Algerian red wine by the carafe, probably drained from the same barrels used by the Corsicans who owned the pizza restaurants in town. The newly rich Saigonese society people went to Maxime to see who was sleeping with whom, which general or politician had a new mistress, or who had recently completed an illegal deal that allowed him to waste his money freely.

The nightclub, owned by a group of Vietnamese army generals who financed it by falsifying pay rosters, functioned as a front for military officers to steal from the government. Wives of high-ranking officials had unlimited travel outside the country, and they were smart enough to spend their money in Hong Kong, Bangkok, or Singapore. I heard that confidants of President Thieu received a cut and that a leading senator in the National Assembly also received large payoffs. No matter how it worked, the people who owned Maxime made a fortune. On the rare evening when the club was only half full, the waiters would be mean, surly, and nervous. Oddly, despite the opportunities afforded by the planned power black-outs, the Viet Cong never bombed or sabotaged Maxime. The accepted wisdom was that the VC were smart enough to let a good enterprise flower. Maxime took only cash, no checks. That meant the Viet Cong could collect protection money—or taxes, as they preferred to call it—from Maxime to fill their frequently depleted coffers. Maxime was in the unenviable position of making money and providing it to everyone who had demands. Everyone.

By April 1985, Maxime had become a state-run restaurant. At almost any time of day or night, I could find NBC staffers eating a bowl of noodle soup, sipping tea, or drinking cold beer. I met a man I had known as a waiter at the Blue Diamond, the restaurant on Tu Do Street that was a hangout for journalists. He now worked at Maxime as the unofficial manager. Though he had not spoken it much in the years since we Americans departed Vietnam, my old friend's English had not grown stale. Like many Vietnamese Buddhists, he had had enough pain in his life to last into his next existence and the one after that as well. He told me he prayed that whatever place he would dwell in would be better than where he was now.

Several nights a week on my return visit, the orchestra at Maxime played its version of popular music. Awful, perfunctory, and emotionless, it was a rinky-dink ballroom trip to a past that was already musty in the 1960s. All the songs, whether ballad or upbeat, sounded the same. The music, plucked out on lifeless strings badly in need of tuning, moved to a strange beat hiding somewhere in the musicians' hearts. "Tenderly" and "Yesterday" were the highlights of each set, yet it always took a few minutes for the audience to figure out exactly which number was being played.

17

Courtship

SEVERAL WEEKS after my return in 1985, I took a long cyclo ride to what had been Josephine Tu Ngoc Suong's family home out past the Central Market. I used my regular driver, Quy, who never stopped talking, his singsong patter lulling me to sleep as we whipped through the streets. Quy was a good driver, strong and responsive though already well past forty. I had one major problem when I rode with him. Everywhere we went, he told people I was "lien so," Vietnamese for Soviet, for Russian. I told him to say, "khong phai lien so," which meant, I am not Soviet, not a Russian. Though he was surprised to hear I had some knowledge of Vietnamese, it did not stop him from trying to have his way. He did not know I took the phrase with me from New York in case I needed it.

"Sir," he said, "I hope not to insult you. I know you are 'my'—American in my language—but if I told people you are American, they would be happy. Crowds would follow us on the street." I found that hard to believe, but I did not argue with him.

Josephine had lived with her father; her mother, whom everyone called Ma Tu; her four brothers, when they were home from the war; her younger sister, Hoan; her grandmother; and, at different times, several uncles in a big, sprawling house on Phat Diem Street, near the Nha Tho Cau Kho Catholic church, off the main avenue leading to Cholon. The house had stood on a corner, next to a small, busy marketplace that was open on all sides and where the local people bought fresh fruit and vegetables and, when available, pork. Dried fish was plentiful then, and live fish caught in the Saigon River swam in old wood barrels, waiting for a buyer. Called Cho Cau Kho, the market was the Vietnamese version of an American supermarket, but without its strict organization or discipline.

When the cyclo stopped in front of what had been Josephine's house, I found myself back in 1966, hearing the old voices in the street. I saw children at play and watched lean, barking dogs roaming the street. I smelled the delicious odors of Ma Tu's cooking and the not-so-pleasant odors of the street littered with dirt and refuse. American music cascaded over the neighborhood from inside Josephine's house. The sounds came from my future wife's rock and folk band, The Free Ones, or, in French, La Liberté. Josephine managed the band and owned the instruments, sang lead, and negotiated engagements in American enlisted men's clubs in Saigon, Tan Son Nhut, Long Binh, and Gia Dinh. Her band of lead guitar, bass, rhythm guitars, and drums was rehearsing the songs of the Beatles, Herman's Hermits, and Nancy Sinatra, with a sprinkling of Joan Baez. The Free Ones' Western music filled the street, its rocking sound floating out through the open windows. Nineteen-sixties rock and roll mixed with the sounds of traffic outside, the spitting, coughing motorbikes and scooters zipping by the house. Many youngsters below the age of conscription were in the Tu house, sitting on the stairs and in the huge, dormitory-like room on the second floor, listening to the music, enthralled with American culture. Adults sat on the patio, where my future mother-in-law had her restaurant. She opened only for breakfast and served her faithful customers shrimp omelettes, French bread, coconut chicken, flan, and Saigon coffee made with chicory and sweet condensed milk. Neighborhood people, including the local police and the pilots who steered barges on the Saigon River, ate and drank while they chatted, smoked harsh French cigarettes, and gossiped freely about their lives and the war.

Josephine's family suspected that the cyclo drivers who waited for customers near her corner were Viet Cong sympathizers and spies. Neither I nor anyone else ever knew who they worked for, the Viet Cong, the National Police, or both. No doubt, they were in one pocket or another. Even if they were not working against the South Vietnamese and the Americans, they probably gave information to anyone who would pay. Some were pimps. Others steered for drug pushers or worked for black marketeers and money changers. Rarely did you see a young driver. Most of them were away in the military. If the military police found a young driver, they drafted him on the spot. At times when the bureau's cars were not available, I used cyclos to get to the scene of a terrorist bombing or riot. The drivers knew their way around the city and usually knew something about the story even before we arrived.

During the war, people of all ages, especially children at play with their mangy dogs, filled the nearby church, which was an informal child care center that allowed parents to seek work and earn a living. Old people sought solace and respite from the war within the high-domed, austere, cool interior. Now, in 1985, the church was empty and its lawn had turned brown, the grass gone to dust amid potholes full of muddy water. Once, the church grounds had been neat, well cared for. Now they were in need of serious grooming. Weeds replaced the blooming flower beds that had encircled the building. The stone facade cried out for sandblasting; the wooden trim needed a fresh coat of paint. The street had not changed, but the Tu home had new occupants. Troops of the Vietnamese army— their accents northern, according to my driver—now lived where Josephine and her family once lived. I thought back to how my life with Josephine began.

After I settled into the routine of running NBC News, Saigon, it did not take me long to realize how my life had changed. The climate, with its sustained heat and sudden rain, especially during the monsoon season; the noise, dirt, and truly foreign smell; and a difficult language I had never before heard all presented problems unlike anything I knew growing up in Brooklyn or afterward. Despite traveling extensively in the United States, Europe, and Central and South America, I had an enormous adjustment to make and much to learn about Saigon and Vietnam. I often wondered if I could ever bridge the divide, the vast difference between the two cultures. I could not do it alone. Josephine became my willing guide and mentor, walking me through the nuances and labyrinth of Vietnamese life. Out of her natural warmth and graciousness, Josephine held out a hand of welcome and comfort to me, a stranger in a strange land. Then, something unexpected took hold: love. It began, as do many romances, innocently. That it flowered into love was an unexpected gift.

Courting a Vietnamese woman was difficult for anyone not of the same race. During World War II, when the Viet Minh took on the French, then when Vichy France and the Japanese ruled the country, and after the war when the Vietnamese threw the French out, men and women of different cultures had an immensely difficult time having an honest, heartfelt relationship. During the Vietnam War, the open distrust and dislike that Vietnamese men had toward American men, and the fear that Vietnamese women had of all foreign men, made it doubly hard to pursue a woman seriously. When the French ruled Indochina, most Vietnamese women learned to steer clear of Frenchmen and to distrust their intentions. The French looked on Vietnamese women as chattel, something to dispose of after use, which was usually only sexual. And many Vietnamese refused to mix with the Chinese because they feared and distrusted them, believing their god was mammon, not anything pure, and their allegiance was strictly to China, never Vietnam.

When Josephine agreed for the first time to have dinner with me, she told me she was breaking her rule never to date anyone from the office. Perhaps I had a chance, I thought. Fortunately, our relationship progressed. Because of the times and of circumstances not controlled by us, our courtship had its imperfections from my point of view and was alien to how men wooed women in New York. We never went to a movie, a show, even the rare concert. Instead, we dined in the biggest restaurants in Saigon. I always had one of my drivers pick Josephine up at her home. Sometimes I met her at the restaurant. Other times, I came along for the ride. The driver took us to the restaurant of our choice, often Arcenciel in Cholon, where they had excellent food and diverting floor shows. We would have dinner and talk. But we never held hands or touched. Even in a darkened restaurant, there were too many people for her to feel comfortable. We could never stay long because we both had to be off the streets at curfew.

Without meaning to, I put Josephine in an untenable position, especially when we were together in public. When we went out to an occasional lunch, Josephine often in the traditional *ao dai,* we rarely walked side by side. She usually walked behind me, or me behind her. When we started dating, every man in the street, from the police to the cyclo divers, from the vendors to the soldiers in their skintight uniforms, ridiculed Josephine. They called her a whore and a disgrace to her race because she appeared in public with an American. I became angry, adrenalin coursing through my body, wanting to strike out at their stupidity. Josephine quickly defused my fury and I began to understand the fear of the Vietnamese. To them, American men had only one thought in mind: sex. They thought Americans were out to steal their women and sully the race forever. Sex for sale could be found everywhere, and there were American men who did have only that on their minds. Vietnamese on the street had no way of knowing my intentions were serious. In time, the neighborhood people left us alone. Soon the bureau knew about us, as did the rest of the press. Then we could relax in the company of other journalists, but still we kept our distance. In the office, we were proper, boss and employee. Josephine did her work and I did not exceed my authority. Never did she feel cowed by my gaze, nor did I look on her as less than a serious worker.

Whenever I visited her busy home, her neighborhood viewed me with distrust. Her mother became my champion, her father my supporter. Many a night, Ma Tu sent stacked trays of hot, delicious food to my office. Sometimes when I picked Josephine up for dinner, I would get out of the car, wave to the family, and wait for Josephine. She would walk quickly from the entrance and enter Mr. Long's car, and we would drive to a restaurant. The neighbors thought that I, an American coming to visit a Vietnamese woman, and a beautiful one at that, had to be up to no good. And Josephine and her family, they also had to be up to no good. Why else did I visit there? The neighbors could not believe that a family with four sons in the military, two of whom were officers, was actually letting me court their daughter. They could not understand that, as my father would have said, my intentions were serious—so much so that I bought Josephine a diamond engagement ring that I found with the help of a Chinese friend's wife when I was in Hong Kong for a rest in the summer of 1967. I gave it to Josephine and asked her to marry me. She said yes, but we would not become husband and wife until my assignment ended and we left Vietnam.

In late December, I returned to New York for a discussion about my future. My tour was due to end but I decided to stay in Saigon an additional six months, suspecting, as I told anyone who would listen, that there would be a major change in the war. Too much was happening on too many fronts, including, in November, major battles at Dak To in the Central Highlands and a North Vietnamese troop buildup along the DMZ. The extension would also give Josephine more time, in her words, "to learn more cooking and sewing" from her mother. Her parents understood she would leave Vietnam with me and we would marry elsewhere. After my meetings in New York, I went to Mexico City for a short rest. I planned to join Reuven Frank in Los Angeles and then tour the Far East with him by visiting NBC Tokyo and Hong Kong, with Saigon our final destination. He and I talked of my staying in the Far East after leaving Vietnam as NBC was considering upgrading its presence in that part of the world.

On the night after I arrived in Mexico City, the phone rang in my hotel room about two in the morning. I woke from a deep sleep. On the phone from New York was Lois Marino, a good friend and Reuven's assistant. Because of our long relationship, she took it upon herself to give me the terrible news that Josephine had been shot by a stray bullet accidentally fired in the office and had suffered a serious head wound.

Josephine had been in the bureau on a Saturday morning doing paperwork. In the maintenance room behind her desk, an American soundman was attempting to unload a North Vietnamese AK-47 rifle he had brought back from Dak To as a souvenir. He could not get the bolt open, and set about dismantling the weapon. He knew a bullet was in the chamber, and was determined to remove it. He removed several pieces, including the spring that held the bolt tight against the cartridge. He put the weapon on the floor with the stock down and the barrel pointed upwards, put one foot on the bolt, and tried to release it. It still held tight. In his words, "I all but gave up and set the gun back to rest on the table. It was then the gun went off." The bullet glanced off the workbench, ricocheted off a box of rubber stamps, and flew through the open door between the workshop and the outer office. At just that moment, Josephine was passing by, and the bullet hit her, slamming into the left side of her head.

Howard Tuckner was in the bureau when the bullet struck, and he ran to JUS-PAO across the street to have them summon an American ambulance. He knew a call from JUSPAO would carry more weight. Because Josephine worked for an American company, she received the kind of special attention rarely given a Vietnamese civilian. She was rushed to the 17th Field Hospital in Cholon, where her doctors realized she needed neurosurgery and sent her to the major field hospital in Long Binh. Fortunately for Josephine, one of the top neurosurgeons in Vietnam, Dr. Justin Renaudin, Captain, United States Army, happened to be at Long Binh that day, operated, and saved her life. Had she gone to a Vietnamese hospital, she probably would have died or ended up paralyzed beyond hope of recovery. I knew none of this when Lois called.

I found it impossible to process the shocking news from Lois. I did not know what to think. Lois kept repeating that Josephine was alive. The wound was serious, she told me, but Josephine would live. I do not recall everything I said to Lois, but I knew I had to get out of there and back to Saigon. I hung up, dressed, and went to the nearest ticket office. With the new year about to arrive, I knew it would be difficult to leave Mexico City. It took me several hours to book and then board a plane to Los Angeles. In Los Angeles, I had nine hours before my flight to Saigon, so I called Bill Wordham, a correspondent who had worked for me in Vietnam. Through the goodness of his heart, he spent the day with me and helped me through those difficult hours.

I finally boarded a Pan American flight and arrived in Saigon on January 1, 1968, at 10:45 in the morning. In what may have been the longest flight of my life, I wrestled sleeplessly through the many time zones across the Pacific until we finally landed at Tan Son Nhut. I remember wearing a double-breasted wool blazer. Though I liberally perspired, I was too preoccupied to remove my jacket. Mr. Long met and cleared me through customs and we drove silently to Long Binh Hospital where Gary Bel, my assistant, had been staying with Josephine through her ordeal. He told me that soon after the operation she managed to convey that she wanted a pencil and paper. He gave it to her and she wrote my name, Ron. I still have the scribbled, nearly illegible page. Her head swathed in bandages, intravenous tubes in each arm, Josephine looked terrible. When she saw me, she managed a smile, and I could only cry.

Her doctor said she would never walk again. He said she would have little or no use of her right leg, right arm, and right hand. He advised her to make a choice about which language would be her main one. With her knowledge of Vietnamese, French, English, and a smattering of Chinese and Japanese, she faced what the neurosurgeons called the Babel effect. The damage to her brain could cause her thoughts and words to become jumbled when she tried thinking or speaking. To my pleasure, she chose English, which meant she still chose to have a life with me.

Josephine was transferred to the Third Field Hospital at Tan Son Nhut, closer to home. Fourteen days after her wounding, holding my arm as tightly as she could and refusing to use a wheelchair, she walked out of the hospital and returned home. She started twice-weekly physical therapy at the Third Field Hospital at Tan Son Nhut with the gracious help of U.S. Air Force therapists. Now she was told her recovery would be long and laborious but she would walk again, talk again, and have a mostly normal life. One year later, when living in Hong Kong, we married and then went on to live in London, Washington, D.C., and New York, where we watched our two sons and daughter grow into lovely adults.

In Vietnam, reality always intrudes, forcing its way back when reverie fades. My thoughts returned to the present that morning on Phat Diem Street. I still sat in Quy's cyclo. The Tu home had become a police station or army headquarters, possibly also a communications post and housing for officers. Warning signs and flags with red stars plastered every wall. Suddenly, Quy became very nervous and stopped his constant chattering. Sitting on the seat in front of him, I could feel his tension running through the cyclo's rusting metal like an electric current. Bending close to my ear, Quy whispered, "The *bo dois*," meaning, the Communist soldiers—they did not like my being there. I counted a half dozen sinewy, hard-looking men standing outside the house. A few men leaned out the second-floor windows. Others sat on the patio where my mother-in-law had run her restaurant. The soldiers looked us over carefully. Faint smiles crossed their tight, wary mouths. I quickly decided that for once I would be happy to be "lien so." If there was to be trouble, it would be easier to be Russian, not American, at least at the start when we might need a moment to think or time to get away.

We moved twenty feet away from the front of the house and had reached the entrance to the outdoor market when I told Quy to stop. The potential for trouble did not keep me from slowly getting out of the cyclo. Quy was shaking his head wildly and whispering, "No, no." My camera at the ready, I turned and quickly started taking as many pictures as I could so I would have a record for my in-laws of the house where they once lived.

Deeply tanned men in army fatigues now stood in the unpaved road watching us, probably wondering why I was taking pictures of the place where they lived and worked. Many of the neighborhood people had come out onto the street. The curious smiled; others watched with stern faces. Quy had had enough and urged me to get moving. Panic filled his gruff voice and he announced that we had to leave. Realizing the urgency of his cry, I climbed back into the seat so fast I almost caused the cyclo to tip over. In my hurry, I did not get all the shots I wanted. Quy started to pedal casually, methodically, but as fast as he could, away, away, back down the street we had come from. Once we were on Tran Hung Dao, he pulled down a side street to the right. Then he turned onto another street to the left, then into an alley to the right. He drove with as much power as his legs could generate.

"Sir," he shouted, "they are following us. Let me see how far they get and how much strength they have to chase us. I know the streets. I do not want them to catch me."

I had no choice, so I kept quiet, tightly holding on to the metal armrests, letting him do as he thought best. I looked behind, but I could not see any soldiers chasing us. I did not question my guide, though I believed he had a good imagination. I did not live in Saigon. He did. He could be right. I assumed he knew his business and we would either get caught if he stumbled or slowed or would manage to escape by virtue of his fancy footwork. I decided that no matter what happened, he would end the day with a world-class tip.

We moved steadily through a once middle-income neighborhood that was now poor, no different from most of Saigon. At times we were less than fifty feet from the Saigon River, which made me think of my wife's home, also close to the river. I realized we were making a kind of horseshoe turn with a twist, and the longer and harder Quy pedaled, the more distance we put between the house and the soldiers who might be chasing us.

The streets over which we raced were in miserable shape. Obviously, the committee that ruled Ho Chi Minh City never came near this area. No blacktop. Pits and ruts beyond repair everywhere. Pools of stagnant water on every corner stared at us like empty eyes. The people looked more ragged than others I had seen in the city. Once these streets had many small shops and factories, and heavy traffic made them impassable. Now they were empty. Too many men and women sat around doing nothing, more proof of the unemployment problem facing the Vietnamese government. If anybody noticed us, they didn't seem to care. I thought that was a good sign.

Garbage was piled on every street corner. Women garbage collectors were pulling large two-wheeled wagons, wearing faded yellow, Japanese-style gauze masks to ward off the smell of decay and to help filter out the germs rising from the rot. But there were too few wagons and too few women to do the job. Their work would never end. Shaggy, sickly dogs, some with running, ulcerated sores on their thin legs and hairless haunches, barely snarled at us as we moved rapidly through the potholed roads.

Nothing happened during our return to the Cuu Long Hotel. I never felt that the Vietnamese soldiers were following us. My driver thought so, though, and without actual proof, his fears were good enough for me. If we were "scouted" as he contended, then he did an excellent job of losing them. The roundabout route to the hotel took an additional twenty minutes. On Quy's automatic foot meter, it cost me an additional three hundred dong for the trip, and I gave him a tip equal to the total fee. Not much money to me, but as a week's worth of milk for his kids, a successful day for Quy. He had a story to tell the other cyclo drivers, which raised his stature. My trip to Josephine's home had ended in a dash of excitement but, in truth, without incident. Despite the war, I had fond memories of those heady days, and it made me sad to see how things had changed. Those memories only increased my sadness beyond my emotional control.

18

Laurie and Lan

BORN IN THE United States in 1975, my Vietnamese niece Laurie was ten in 1985 and had never seen her father. Hoan, her mother, known as Agnes, was pregnant with her when the war raced to its swift end. Her father, Nguyen Van Lan, a graduate of the Dalat Military Academy and a handsome young lieutenant colonel in the elite Ranger-Airborne known for his bravery and ability to command, had his chance to leave the country but he did not.

President Nguyen Van Thieu, also a Dalat graduate, gave up the fight early without telling his generals or the people. He fled his dying country before it fell, deserting his people and his supposed ideals. Thieu took with him gold ingots worth millions. Other members of his corrupt household eagerly filled the seats of his airplane as it departed Tan Son Nhut Airport before dawn, days before the victorious North Vietnamese marched into Saigon.

Because of their close connection with an American and their fear of North Vietnamese reprisal, my in-laws had also made the decision to leave the country. From my post in New York, I made a last-minute appeal to a CIA agent at the U.S. embassy to get them on the departure list. On a designated Saigon street corner, as the family waited for the bus that would take them to Tan Son Nhut Air Base, Lan told his wife he would not be going with them. Ever the dreamer, the romantic warrior, he wanted to stay and fight the advancing North Vietnamese forces. He thought he could use his fighting skills and prove again his ability to lead. A barely workable bus arrived and Hoan cried, reluctant to leave her husband. He told her she must go and gently pushed her away from him onto the bus, forcing her into the arms of her father and the other members of the family. Each carried a small bag with a few personal possessions and had gold, jewels, and new South Vietnamese banknotes concealed on their persons. The notes became worthless overnight. The nervous bus driver told Hoan that they had to leave. He had a schedule to meet. At Tan Son Nhut, the family boarded an American Air Force C-130 airplane that flew them to the heat-racked processing camps of Guam. They were among the fortunate who got out before Saigon collapsed.

His wife gone, Lieutenant Colonel Lan, not yet thirty, stayed behind to fight, but for what? There were no men left to rally. South Vietnamese soldiers had tossed their weapons casually into the streets. These demoralized and defeated troops shucked their uniforms in favor of underwear. They would rather have faced capture than fire their weapons in a lost cause. Few soldiers cared to keep fighting. The years of struggling for survival had sapped their desire for war. Lan, though, had another reason to stay. He thought he could get his parents, who were living in Hue, out of the country. But he misjudged his ability to move around the country. With the war over, it became impossible for South Vietnamese to leave, especially those not connected to an American. That would change several years later when desperate South Vietnamese started fleeing to freedom by the thousands in boats, making a mockery of the new order in Vietnam. Lan's parents, however, were too old for a dangerous journey, so they stayed behind in Vietnam.

The end for South Vietnam had come quickly, too quickly for anyone left hoping for better days. The South Vietnamese Army had crumbled. Nothing remained of the Thieu government. All former soldiers had to report to North Vietnamese officials in their home district. Showing how dutiful they could be, they appeared on schedule, to the surprise of their new leaders. They understood they would enter reeducation camps where they would stay for thirty days. This is what the victorious Communists claimed Lan, and others like him, needed to become model citizens. Thoughts of insurrection still whirled in Lan's head, but not as strongly. He kept alive his hopes that he would soon be free of the Communists and be able to join his wife in the United States. Maybe, he thought, the ravages of war would end. His dreams were not to be. Bad luck and the new Communist government took a powerful and disastrous hold over the lieutenant colonel's life.

By the time I returned in 1985, Lan had been a political prisoner for ten years. Since 1975, year by year, his patient wife, now working as a chef in Maryland, had traced his journey through the Vietnamese gulag. Hoan had followed his path from prison camp to prison camp, starting outside Hanoi where he and other high-ranking officers were first transported. Lan spent hard time in many different camps all over the newly united country. From what Hoan could learn, his jailers were not able to change the way he thought. They could not retool his mind. They found it impossible to make Lan believe they were good and he evil. He had become as unbending as they. So they shipped him from camp to camp, warden to warden. He never stayed too long in one location. Eventually he was sent to the deep south and then to a camp northeast of Saigon. He sent infrequent letters, and in those Hoan received from his friends and family in Vietnam, they wondered how he, and others like him, had survived. As did any Vietnamese political prisoner, he had a series of continuing and damaging health problems. Not enough green vegetables; he had only the occasional weed to eat. Not enough protein; he had almost no meat for months at a time. Not enough natural vitamins. Hardly any fruit. No pure water, ever. Almost no rice. Too many parasites. Too many insects. Vermin. Who knew how many beatings he had experienced in his ten years of imprisonment? Who knew or could calculate the extent of his mental torture?

Hoan's appeals for help to Hanoi and to Washington, including several members of Congress, went unheard. Hanoi did not care. Washington had no power. The politicians wanted nothing to do with the Vietnam War. It was easy to ignore one Vietnamese immigrant and her pleas to have her husband freed from political prison. Hoan became an American citizen. She lived with her daughter, Laurie, and other members of her family in Rockville, Maryland, outside Washington. She sent Lan pictures of their daughter, lovely, intelligent, lonely. I believe those visual progress reports on a life free of fear helped to keep him going against the mighty and nearly insurmountable obstacles he had to his survival.

When I told the family I would be going to Vietnam, I said I would try to deliver needed medical supplies to Lan and would work to free him from his long imprisonment. Every Vietnamese I knew urged caution for Lan's sake and mine. Many months before my visit, I entrusted the location of Lan's prison camp to a friend and fellow journalist, Jon Alpert, who was going to Vietnam for NBC News. In retrospect, it proved to be a mistake. My colleague, through no fault of his own, could not break through the wall of silence about Lan. Jon's persistence only served to anger the authorities. I had no doubts that my brother-in-law's chances for freedom had been set back because American television wanted to do a story about him. Only in his early forties, Lan had already spent almost a quarter of his life in prison camps. The conditions were terrible and demeaning. Telling his story to the outside world would not be positive propaganda during an anniversary that the Foreign Press Office in Hanoi was eager to celebrate with pride. Though well documented on paper, in 1985 there was still almost nothing on film or videotape about the Vietnamese gulag. A television story on Lan would damage the country's image as a socialist revolutionary leader in the too-sensitive third world.

If I tried to free Lan, I feared he would suffer further at the hands of his captors in ways I could not imagine. Could he endure more physical torture and mental pain? I did not want that on my conscience but I had to do something to help him survive. Hoan and the others in his family agreed I should simply try to get him money and medicine.

Vietnamese living in the United States and Paris, as well as other journalists experienced in Vietnam, U.S. officials, and members of Congress, warned me how dangerous it would be to try to help Lan. If I were caught trying to reach him through bribes, payoffs, or anything else illegal, I would be in serious trouble. At best, the Vietnamese would throw me out of the country. They could detain me, which would embarrass NBC News and the United States. At worst, they could jail me, something I feared. Warned to be careful no matter what I did, and with all these possibilities on my mind, I packed the antibiotics, stomach medicine, and mild painkillers I knew Lan needed. I would take a chance and test my luck. I would go to Vietnam to cover the anniversary story and to find Lan. If I did, I would help him, maybe free him, if I could. I warned my wife and her family to make her sister understand that I could not work miracles, but I would do my best.

The best advice I received was to use official means first and send Lan the package of medicine through the Vietnamese post office. I did not believe that would work. After being back in Saigon for only a few days, I found it impossible as a foreigner to mail anything inside the country. Any package or letter mailed in Vietnam was opened somewhere for inspection. Everyone was under suspicion and everything a foreigner did was carefully scrutinized. Being a journalist did not help, nor did being an official guest of the government, which I was. The watchful eyes of my minders kept me under constant surveillance. I decided that subterfuge was my only course.

My plan was to send the package and a letter from Hoan and Laurie to a third party who could then get them to my brother-in-law. A sympathetic Vietnamese told me not to trust anyone from the North. Their loyalty, naturally, would be to Hanoi. Someone from the center of the country, Hue or Danang, might be acceptable, but no one from above the old DMZ. Someone from the South would be best. He advised me to find a southerner who was as willing to gamble as I was. I did not believe all southerners were trustworthy just because they came from the South and still mourned the former Saigon. I could not forget that the Viet Cong came from the South. The few surviving VC held minor positions of power in the new regime. The Cuu Long Hotel gave me many openings, however, to people who wanted extra money and would take a chance to line their pockets. Shortly, I found someone willing to address an envelope and put on a false return address. I might get lucky with a letter addressed by a Vietnamese in their curious script, I thought. It might have a chance of getting through. A package, though, would be difficult. A package faced being opened officially or stolen by an underpaid, corrupt government employee. No matter how it was handled, a package would be a problem. I decided to drop this plan because I realized it would not work.

Getting money to Lan proved even more difficult. Sooner than I believed possible and much to my delight, I found someone willing to act as a go-between. Ultimately, there would be many steps. He had to be certain that he would not be seen taking the package from me, from my hand. No Vietnamese could be seen taking anything from a foreigner, especially if he worked for the government. Too dangerous. His life and work, in that order, were more valuable than a new friend. All contact between visitors and Vietnamese was limited, governed by the Vietnamese people's fear of reprisal. Informers were the biggest threat to me, more of a hazard than the formal system of secret police or the freelancer looking for fast money. Informers organized themselves around interlocking cells. The person originally receiving and processing information for me remained in deep cover. I could not identify him as the first link in the chain. It would be the system I eventually used for my amateur operation.

My new intermediary told me he would attempt an exchange sooner than I expected. The drop would take place in a small coffeehouse on a moderately busy street in the center of the city. In the privacy of my poorly lighted hotel room, I rehearsed my moves carefully. My only audience was a horde of crickets entrenched in one corner of my large window, crowded between the curtain and the windowpane. Together we listened to a cassette of Sonny Rollins's "Freedom Suite" as I went through the motions of delivering the package.

On the appointed day, I carried a black canvas shoulder bag containing a package, small and neatly wrapped. I entered the café and sat at an empty table. I ordered iced tea with lime, to all appearances a tourist trying to escape the heat, looking for something to wet my dry throat. I was carrying a camera and wore faded blue jeans and worn running shoes. I could feel the careful scrutiny of many eyes watching my every move. More than one person kept me, a stranger, in view, there being no other foreigners in sight. They had to have wondered why I sat there. I had seen my share of spy films, read all the required spy novels and then some. I had had the good fortune of spending time in Communist Eastern Bloc countries. I did not doubt my fear. Too much could happen to me if I took a wrong step. I wanted to break through the impossible barrier placed in my path, but I had to be careful. I had always been successful when I rehearsed it alone. I never missed a beat when I made my fake delivery.

I had to stay in place long enough to allow people to get used to my being there. I hoped they would soon ignore me, taking me in as part of the scenery. I drank my weak iced tea and ordered another glass. I added so much unrefined sugar to the drink that it tasted more like sugar and lime than tea. I opened and read from my book of John Cheever short stories. From time to time, I looked at my map of Ho Chi Minh City provided by what was still called the Saigon Tourist Bureau. I ordered and ate a reasonable copy of a French pineapple tart and watched the people passing in the street. In my mind, I wanted to be anywhere except that place. My contact sat inconspicuously across the room. I did everything I could not to look in his direction. I may have been too obvious about looking the other way but it caused no trouble, or none that I knew. Eventually, I had enough courage to depart. As I rose from my seat I left the small package behind me on a chair tucked under my table, hidden from view.

I walked slowly from the café into the midday sun, moving deliberately down the street. When I was no more than fifty feet from the restaurant, I felt a tap on my lower back. I jumped, and then froze. Turning around, I saw a toothless old woman, her graying hair pulled tightly back from her head, a large grin splitting her heavily lined face. She held my package out to me, imploring me to take it. She probably picked it up thinking I had left it behind by mistake. Traditionally honest, she was returning what she thought I had lost. I could not believe what was happening. I had no choice but to take the package with gracious thanks. I tried tipping the old woman but she refused my money, acting as if I was insulting her. She said nothing, smiling happily as I took the small package from her tiny, arthritic hands. I hoped it appeared to her that I was a careless Westerner. Maybe she knew what I had done and in her way had become my protector. It would be a question I posed to myself frequently throughout my stay in Vietnam, one I could never answer. Meanwhile, my contact quietly, quickly departed the now-busy café. I did not see him leave. After that initial failure, we decided that if we were to succeed, we had to find a better, safer way to make the exchange. I was frustrated and angry and it was difficult to mask my feelings in public and among my coworkers, who had no hint of what I had gone through.

At the Cuu Long Hotel, my contact and I never spoke about anything other than, "Are there any messages for me?" Our conversations with each other seemed never to be about anything, yet were always about something. We used "spy talk" and communicated with each other by combining portions of various dissembling conversations. We decided that for the next step I would not take part in any direct transactions. However, I could not wait for something to happen. With great difficulty, I made a new contact in a way that surprised even me. But I cannot hint at how I did it. Even now, I must protect someone still living and working in Ho Chi Minh City. I finally had a legitimate third party. I had a middleman, a true fixer. This person, who I called "O," was someone who would set up a meeting for me without me being anywhere near the designated place. It cost a little money for expenses. No surprise. I agreed to pay in ten- and twenty-dollar American bills.

The money had to be as new as possible. The Vietnamese did not like soiled money, because new bills meant good luck. The person did the work for cost. I reimbursed him for his expenses. No money went into his pocket. My contact, my friend, was a kind man who was sympathetic to my situation. Empathy was his only reason for becoming involved in something so dangerous. The money he received was not worth the pain he might suffer if he were caught helping me.

Within hours of his joining my cause, I passed to him an address outside the city where a sister of Lan's lived. We were finally moving. The next day, a woman he enlisted took an all-day bus ride to connect with the last link ninety miles northwest of Ho Chi Minh City. She would tell the sister that I had arrived and was staying at the Cuu Long Hotel. She would tell her I had a package of medicine, important documents and letters, photos of Lan's wife and daughter, and money. I wanted all of it passed along and out of my hands soon. We would soon be four layers deep. No two layers would know what any other layer was doing. I could do nothing directly or by myself. I felt more helpless with each passing hour. Everyone was afraid, including me. Everywhere we turned, we were breaking a different law. We were driving forward nevertheless, for humanitarian reasons.

The project took on its own life, its own momentum. No one I worked with at NBC suspected anything unusual. None of the other members of the press covering the anniversary story knew what I was doing. I kept reminding myself of the warnings I had heard before departing New York: If caught, I faced jail or, if lucky, expulsion from the country with appropriate noise. I knew Hanoi would accuse me of betraying the trust it put in me when it granted me a visa and permission to work as a journalist in Vietnam. The government would probably devise a phony espionage charge as well. Knowledgeable folk would laugh at that because there were no secrets worth stealing from Vietnam. But NBC would be furious with me and I did not know what else they would think or do. I could only guess. My primary Vietnamese contact, if caught, would definitely find himself in prison without a trial, and for a long time—possibly in the very camp we were trying to penetrate. The risks were great, but the rewards were greater.

Meanwhile, I continued my overt attempt to free Lan, approaching every government official I met about getting him out of the concentration camp. My pleas went unheard. They ignored me. Most cadres would not even discuss the issue. For them, the camps did not exist. Worse, political prisoners did not exist. They were considered a figment of the fertile Western imagination and, in particular, the United States. Of course. I knew that pride and fear did not allow the ruling clique in Hanoi to admit any wrongdoing. To admit to the outside world that they were perpetuating a crime against humanity would be a terrible loss of face for the Communists. Ten years after the war, very few prisoners were free. Officers of rank were still in the camps. Most of those released were low-ranking soldiers who did not matter anyway.

Political prisoners were nothing new in Vietnam. The French had them before World War II. The Japanese had them during World War II. The French had them again after World War II. All the so-called democratic South Vietnamese governments had political prisoners before the fall in 1975. Now the Communist government had its own brand of political prisoner, the exact number we will never know. Reeducation became another name for brainwashing. All physical, emotional, and spiritual benefits were denied the prisoner. The ancients running Hanoi saw no evil in forced reeducation. The good of the party mattered most, followed by the emerging nation, and the people last. The Communists did not care about my brother-in-law's problems, the daughter he had never seen, his wife surviving in the United States without her husband. Once I thought I might be on the verge of a breakthrough when a Vietnamese official said he thought it was too bad that Lan languished in a camp. Then he said, "Perhaps his wife should never have been disloyal" enough to leave the country in its moment of supreme triumph. Are you suggesting his suffering is because of her, I asked? No, no, he said. The conversation abruptly ended. He had offered a reason that I thought too simple and a ploy I thought too crass even for a well-trained Communist functionary.

Another time, someone in power wanted me to tell him more about the stubborn lieutenant colonel. Maybe, just maybe, he said, we can then help you and, of course, him. Another hint. Tantalizing. Vague. But I thought it was my turn to freeze up. I decided not to divulge anything more until I could be sure help would be forthcoming. It became a game of the child and the cricket. I refused to be the cricket, caught and played with before my captor finally crushed me, even if accidentally. I decided to be tightfisted with my information until I found someone my heart told me to trust. My pessimism paid off. I never found anyone, but I stayed a cricket with wings.

Days passed. I helped to prepare stories for *Today*. My contact stayed away. Nothing was happening with my effort for Lan. Security increased proportionately at all the hotels as more foreign journalists arrived for the anniversary celebration. Every hotel, restaurant, and café had a soldier out front. More soldiers and police patrolled the streets. The large number of Foreign Ministry and Foreign Press Center officials in from Hanoi made everyone jumpy. Secret police in white shirts and blue trousers were everywhere throughout the city. They made no effort to hide their identity. Additional police were in the city from the provinces. We knew who they were by their ill-fitting, polyester uniforms in deep olive. These "country" police stood two or three to a corner near every hotel we journalists lived in and every restaurant in which we ate. They were never alone because they might get lost in the big city. We were never alone because they did not know what to expect from us. When I saw my contact, he became increasingly nervous, even within a hundred feet of me. We had no more conversations. Occasionally we exchanged a casual nod, a brief wave of the hand.

I had been trying to find Lan's sister for more than four weeks. When I least expected it, I received a message that my party had been contacted. I was passed a sealed note, and my hands shook when I opened the envelope to see an old photo of Lan and his family outside my mother-in-law's former restaurant. The confirmation I required that the right individual had been found had finally come.

Lan's sister arrived from the country the day before the anniversary celebrations. She came at great risk. She would be in the city less than twenty-four hours but she did not want to see me because she thought it too dangerous. We were too close to success to fail now, so she had to be careful. Besides, she spoke no English, making it more difficult for us to meet. Surprisingly, she sent a message that she did not want the package of medicine. I assumed she feared that she might be caught carrying it on her return journey or after she arrived home. As I have said, moving and receiving even a small package through the post office could be dangerous. On the bus and in the provinces, she faced the greater threat of a sudden search and tough questioning. The authorities would tear the package open and confiscate its contents, keeping everything for themselves. Her arrest would follow and her family would suffer. Lan would be in more difficulty than he was before the incident—terrible to imagine that happening, but not an unthinkable scenario. Through my contact, the woman made it known that money would serve everyone best. It could be hidden and transported, probably on her person, with relative ease. She could manage to carry the money most anywhere without any suspicion. Her need seemed great and time had become short. My stay would soon end and I felt pressed to do the best I could under extreme, sometimes bizarre, conditions.

She would be in the city for three more hours. If she missed her bus, she would have to stay an extra day. I went quickly to my room and took all the available cash I had in Vietnamese dong and U.S. dollars. I wrapped it up together with the photos and the documents my in-laws wanted passed to Lan. They hoped those pieces of paper would speed his freedom. I wanted to send more money, but I would have to get into the hotel safe where I stored my cache and I did not have enough time to get to those dollars. If I made the desk clerk hurry, she might wonder why I needed it so fast. I did not want her to think my actions were unusual. I did not trust the desk clerk because I felt she did not trust me. I decided to go with what I had, knowing it would be substantial though not as much as I would have liked.

Thirty minutes later, I met the person I called "O" on a street corner several blocks from the hotel. I delivered the medium-sized envelope, neatly wrapped and heavily taped, to my contact, who hid it in his shirt. We discussed some business to make our meeting look and sound official. I walked back to the lobby bar of the hotel and had a lime juice and vodka, no ice. My long wait began. I worked through the day and into the night. I ate dinner with friends, bathed, worked again, read, had another drink. I spent a fretful, restless night looking forward to hearing if and how the money had been delivered. The next morning, the delivery was confirmed in a typical, businesslike Vietnamese way. At breakfast, a waiter handed me a small envelope. Inside was a neatly scripted note in Vietnamese listing the serial numbers of the American bills accompanied by another photograph of Lan that further sealed the legitimacy of the transaction. Though limited by circumstance, I had completed my job.

Several hours later, my contact told me that he, too, had been very nervous throughout the proceedings but felt good he had helped me accomplish my mission. I never saw the last part of the deal, but he said it took place in the back of a small shop near the Central Market bus terminal. The shop faced the street and sold imported shoes and baskets of all sizes, colors, and shapes. My contact met the woman. At first, they said little. He handed the envelope to her. She held it at a distance from her face, gingerly touching it, turning it around and around in her, small, broken-nailed fingers. It was only then that she showed her first sign of excitement but she looked around the small back room to make sure they were alone. Then she opened the envelope swiftly, as if to make sure nothing inside had the chance to fly away. Her eyes opened wide. Slowly she took out the money and carefully began counting it. She put the bills in the curious piles of tens the Vietnamese use, folding one bill in half over nine others. Tears filled her eyes. Then she openly wept. Finally, smiling shyly, she wiped the tears gently and swiftly from her smooth, young skin, happy, pleased, touched. Someone had thought to help her and her family. Although she had not seen me, she knew she had real contact with the outside world, with America.

Later that day when there was a break in our coverage, I opened the bundle of medicine. I made two smaller packages and wrapped them in Vietnamese newspapers and garish gift paper. I stashed them one in my luggage and one in my closet. Now I had to find a Vietnamese willing to address them and mail them in a way that would ensure delivery in one piece without being traced. But no matter how I pleaded, no matter how much money I offered, no one would take the chance. Before departing the country a week later, I broke open the packages and gave the over-the-counter drugs as tips to the hotel staff, except to the desk clerk I did not trust. I carried the prescription drugs back to New York. I would have to find another way to deliver them.

I had accomplished only a small part of my mission. In a sense, it was the least important part, because when I departed Vietnam, Lt. Col. Nguyen Van Lan still languished in prison somewhere on the coastal plain north of Saigon. A few years later, I learned that his sister had delivered most of the money to Lan. I had expected that she would keep some of it for her family. Everyone in his family needed help. But Lan still lived behind bamboo bars in intolerable conditions. I never found any official who could explain clearly why Lan remained in prison. Perhaps once a political prisoner, always a political prisoner, a symbol for all of us, a reminder of what freedom really means. When I saw Lan's ten-year-old daughter, I had no words to explain why her father remained behind locks of steel, embedded in concrete, guarded by humorless teenaged boys carrying loaded rifles—in the end, it was all ideology.

In early 1988, Lieutenant Colonel Lan was finally freed after almost thirteen years as a political prisoner. By 1989, under the orderly departure program, he was allowed to leave Vietnam. He now lives and works in Maryland with his wife and daughter, who is a graduate of the University of Maryland.

19

Happy New Year
1968

JANUARY 19, 1968. I sent a message to director of news Bill Corrigan that we were approaching Tet, the Vietnamese lunar new year. This is the most important holiday for the Vietnamese, a three-day celebration filled with bright, yellow flowers, specially prepared foods, and prayers for a fulfilling new year. The events of the first hours of Tet are thought to foretell the future for the rest of the year. A Vietnamese tradition says the first person who steps over the threshold of your home in the new year will be someone who will bring you good luck.

Each year at Tet, NBC, as did all companies, gave bonuses to its Vietnamese staff, usually one month of additional salary. I included everyone: the drivers, workers at Pan American Airlines, government officials who regularly helped us survive mountains of paperwork, tipsters, sources, and many others. All the Vietnamese who worked for NBC had three days off to celebrate the new year and perhaps forget the war. President Thieu announced he would give three days off to his government and the army. The Viet Cong and North Vietnamese said nothing, giving tacit, silent support to the celebration as it had done for all the years of the war. Tet was traditionally the quietest time of the year. Official life in South Vietnam would come to a standstill during the holiday. Our Western staffers would have light duty and would be available in an emergency. Everyone went to bed on the eve of Tet thinking good thoughts, hoping for a better year.

Twelve days after my note to New York, on Wednesday, January 31, 1968, the Tet Offensive changed the war. When the Viet Cong guerrillas and North Vietnamese regulars struck, the attacks were swift and damaging. Nothing in Vietnam, including life in the bureau or our coverage of the war, would ever be the same again. Before that first day of what we immediately called the Tet Offensive, I had enough staff to cover the war and satisfy the needs of the producers and programs in New York. I had the people to handle a mixture of combat, terrorism, politics, religion, the occasional social story, and the rare cultural event. I usually had four or five correspondents but that week I was down to three, Howard Tuckner, Wilson Hall, and Ron Nessen, who was covering our bureau in Danang up north. Jack Russell worked as a full-time radio reporter. Gary Bel, the assistant bureau chief, also reported for radio. Hoang Trong Nghia and the brothers Vo Huynh and Vo Suu were the Vietnamese cameramen in Saigon, and Phil Ross was the American cameraman. Doron Pollak, an Israeli cameraman, was working in Danang with Nessen, along with two other Americans, Dennis Moore on camera and Marvin White on sound. Vi Giac, Phan Bach Dang, and Le Phuc Dinh were the Vietnamese soundmen. Detlev Arndt, a West German soundman whom I sometimes used as a cameraman, could handle the 16-millimeter Bell & Howell camera with skill. Others in the bureau were Dennis Freppel, a soundman from France, and Lutz Gruebnau, a talented engineer who maintained and repaired the equipment. Lutz sometimes worked as a soundman, sometimes as a cameraman, which gave me an extra pair of hands when needed. I had three drivers on staff, Mr. Long, Tam Coi, and Mai Van Ngoi, whom we called "Ut." They owned their cars and I paid them a small salary plus expenses to drive the crews everywhere, sometimes even to combat. Denise Hanh, a close friend of Josephine's, ran the office in place of the injured Josephine, interpreting when needed, interceding with Vietnamese officials as required. Including myself, there were twenty-four people in my bureau on the first day of Tet. Throw in my two Vietnamese reporters and the number rises to twenty-six—not excessive, but enough to do the job, I thought. That changed as the Viet Cong and North Vietnamese struck with impunity across South Vietnam.

Saigon had always been noisy. There were too many people and too much traffic in too small a place. Certain sounds, however, always cut through the usual symphony rising from the crowded streets: sirens, mortars, machine guns, explosions, helicopters churning overhead. The night before Tet was no exception to this rule, but the sudden ferocity of the attacks rudely awakened me. I had gone to bed before midnight, early for me. Sirens screamed past my windows. I heard the steady thumping and popping of falling mortar shells. MP jeeps, radios blasting, sped down the street toward the American embassy and Independence Palace, where President Thieu lived and worked. Bright yellow fiery flares illuminated the black sky. I heard the rapid crackling of automatic weapons firing in the distance. Something serious had happened. But something was always happening in Saigon, so why consider this night any different? In any case, it was dark, difficult to film, and it was dangerous for my crews to be out where they did not have the advantage of seeing, at the very least, what moved before their eyes. I rolled over and went back to sleep.

Several cities were attacked, and all U.S. units were put on maximum alert. But we did not know the extent of what was to come.

On January 31, at approximately 12:30 A.M., my phone started ringing. The first call came from the American embassy. The voice at the other end gave me many details about the attacks. By 3:00 A.M., U.S. military intelligence called to say all hell was breaking loose and we should be prepared for a long week. They did not know, of course, that it would be a very long month. Surprisingly, even various Vietnamese sources called to say we should expect nothing but the worst.

The situation exceeded my worst expectations, unlike anything I had ever covered, and it was incredibly exciting. In defiance of their own national and religious holiday, the Viet Cong and their masters, the North Vietnamese, had breached the wall of the American embassy, entered the grounds, and tried to capture it. They attacked all the major cities in the South, all the major military bases, and everything else in their path. In Saigon, they attacked Tan Son Nhut Airport and Independence Palace. They partially destroyed the South Vietnamese government radio station. They also hit the Joint General Staff Headquarters of the Vietnamese military, many other major installations in the city, and, of all things, the Philippine embassy, a usually peripheral location.

All the Vietnamese in the bureau were off for Tet. I had a small staff of Westerners available, but they, too, were taking it easy. Despite my lack of people, by five that morning I had our coverage organized. I knew where I had to send every crew I could muster. I called Howard Tuckner in his room at the Caravelle Hotel. Without any preliminaries, I told him to come to the office. "There's fighting at the American embassy. That's where I want you to go." Howard later told me he thought I was pulling his leg, but before he could say anything, I said, "And I'm not kidding." He dressed quickly, putting on a yellow shirt. Hours later he realized, in his words, "it was a stupid thing to have done." Yellow, too bright for war, made him a potential target.

At first light early that first morning of Tet, Howard and his cameraman Phil Ross, a Midwesterner with great courage, headed to the American embassy. I moved them before a soundman arrived. The story could not wait. When they arrived, daring Viet Cong sappers were fighting inside the compound and enemy snipers were everywhere, firing at anything that moved. They heard the military police would have to break though the embassy's main gate to assault the Viet Cong inside, so that is where they headed. As they started down the street, Phil discovered his sound gear did not work. He and Howard decided to handle the sound together as best they could, using a small tape recorder.

Less than a block from the gate, they saw the MPs covering themselves from the snipers by hiding behind the trees that lined the boulevard leading to the main entrance. They worked out what they called "a small plan." Howard would move three trees up. If he took no fire, Phil would move up four. Then Howard would move six trees up. Phil would go seven, and so on. They encountered enemy fire as they ran. At trees number four, nine, and thirteen, they encountered heavier fire. Howard's yellow shirt had become the obvious target, as he feared it would.

The two men finally reached the main gate and started filming the MPs crawling and running through the gate and onto the grounds of the embassy. Just as they were to follow the MPs onto the embassy grounds, they saw, to their amazement, their soundman, Dinh, coming toward them, hugging the embassy wall and carrying a big Auricon sound camera, a battery power pack, and six magazines of sound film. Each magazine had four hundred feet of film, about twelve minutes' running time. I had loaded him up and sent him to meet Howard and Phil. No bigger than the average Vietnamese, and possibly slimmer, he was lugging more than forty pounds of equipment as if he were a locomotive. "The thing that struck me at that moment," Howard later said, "was not only that he had gotten through, leaving other film crews a block behind, but that he did it on his own. Going with another man or with two others, the way we usually travel, is one thing. You feel less frightened when others are with you. But doing it on your own is quite another thing."

I found it remarkable that Dinh, born in Saigon and married with two children, had showed up at the office that morning at all. Some surprise attacks had taken place in his neighborhood shortly after midnight. The Viet Cong were entrenched for four hours in his neighbor's house about a hundred yards away, and the only way to root them out was to bomb them out. The residents of the area were warned that rocket attacks were pending and that they were in the line of fire. Dinh moved his family out minutes before the airplanes arrived to obliterate the area. Jet planes sent rockets into Dinh's house, smashing his kitchen and back room, destroying most of his furniture and possessions. When he had made his family safe, Dinh made his way to the bureau, arriving before dawn. "I thought you might need me," he said.

Dinh had served in the South Vietnamese Army for five years and had seen action in Vietnam and Laos, but he said later, "In Saigon it's more dangerous because you can't see the VC anywhere. It was unbelievable to me that the VC could get inside the embassy. How could so many VC get inside the city so easily? I was very surprised." As we all were.

By the time the MPs were deep inside the compound, many other newsmen were also there, but our team had gotten there first. Suddenly, a Viet Cong in the consulate house tossed a grenade from a window. Several cameramen and correspondents, including Phil and Dinh, and ten MPs were within five feet of where the grenade landed. Fortunately, it did not go off. It was a dud. Phil, who, like all our cameramen, was carrying about fifty pounds of equipment—including film magazines, extra film, extra camera batteries, cables, and plugs—felt at a disadvantage. From a distance, crews often looked like soldiers carrying medium-sized weapons. As Phil put it, "A guy in the field can shoot back. I can't." He, as did all my cameramen and soundmen, knew he had no way of getting the story without exposing himself to danger. He told me, "If you are not with the lead element, you don't tell the story. It's what we do that determines the story. The fact that five or six MPs went into the embassy . . . that's the story visually. That shows we have retaken the embassy. If you stayed back, it's like any other day . . . a lot of guys standing around."

Phil was the only newsman there who captured one particular moment on film. George Jacobson, an embassy employee and retired colonel, had been asleep in his room on the second floor of an old French villa on the embassy grounds when the Viet Cong broke through the outside wall. He heard one of them enter the ground floor and start moving from room to room, obviously looking for people. Jacobson started searching for a weapon with which to defend himself, and found a hand grenade. Just as he heard the Viet Cong start up the stairs, a unit of MPs arrived. Jacobson called down to an MP, who tossed a .45 caliber pistol through the open upstairs window. A few minutes later, shots were heard; Jacobson had killed the Viet Cong. The ever-alert Phil filmed the entire sequence with Jacobson at the window and the MP tossing the pistol, including the sounds of the gunfire that followed. NBC was the only network with film of this incident.

Gary Bel, my assistant bureau chief, saw more action that day than usual. Gary normally helped me administer the bureau, rarely getting into the field. He was usually deskbound, filing radio stories when he had time. However, these events saw the end of his routine. It had never been easy to ship film from Saigon, but the attack on the city and its airport presented us with almost overwhelming problems. In Gary's words, "No film, no matter how spectacular, is of any value unless we ship it out of Saigon for developing and broadcasting. It meant I had to jump on a helicopter on the roof of the U.S. embassy while under sniper fire. It meant I had to fly over the city because the streets were crawling with Viet Cong. It meant I had to throw our film on board the huge C-141 MedEvac jets heading for Japan with wounded American troops. Those planes kept flying because they had to."

We never stopped shipping film. The air force managed to give us and other news organizations space on one of its flights each day. Though the streets were passable, they were not safe. Squads of Viet Cong were everywhere. Snipers could be around any corner. Every day, my drivers rode bravely rode through the city up to the gates of Tan Son Nhut. No Vietnamese, even our well-known NBC bureau drivers, could drive onto the base during the crisis. But Seventh Air Force personnel met them and took our red NBC onion bags to ship without hesitation, no questions asked.

I called Wilson Hall and woke him from a deep sleep, shocking him into the reality of this new dimension to the war. At one point I looked up and saw Vo Huynh at my desk, ready to work. When Wilson arrived, I sent him and Huynh to the Independence Palace, which was under siege. Once they had that story, their next stop would be the heavy fighting at Tan Son Nhut Air Base. Other Vietnamese staffers drifted in, dazed and confused by the attacks. I put each man to work covering anything that moved. They realized the gravity of the situation and had come in to help on what they knew had to be the biggest story of the war. Without their dedication, I could not have covered the attacks the way we did.

By six that morning, NBC News had awakened on both sides of the world.

Messages started flowing freely between Saigon and New York. Telephone calls were almost impossible to make or receive under normal wartime conditions. This happened to be worse. Our rickety and slow-moving telex system saved the day. I organized a newswire with Gary's help. We fed continuous stories to New York over the direct, closed-circuit telex. The information would be used for television bulletins and for frequent updates on NBC network radio. To support our own reporting, we used the wires of our neighbor down the hall, the Associated Press, and our sources in the U.S. military and at the U.S. embassy. Jack Russell, our radio correspondent, did the bulk of that work. I edited and added to his copy, dispatched crews, chain-smoked, and drank endless cups of tepid jasmine tea.

Every message we sent to New York was headed "Johnson" for Mac Johnson, the director of foreign news. Sometimes I prefaced his name with "pro," meaning "for." Once each message arrived, a copy was delivered to the desk of the appropriate producer, such as Shad Northshield, the executive producer of *The Huntley-Brinkley Report,* and Les Crystal, that show's producer. Executives such as Reuven Frank, executive vice president of news, or Bill Corrigan, director of news, received a copy of every message. Everything New York sent my way had the heading "natbrocast saigon steinman."

As I've mentioned, I have most of the message traffic from my years in Saigon. It came into my possession in the 1980s when a clerk in NBC News archives happened on several cardboard boxes with my name on them among many that he planned to destroy. Many years later, I finally looked inside the boxes. Some pages were missing from the first day of Tet. The pages from the newswire I created no longer existed. Almost everything else I wrote to New York or edited for New York, and what New York wrote me, remained intact. We numbered each telex message consecutively, with the number followed by the date. 1–30 was the first message from Saigon of January 30, 1968. 2–30 was the message that followed, and so on for each day.

> 1–30, JOHNSON FYI WE HAVE FILM OF LAST NIGHTS ROCKET ATTACK AGAINST DANANG DUE IN SAIGON LATER TODAY. AS YOU KNOW OUR VIET-NAMESE STAFFERS ARE OFF FOR TET. I AM TRYING TO DIG UP STRINGERS TO GET THEM WHERE THINGS ARE POPPING.

Detlev Arndt arrived in the office early enough for me to thrust a 16-millimeter silent camera and ten rolls of film in his hands. Each roll was a hundred feet in length, approximately three minutes of real time. I gave him a small audiotape recorder and audio cassettes for natural sound. I told him to board a waiting army airplane at Tan Son Nhut Airport and fly with a few other journalists to Ban Me Thuot deep in the Central Highlands. I had information the Viet Cong had attacked with a small force and raised its flag after destroying most of the town. Anticipating many questions, I sent the following message to New York:

> 2–30, JOHNSON PROCORRIGAN ALL HANDS SAFE SO FAR. HAVE BEEN IN PROCESS OF ROUNDING THEM UP (THOSE WE CAN FIND) AND DISPERSING THEM. DOING WHAT WE CAN AND WILL DEFINITELY HAVE SOMETHING BUT I DONT KNOW WHAT. WILL SHIP TOKYO AND ADVISE ALL POINTS ACCORD-INGLY.

The first stories from the field started to arrive. I looked at the scripts and production notes and sent preliminary messages to New York to advise them on what they should expect. The two bulbous telex machines several feet to the left of my desk were in constant use throughout the Tet Offensive. We typed our messages on half-inch-wide yellow tape in perforated symbols, almost as if they were in braille. We then fed the tape into the telex and waited for the telltale clicking to begin that signaled the tape was feeding to New York. When the information reached its destination, a tape printed out in New York that was then fed into a reader that retranslated the symbols back into words in real time. Despite my hunt-and-peck typing, I produced the tape faster than it arrived in New York. Others who used the telex typed faster than I. Sometimes we waited an hour for a ten-line message to get through.

Stories from Danang also started arriving in Saigon. I sent a driver on a dangerous mission to pick up the material at Tan Son Nhut. The notes from the crew said they had filmed night scenes of still-smoking, damaged aircraft, refugees fleeing a village near a military compound, ARVN troops in a firefight, and dead Viet Cong. I had to get on the air with their footage but I did not know how. Normally we shipped film to the States for developing and editing in Los Angeles, San Francisco, Chicago, or New York. Searching for a faster solution, I suggested to New York that we ship to Tokyo for the rarely used and very expensive satellite. I had no idea of the cost for the satellite from Tokyo or anywhere else. Money was the farthest thing from my mind. If we did send the film by satellite, we could be on the air for the Huntley-Brinkley show a full twelve hours before *Today* the next morning. I knew we had strong material, though no one, including American officials, the American and the Vietnamese military, and the Vietnamese government, knew how big the story would become. We were highly competitive and being first on the air was paramount. We owed it to our audience to provide the fullest coverage possible. Also, I had heard that CBS was using the satellite and I did not want to lose to our prime competition.

The New York news desk responded quickly and said we should send the Danang rocket attack and anything else we might have to Tokyo for the January 31 satellite feed. We were pleased that new ground rules were in place, if only for the moment. All of us wanted our stories to be available as soon as possible to the New York producers and editors. Satellites were still new and very costly. New York ordered and used the satellite only for the biggest breaking stories. We in the bureau felt we were on the verge of the war's biggest story.

I told New York we did not yet know the meaning of the Communist attacks, but we expected there would be more. I could not predict what would happen, but my sources told me Khe Sanh still loomed large, the DMZ appeared at risk, and the Central Highlands would see very heavy fighting. I had not heard from Arndt, and knowing of the fierce fighting in the Central Highlands, I hoped that I had not made a mistake in sending him. I ended a message by saying, "Be prepared. Anything can and usually does happen in this place."

In my first message on January 31, I tried to give some perspective to the difficulties we already faced. We were unable to get around the city by car as we usually did, though the drivers bravely drove to Tan Son Nhut. Our three-man crews went by foot and lugged their heavy gear with them. During the night we did not get any film, though we tried. At times the rightfully nervous MPs were more of a threat and danger than the Viet Cong suicide squads. We understood that, because they were the only American troops inside the city. In accordance with an agreement with the Vietnamese, no American troops were in Saigon, so the MPs did the initial fighting until later in the week when American forces moved in to help. Under those circumstances, I did not again risk getting nighttime action.

Howard Tuckner, Phil Ross, and Le Phuc Dinh were still at the American embassy and Wilson Hall and Vo Huynh were at the Independence Palace, where fighting was continuing outside the main gate. I had no way of contacting the other Vietnamese staffers. None had phones and we did not have a walkie-talkie system. I hoped they would start drifting in when they awoke to the sensation of the story. Arndt was still missing, but the army told me the plane carrying him and several other journalists had arrived in Ban Me Thuot after first going to Nha Trang on the coast, another important city attacked in the early fighting. Our telephone system had become useless. It was impossible to get calls though to Danang, but I knew and trusted Ron Nessen and his two crews to get to the action where the city was under enemy attack. In the middle of the chaos, we continued to file regularly for radio. Jack Russell was ready to work around the clock to satisfy radio's needs.

I received a message from Reuven Frank saying he wanted to start using the satellite only if we could get film of the embassy battle to Tokyo:

MY OWN FEELING IS THAT DAYTIME SATELLITE SPECIAL FROM TOKYO JUS-
TIFIABLE ONLY IF SAIGON AND EMBASSY MATERIAL CAN BE INCLUDED BUT
THAT IS SOMETHING WE REALLY WANT TO DO. THIS ADMITTEDLY OVERBUR-
DENS YOU WHEN YOU LEAST NEED IT BUT NEWS OF THIS MAGNITUDE MAKES
PROBLEMS OF THIS MAGNITUDE ESPECIALLY FOR THE MAN IN THE MIDDLE

WHOSE NAME HAPPENS TO BE STEINMAN. SO CHARTER IF NECESSARY, SPEND
WHAT YOU NEED TO MAKE THIS SCHEDULE AND SOMEHOW WE'LL MAKE IT
UP TO ALL OF YOU. ALL BEST REUVEN.

It was reassuring that New York understood and appreciated the importance of
our situation. Within hours of that message, I told New York we had two excellent
pieces of film. We had the story of American MPs storming the American embassy,
the firefights in and around the embassy, and the retaking of the embassy compound. The other story took place outside the gate of Tan Son Nhut, next to an
American officer's billet, where our team witnessed an intense firefight between
American military police and North Vietnamese troops that involved machine
guns, automatic weapons, small arms, and helicopters. However, we had a major
problem: Tan Son Nhut and the American base at Bien Hoa, where we occasionally shipped from, were on red alert and no planes had arrived or departed. We
were trying to get an air force plane to Tokyo. The air force did not know if it
could get the material out for us. They were working on it and they promised to
let us know soon. I told the air force that NBC Tokyo needed the footage to arrive
at least ten hours before the feed time. I stayed in touch with the embassy to see
if they could help in getting our film out, but they could not. They suggested we
use the Thai International flight to Bangkok, which was very risky because we
had no one there to transship. So we were still trying to ship the embassy footage
directly to Tokyo with several other stories. We had the aftermath of a battle and
the continuing explosions at the Saigon radio station with dead Viet Cong on
the ground. We had aftermath footage of fighting at the Philippine embassy. As
the Vietnamese staff arrived in the bureau, I sent another crew to Independence
Palace to cover the action there.

In my twentieth message of the morning, I told the news desk that we were
preparing to ship the film stories we already had in the bureau. These would
go by chopper from the top of the recently liberated American embassy to Cam
Ranh Bay on the coast. From there, our shipment would go by jet to Tokyo. I did
not think an afternoon arrival was possible, but we would try. I knew that CBS,
ABC, and the AP would also ship the same way. We all agreed that Tokyo had to
be our destination. We planned to ship five pieces in two red NBC bags. Then
another strong Tuckner and Ross piece arrived in the office, this one on more
fighting in the city, in a populated area near Tan Son Nhut Airport where American forces were using tanks and machine guns against enemy positions. Clearly
the Viet Cong and North Vietnamese wanted to seal and, if possible, capture the

base. If they could, it would be a major victory. Hall, Huynh, and now Nghia were covering the siege of the Independence Palace. They already had good action and were staying there for more. I had a tip from an ARVN source that they planned to bomb an area near Tan Son Nhut. The government would evacuate the residents before they destroyed the neighborhood. When I could, I would send a crew to cover. As the minutes passed, I still did not know when we would ship but I hoped it would be soon. As it happened, four hours went by before I had the details.

Despite its importance, radio never had the priority of television, remaining a poor second cousin, though never far from my mind. During the war years, the NBC radio network broadcasted five-minute newscasts every hour. A major morning news roundup ran for fifteen minutes and an evening newscast also ran fifteen minutes. Radio, with its insatiable appetite—and the news division's belief that we never gave radio enough—was a problem. It always demanded more material than we could provide. Besides my full-time radio reporter, television correspondents filed stories for radio when they had the chance. But as many spots as we fed, they were never enough. Television kept us very busy because that was our main audience, and our reporters did not have time for radio.

We did our radio broadcasts from the PTT, the phone company's main office. PTT stood for Post Telecommunications et Telegraphes, the center in Saigon for commercial telephone, cable, and telegram traffic. For radio feeds to New York, the three major networks were given fifteen-minute blocks, the order of which rotated each day. On January 31 we were first, with CBS and ABC to follow. Sometimes WOR would also feed, and that complicated matters because it cut into the minutes we needed for our feed. NBC had the option to take another circuit that first day of Tet. When everyone else finished, we used our second circuit. We fed several spots, including live elements and audiotape—what we called an actuality. These were sounds of the battles and excerpts from a news conference by Barry Zorthian, who, as the director of JUSPAO, ran public affairs for the United States in Vietnam.

The PTT was normally a drive of fifteen to twenty minutes from the bureau. Suddenly a routine trip had become dangerous, but then so was everything else. You could no longer safely cross even narrow streets, especially at night. Our neighborhood had become no-man's-land, with nervous American MPs, Vietnamese sentries, and National Police everywhere. We heard sporadic firing, at real and imagined targets, everywhere in the city. Our local phones continued to work, though intermittently. In one corner of my desk, next to a small, moderately sophisticated phone system, was the ancient French upright rotary phone that I used for Saigon calls. But early on that first morning, our telex circuit went down for more than four hours and we had no way to send fresh information to New York. However, we never stopped preparing messages for the moment when we could feed them again.

With so much information being passed along so fast, New York had rightfully become concerned about accuracy. In answer to a query from New York, I said that technically the VC had not gotten into the embassy. That is, they did not get into the embassy building. They were in the compound. They got through holes in the wall, and probably over the wall. The Viet Cong soldiers were on the embassy grounds and inside a building in the compound. That was the embassy for me. And it would probably be the embassy for most of the American people. To clarify, in our later spots and TV copy, we said the VC got into the embassy compound. But I did not believe then, nor do I now, that the American people knew the difference or cared to know the difference. Could anything be more insulting to American presence and power than enemy troops breaching the walls of the embassy?

There were mistakes made in stories that were written in haste and, admittedly, proofread faster than I would have preferred. That we made very few errors was a testament to our knowledge of the story and the care we gave to it. When we found errors, we corrected them quickly, as witness this message I sent New York:

> 12–2, URGENT JOHNSON PRORADIO HOURLIES IN HALLS SECOND SPOT TONIGHT THERE IS A GOOF. ABOUT MIDWAY HE SAYS QUOTE BY UUSS FIGURES THIS WOULD MEAN THAT FOR EVERY ONE SOUTH VIETNAMESE OR AMERICAN WHO DIED, 100 OF THE ENEMY WERE KILLED ENDQUOTE. 100 IS THE WRONG FIGURE. IT SHOULD HAVE BEEN TEN REPEAT TEN. HALL TIRED. ME TIRED. FOUR EYES NOW WORTH ONE. IF YOU WANT TO USE SPOT PLEASE CUT OUT THAT GRAPH.

Two hours after we placed our material in air force hands, I learned that the two NBC bags, tagged with Japanese custom forms, were on their way to Tokyo in the army mailbag. The army suggested we get an American military postal inspector to unload the bags and shepherd them through customs. The NBC bureau in Tokyo took care of that detail. In the field and on the ground, the American military was not the enemy to the press that it would become in later years. We were not in the same business, but we were all part of the excitement generated in the moment. Never did the military, whether army, marines, air force, or navy, give us any problems in getting to a story or getting that story out for broadcast, even during the Tet Offensive. To a man, noncommissioned or officer, they were usually willing to lend a hand. There were times in the field when news crews were in the way of the fighting, but during Tet it rarely happened because our teams conducted themselves with dignity and professionalism.

When I had the details about the shipment, I gave them to New York, including the plane's tail number, N-GR-57, the final piece of information that would ensure our people in Tokyo met the right airplane. I reminded them to process all the footage. We easily had the best material of any network because we were at most actions first, and I did not want New York to neglect the importance of anything, especially the American embassy story, where we were not only earlier than anyone but closer to the action than anyone.

Getting that last piece of information through to New York took longer than expected. The circuits that carried our messages frequently broke down for many reasons and this day they did the same. Mostly the problems were technical, such as a break in a cable under the sea. Sometimes sunspots or other weather patterns like heavy storms created havoc on our lines. My messages often arrived in New York garbled and had to be painstakingly decoded character by character in order for the editors on the news desk to be able to read and understand them. Common punctuation was rare when I sent messages to New York. I included full stops but rarely commas and never apostrophes, colons, dashes, or semicolons if I could help it. They took too much time to write.

In my messages, to save time in processing the film and thus getting on the air, I let New York know which were the important reels to develop. (I could not contact Tokyo directly at this time.) We always numbered each film story according to when it was sent from the bureau. I did not create a special numbering system during Tet, but continued to number the stories consecutively. On advice of the crews, I told the desk the emulsion speed of the film, which was dependent on the amount of light available when shooting. Less light meant longer processing. I advised which stories I believed should get special handling. I also alerted New York to the stories our correspondents and crews were covering that were not yet complete or ready for shipping. It took eighteen to thirty hours from the time we completed a story until it was shipped, developed, edited, and aired. I updated my messages with detailed information and assessments of what we were covering.

In my cables, I used the abbreviations SIL and SOF. SIL was shorthand for film that was silent and had no sound track. The cameraman recorded the accompanying sound on an audiotape cassette with a small, handheld machine. SOF meant "sound on film." Sound film was in magazines of either four hundred or six hundred feet. Each roll had a magnetic stripe running the length of the film. Recorded sound was in synchronization with each frame of the film as it was shot. With magnetic striping, matching the picture to the sound was always perfect, unless the battery was running down. Film editors did not have to worry about synching what we called "wild sound" to the picture.

In many messages, I doubled the letters in acronyms. That made them more like words and assured they would be understood. NBC became NNBBCC. CBS became CCBBSS and ABC was AABBCC; sometimes we referred to the other networks as "brandex." The Associated Press was AAPP and the Voice of America was VVOOAA. United States became UUSS. For the Viet Cong, we would write VVCC. GI was GEEYE, to make sure it stood for an American soldier. I Corps was EYE Corps. Doubled letters and repeated words were common when cables and telex messages were the only means of communicating between distant points, a device that made them easier to understand.

With so much going on, I found it difficult to make objective judgments, but I knew we had the best footage of the battle at the embassy. First, we were there earlier than anyone else. Second, we were closer than anyone else. Third, we were inside the compound first. I repeated to the producers they should process all the film. After a careful debriefing of the crew, I knew the film contained various shots of American troops hiding behind trees, running on the street toward the embassy, and firing at the embassy. We had the American troops shooting open the gate of the embassy and American MPs crouching, moving through the gate, getting behind trees, and firing. We had shots of the assault on the embassy, the holes in the embassy walls, and dead American marines and Viet Cong in the compound. One sequence had a wounded VC reaching for his rifle before being shot to death by two MPs. This took place eight feet from Ross and Tuckner. Ross also had shots of CIA agents in civvies rushing into the compound, American troops in gas masks, and a trooper running and yelling for more gas masks. Other film showed MPs breaking windows with their rifles and then firing through those windows into the building. CBS and ABC were there, but Tuckner and Ross were in the lead.

There was never any doubt in my mind that we had to ship to Tokyo for the satellite. After the attack on the American embassy and its being held for seven and a half hours, U.S. troops in the streets of Saigon counterattacked and took back the embassy. With the great help of the Seventh Air Force we shipped to Tokyo. And with NBC's staff in Tokyo doing all it could, we made air on *Huntley-Brinkley* Wednesday night. It was the first raw film, not edited, of the storming and taking back of the embassy in Saigon.

Almost immediately after the story appeared as the lead on *The Huntley-Brinkley Report,* the following message arrived that I posted for all to see. Keeping morale high was essential during those first hours of our coverage.

> NATBROCAST SAIGON STEINMAN GOD KNOWS YOU HAD TROUBLES AND SO DID WE. YOU ALSO GOT FILM AND SO DID WE. HUNTLEY BRINKLEY MADE UNEDITED AND RAW ABOUT EIGHT MINUTES OF EXCITING FILM FROM EMBASSY INCLUDING THROWING JACOBSON HIS PISTOL. CRONKITE MADE NOTHING. AABBCC MADE PRETTY GOOD PIECE BUT WE DID BETTER. SHAD, AND REUVEN.

February 1. The story continued fiercely. There had been no letdown in the action or our coverage. Barely able to take a breath, it hardly mattered that we were not sleeping, eating, taking time for a drink. We had a mission to tell an unbelievable tale.

I sent six more stories aboard a MedEvac flight to Yakota, Japan. The flight would take close to six hours. The film, in our usual red mesh bags, was in the capable hands of an air force courier.

One story, from Hall, Huynh, and Nghia, was about the storming and taking of a building across from Independence Palace and the subsequent rooting out of the Viet Cong holed up there. There was a Tuckner and Ross piece on fighting in the streets where tanks were opposing some well dug in VC, with plenty of action in that one, too. Tuckner and Vo Suu provided a story from the outskirts of Saigon showing villagers evacuated before troops moved in. It had pictures of fleeing refugees and a hectic firefight between U.S. First Division troops and the Viet Cong. We also had an Ambassador Bunker news conference from Bel and Ross which, as expected, said little. There were two pieces from Nessen and Pollak, one of which Ron said was good. It took place in a town called Nam O, south of Danang, where the VC had raised its flag. The ARVN mortared the town, causing more refugees to flee. The Viet Cong were forced out, but not before they had destroyed everything. When the ARVN took back the town, there was hardly anything left.

At NBC News, radio and television worked separately, although each was part of the same operation. Radio, with its low budget and often below news management's sight lines, but never out of its thinking, learned to depend on the largesse of the television reporters. In our bureau, radio got more than what many other bureaus gave, but, as I've said, it still was not enough. Often we received requests that I thought were outrageous or just thoughtless. One came on the second day of Tet, requesting that we produce what radio called "think pieces," explaining and analyzing the fighting to that moment.

I told Jim Holton, the New York radio manager in charge, that I didn't think we could fill his request for think pieces. We had a few problems. Time, for one. Another was shipping. A third was finding available people. Fourth, we already had difficulty meeting the radio circuit with the circuit time available to us on a daily basis. If he wanted the correspondents to write more straight pieces about the war in Saigon and the other events around the country, we would have a better chance of getting it done. But if the spots he requested were to be done right, they needed time, and we did not have enough of it. We could barely keep up with covering the story minute to minute. I asked Holton to reconsider or come up with a more workable idea. He soon withdrew his request and we were able to get on with our coverage.

When Tet started, New York did not have anyone around the clock in communications. Finally, to my relief, New York started manning the communications center twenty-four hours a day, allowing us to stay in touch around the clock. For that, I gave a large thanks to New York.

We were covering everything that happened that we could get to and that we believed deserved attention. The correspondents and crews often produced two or three stories each day. Once we established our shipping pattern, we kept making flights to Yakota, Japan. At times, we carried material for other news organization, such as *Newsweek,* with whom we were not in competition. We knew where the airplane would park and who would unload the film. The NBC Tokyo bureau, with the fastest motorcycle couriers in the world, rushed the film to the laboratory for processing. The developed film went to the Tokyo bureau or to NHK, the Japanese broadcaster, for editing and feeding on the satellite to New York.

■ ■ ■

In war, correspondents and crews—those who handled the storytelling, the camera, and the sound equipment—often reacted differently though they were in the same situation. They worked as a team and produced their story as a team, and they seemed always to be together. Unless you asked them, you would never know that different thoughts were in their minds during the coverage of a story.

Wilson Hall had seen combat in World War II as an artillery forward observer in Europe. As a reporter, he had covered the Korean War, street fighting in Santo Domingo, and the Suez War. He told me that during his four years in Latin America he reported "coups, countercoups, and under-the-counter coups." In Tet, though, he said, he saw more action than in any of those wars and police actions combined. He said that in the Saigon fighting, South Vietnamese troops impressed him for the first time with their bravery and ability. All those actions were battalion or company size, led by younger officers who may have had more interest in defending their city and country than their older counterparts.

One afternoon, Wilson and his crew, with radio reporter Jack Russell, walked up a railroad track near Tan Son Nhut Airport to meet a company of South Vietnamese paratroopers who were in position behind a row of huts. An estimated forty Viet Cong were in another row of huts twenty yards to the north, preparing to overrun a South Vietnamese Army headquarters less than a mile away. As the crew moved up the tracks, Phil Ross said the Auricon sound camera was too damned big and heavy for such stuff. Nghia kept telling the others that they were walking through VC lines. No one believed him until it was too late.

The Vietnamese command called in U.S. helicopter gunships to work over the disputed area with rockets and machine guns. Wilson and his crew moved past bamboo thickets to the next row of huts. The Viet Cong were still out there, but not for long. They decided the quickest way out was over and around the paratroopers. Fire came crackling in from the front and on one exposed flank. Wilson and his team hit the hard-packed dirt behind a hut. Bullets were flying everywhere. They could feel the rounds flying over their heads, which meant they were much too close to the action. "Fingernails may be useful for some things," Wilson said. "They are not entrenching tools. We all tried it, trying to dig a hole in the concrete-like dirt we lay on. Nothing worked."

A Vietnamese sergeant passed the word that they were pulling back. "It's amazing how much Vietnamese one understands when necessary," Wilson said. The Vietnamese squad covered the NBC team, firing rapidly and telling them to get out, to move. "We got out, snaking, crawling, running, until we worked our way back to where there was no firing, next to a cemetery, it so happened." A paratrooper grinned at the exhausted, shaken crew and asked in perfect English, "Did you find the operation interesting?" Wilson and the others laughed and carefully walked the mile back to their car. They drove the two miles back into Saigon without saying a word about the action. Jack grumbled about losing his cigarettes. Wilson wondered aloud if the business people would allow him a pair of reading glasses on the expense account since he lost them in the scramble. Dinh suggested he would wait if Wilson wanted to go back and look for them. Wilson decided it was a bad idea. When they returned to the bureau, they were thirsty, but as usual there was no cold water in the refrigerator.

Hoang Trong Nghia told the story from his own perspective. Small though he was, Nghia rarely showed fear. But on that day, he said, he was frightened when they went in without a military escort to join the friendly troops. The area looked like a friendly village, all tree-lined and calm. At the command post, the officer told them to go first to the power station and from there they could easily meet the ARVN. They continued walking alone without an escort. After three hundred meters, they had not found the ARVN. Nghia told the others they were in the wrong place. He felt the area had maybe two battalions of Viet Cong, about 750 men. "No one listened to me," he said. But he was right: Unfamiliar with the location and having no guide, the men had blindly walked down the railroad track behind enemy lines.

Somehow they managed to avoid the enemy and finally joined the ARVN forces. Once there, Nghia saw a squad of VC no more than fifteen feet from where they were standing. He saw one VC running from house to house. South Vietnamese troops fired at him but he fired back and got away. When the VC opened fire, Nghia and the others heard bullets over their heads and around them. Nghia thought getting caught behind enemy lines was more dangerous than anything else he encountered during Tet, which was significant considering he had filmed the fighting at the Independence Palace, the radio station, and the An Quang Pagoda. Phil said the area was more dangerous than Dak To in late 1967 during the hill battles. The Viet Cong had been everywhere.

Usually in the retelling of a shared experience, as with Wilson and Nghia, the correspondent and cameraman see it and feel it differently. In another episode, Howard Tuckner and Vo Suu were on the same story, but each told it from his own perspective. It was late afternoon on the first day of the Tet Offensive. I sent Howard, Suu, and soundman Dinh to a hot zone near a Tan Son Nhut runway that was under siege. Mr. Long was their driver and porter. After parking his car, Mr. Long carried their extra gear and film magazines. They covered the battle and got enough material for a story. There were deadlines for shipping the film and the crew had to return to the bureau, but the firefight was continuing not far from their position. The crew was terrified to realize that friendly troops, either South Vietnamese manning the posts on the road or equally nervous Americans manning any position, could fire at them. The South Vietnamese troops had orders to challenge everyone first, then fire if anyone ignored their commands. Some soldiers, however, whatever their nationality, were ready to fire first and then send a challenge, especially if they saw a Vietnamese. The war in the streets naturally made everyone jumpy.

The four men had another two hundred meters to go on their way out before reaching Mr. Long's car. They had to make their way down a deserted street that had no houses, no trees, nothing for protection. Mr. Long ran first, followed by Howard. "Just about then," Suu said, "I saw three Americans on top of a three-story building wearing fatigues and helmets. Howard waved at them but kept on running. He was tall, obviously not Vietnamese, and was wearing light-colored clothing, his yellow shirt from earlier in the day when he covered the assault at the American embassy. Dinh and me were following Howard, and we had on dark pants and shirts. The troops in the area for sure thought Howard was being chased by VC. Suddenly they opened fire. First three rounds and then the whole magazine. Dinh and me saw bullets hit the ground all around. We kept running. I felt that something was around me, maybe bullets just missing my face or back. If I would have been hit, I would have tried to keep running out of the area and then fall down. We kept running. They were still firing at us when we reached the car. Three of us hit the floor. Only Long had to keep his head up a little so he could see where to drive."

The way Howard told it, they had just finished filming and started to run back to Mr. Long's car, about a block down the street. The firefight was still going on behind them. To his right, about a hundred yards away, Howard saw what he thought were three U.S. soldiers on a balcony. He waved and gave thumbs up to let them know they were okay. The next thing he and the crew knew, the Americans opened up on them, with bullets cutting between them and the pavement. Howard said, "They apparently figured that I was a Viet Cong hostage, that my crew of Suu and Dinh, Vietnamese wearing dark shirts, were really Viet Cong, that Suu's big sound camera with the long lens on his shoulder was not a camera but a bazooka-type weapon, and that my signal to them really meant that all was not well. We ran like all hell. At this point, driver Long dropped his sunglasses. We screamed at him to forget them and keep going, but he stopped to pick them up. More bullets. Then Long ran madly, we jumped in the car, and sped off at about fifty miles an hour. Bullets still followed the car. Long slouched so far down in the driver's seat that his forehead was even with the middle of the wheel. He couldn't see a thing in front of him. Like a good, frugal Vietnamese, Long saved his sunglasses. Now he was about to kill the four of us in a crackup. We all had a few choice words for him. Long didn't drive that way for long."

Suu later told me it happened too fast for them to think. "One hour, I was in the office. The next hour, I was in the middle of battle. The hour after that, I was back in the office. In the jungle or mountains, it usually takes a day to get into battle and you must stay there three hours at least before you get out. And then the only way to get out is with MedEvac chopper or a chopper bringing in ammo or emergency supplies. In Saigon, we had to depend on our drivers. We loved them, but sometimes they drove us crazy."

Sleep was almost impossible during the first three days and nights of the Tet Offensive. Fatigue affected everyone, including me, though I refused to admit how tired I had become. In spite of our exhaustion, we were elated with our showing. Late on the night of February 2, I told the news desk I would try for some of that elusive sleep, a part of my routine I rarely thought about. I left the bureau uncovered for maybe three hours. If something major happened, the phone in my apartment connected to the one in the bureau on the floor below. At that time of night with the curfew on, there would be no way to get to a story anyway unless it was right in front of us. I would hear about it, but I would be able to do nothing. The streets were calm, as far as I knew. The only people moving about were American MPs and the Vietnamese National Police on patrol in four-man teams traveling in army jeeps. Not even prostitutes were taking a chance on that dangerous, unpredictable night.

I thought of the next day and wondered how we would ship anything. Tan Son Nhut, that odd amalgam of a commercial airport and military base, remained closed, which meant that nothing but essential military planes could fly in or out.

The first problem I had faced on day three was that the Saigon government had ordered all telex plugs pulled, meaning they were turning off our conduit to the outside world. Our leased circuits existed with the permission of the Vietnamese government. Vietnamese technicians administered the circuits (and those of the wire services as well) at the main office of the PTT. We faced the possibility of not being able to get any messages through to—or receive messages from—New York or anywhere else. It could not have come at a worse time.

I advised New York that they would have to check the times of all Saigon flights to Yakota Air Base. I was preparing to ship several strong stories, including a remarkable story called "Pagoda Fighting" about street fighting in Cholon. The pagoda story contained the powerful film of the sudden execution of a Viet Cong prisoner by General Loan, an event that everyone in the world came to know from the still photo shot by the AP's Eddie Adams. We also had a story about street fighting in Hue and a story about a napalm dump in Danang exploding.

Some managers in New York thought we could solve our problem by using the Voice of America circuits as backup whenever we wanted—in their words, "verbalizing all the information as a spot if necessary." They also thought it a good idea for us to order radio circuits to replace the telex if it went down. They assumed we could order circuits as easily as if we were placing a call from New York to Chicago. As often as I told them, they did not seem to remember that the radio circuits and the telex circuits were both under the control of the PTT, and if one went down, so would the other. Besides, with the Saigon government in increasing disarray, we could often find no one to take an order or carry out a technical request. The VOA circuits were difficult to obtain, but there were times we could and did use the Voice of America to feed radio stories and narrations for film reports.

As predicted, government troops marched into the PTT, told the staff to honor the curfew, and sent everyone home. They turned off the AP's wire photo machines but for some reason left all our telex and wire service machines plugged in and running. That meant we did not have anyone monitoring our messages that went through the PTT. Better no monitor than no circuit. We expected more trouble, but we could not do anything about it but wait and hope. I told the New York desk that if the troops came back and pulled the plugs, they would be, with us, in the dark. If you don't hear from us you will know why, I said.

As we struggled with the situation, a message arrived from Bill Corrigan that made everyone in the bureau angry. It was not a major problem, but with everything else going on, it hit us the wrong way. It said:

STEINMAN EXCORRIGAN ADDITIONALLY RE TELEX SUGGEST YOU CONTACT UUSS MILITARY ON SCENE AND URGE THEY PROTECT OUR INTERESTS IN THIS MATTER.

I wanted to respond with outrage and sarcasm. In his enthusiasm to give advice, Corrigan overstepped his bounds and showed his ignorance. After all, the

American military did have its hands full. It was fighting a war. The American army had lost many men. Militarily and politically, the Tet Offensive had become an embarrassment to America. We were not part of the military or an official U.S. agency. Though we were getting help from American quarters, we could not be further in their debt. The air force did more than expected by helping us get our footage out of Saigon and eventually on the air. We were walking a fine line. All journalists were in Vietnam technically as guests of the Vietnamese and not under the protection or orders of the United States. If I dared go to the military with our telex problem, they would have run me out of Saigon. Of course, I did not speak to the military. And I did not respond to Corrigan's message. The better part of valor was to keep my mouth shut and my fingers off the keyboard.

Knowing how tired we were and guessing how much more tired we would become, the executives who ran the news division had already started making decisions without consulting me. I could live with that, but barely. They were in charge, but I felt their decisions were often wrong. Another message from Corrigan came in saying that New York, in their wisdom, had decided to add to my overworked staff—but that was not the kind of help I wanted or needed. Assuming planes would be flying again soon, New York planned to send former Saigon bureau chief Jack Fern (the man I had succeeded), correspondent Douglas Kiker, and cameraman Jim Watt for two to three weeks. Their assignment would be to cover political and economic stories for *The Huntley-Brinkley Report*. Under no circumstances were they to go into combat. I wondered how my overworked staff would handle that blatant discrimination. More "help" was on the way with George Murray, my close friend from the *Vietnam Weekly Review,* coming to prepare a special program on the war. His cameraman would be former Far East staffer Larry Travis. Corrigan wanted to know if any soundmen were available. I told him no. Interestingly, he had the nerve to say that neither unit would put any demands on the bureau. But the thought of their arrival already had, and the strain on our limited resources and space would be enormous.

Despite Corrigan's saying he hoped we all were bearing up under the present difficulties and that we should advise him if we needed any assistance, his message set off a firebomb in the bureau. I was of two minds. I needed help, but under my terms. Inside I seethed. I believed that the *Huntley-Brinkley* show had said to my staff, we will sacrifice you on the front lines during the difficult days of Tet. I believed they had said, you have sacrificed yourselves for months covering the war; however, we have concluded that you are not up to providing the more thoughtful stories we need to round out our coverage. *You* who work in the bureau can cover the fighting. *You* bureau members can go and get shot at each day. *You* can watch death and destruction. *You* can lose sleep and barely eat. *We* will do the long, interpretive pieces that will get the attention of the brass and look great on our résumés.

I was not alone in my thinking. The correspondents and crews were equally upset. By sending in another team, New York would be creating two bureaus. Worse, the new demands on our resources would be major. We barely had enough drivers and cars. There were no hotel rooms anywhere. There were not enough interpreters, so I tried to assign a Vietnamese with each team. Management's plan, though obviously made in good faith, was an affront to my bureau and my staff, who made such an effort to provide coverage. But instead of saying no thank you to Corrigan's offer, I sent a message saying, "The upcoming invasion is one I will not try to repulse." I planned to accommodate the invaders, but on my terms. I would not allow our news coverage to suffer—if it did, my "help" would be sent packing. For the time being, I held my tongue. Once they were here, I would figure out my next move, use my wiles, and get them to do as I wished. My immediate concern was morale. I did not want the level of coverage to decline because some executive was pushing us off the front page. I believed then, and still do now, that the story of young Americans dying in a war they did not want, a war in a strange and foreign land, was far more important than economic and political stories.

I sent instructions to New York on how to get the men into the country. With the airports closed and fighting around all the military bases, it would be highly difficult. It could take longer that anyone expected and that, for the moment, was fine with me. After all, I thought, there was a war on and an extreme one at that, and the more time I had to cover it, the better.

As this internecine administrative problem unfolded, we were unleashing a dramatic piece of film on the world, one that showed, and still does, the horror and insanity of the war. During the Tet Offensive, finding stories to cover was easy, though most were dangerous to the men covering them. One action often led to another. If we covered a firefight one day, chances were that some action would follow the next day. We knew the position of all American units. I routinely received calls from the American military directing me to further fighting in a location we had recently visited. Even my Vietnamese reporters and sources called in or dropped by to tell me to watch one area more carefully than another.

Sometimes they had information about where the North Vietnamese or Viet Cong might strike next. The An Quang Pagoda was a good example.

On February 1, the second day of the Tet Offensive, I had arrived, as usual, in my office at five in the morning. Howard Tuckner and cameramen Vo Huynh and Vo Suu were soon there, as was soundman Le Phuc Dinh. As my team prepared for their assignment, AP photographer Eddie Adams stuck his head in my office and said he did not have anywhere to go that morning. He wondered if he could ride with our crew. Eddie was a good friend. I said yes, he could join them. There were no objections from the crew. I told him the crew was heading to the An Quang Pagoda, the seat of Buddhist militancy and a rumored Viet Cong field hospital. I could not promise anything, but my sources said the North Vietnamese were planning an assault and we should be there. Because he was looking for something to do and asked for a ride, Eddie found himself in a position to take his powerful Pulitzer Prize–winning photograph. It was, of course, of General Loan summarily executing a suspected Viet Cong guerrilla. We, too, had the pictures, but on motion picture film. The rest was history.

When the team arrived back in the office, they were in a state of high excitement. As a group and as individuals, they were unable to contain their emotions. The adrenalin rush they were experiencing was obvious. I had to quiet each man down and debrief him separately in order to get a picture of what had happened. On the surface, it was simple. South Vietnamese government troops had gone into the An Quang Pagoda to clean out suspected Viet Cong. The film showed the fighting around the pagoda and the heavy firefight when Vietnamese marines rushed the pagoda and stormed inside. Men, women, and children fled from the pagoda grounds, carrying their belongings. Wounded women and children came outside and received treatment. Then the Viet Cong opened up on the marines and there was more fighting.

The next part of the story was the Loan segment. It was on Suu's sound roll one, and he believed he had most of it. His captions read as follows: "A VC officer was captured. The troops beat him. They bring him to Loan. Without warning, Loan pulls out his pistol, fires at the head of the VC. The VC falls. Zoom on his head, with the blood spraying out like a finger." If Suu had all of it, it would be startling. If he had only part of it, it would still be more than anyone else had.

When I was sure of what we had, I sat down with Howard and we formulated our approach. We decided to play it straight and direct from beginning to end, allowing the powerful footage to tell the story. I wanted the script to be sparse and as unemotional as possible because the film was so strong. Then Howard wrote notes and script to go with Suu and Huynh's footage. He wrote two versions of the story, one with alternate lines in case some shots were different or not there. We made plans to ship the film to Tokyo for the satellite. The story was competitive. CBS and ABC were there, but we were the only ones who had the full execution on film.

If it was working, the telephone would have been the best way to pass the information to New York. I sent a brief telex to let the New York desk know about the story, saying that we would get it to them as quickly as we could. I called the piece "Tuckner's Pagoda Fighting." Over the next several hours, I passed more information along in separate messages. I told New York what we had so they could prepare themselves and start to think how they would present this material to the evening audience, who would be the first people in the United States to view this remarkable story. The American public would soon see something over their dinner they had never seen before and would probably not see again, at least for some time to come. I mentioned the execution in my messages and hoped that the monitors at PTT were either too busy to read it, would not understand it if they did read it, or would did not care. I suggested to the desk that they develop all the film. I told them to read Howard's note about the exact on-camera closer that we preferred they use. It was important because we were dealing with a delicate problem, namely, General Loan, his anger and unpredictability. The message got through cleanly and Tokyo made preparations to handle the film, process it, and feed it across the United States and the world.

The crew knew it had a remarkable, once-in-a-lifetime story when they shot it. But the other Vietnamese staffers understood that the crew was treading in dangerous waters. Their nervousness spread quickly to everyone in the bureau. They feared General Loan, and rightly so, and thought it possible that he might retaliate when the story played on television. He knew every Vietnamese staffer by name and probably had them on file. They worried he might come after them. He also knew me. But to the relief of all of us in the bureau and NBC News, Loan never retaliated. In his arrogance, he believed the execution was moral and something the world should see.

The image of the South Vietnamese—who were increasingly playing a secondary role in the war—was already tarnished, and the story's impact was as damaging to their cause as we thought it would be. But that is not why NBC played it as the lead story that night. The network led with the story because of its expression of war's horror and inherent ugliness. Today, the NBC film and Eddie Adams's graphic stills are as powerful as they were then.

■ ■ ■

Other stories continued to flow in from all over the country. Wilson Hall filed a piece on heavy fighting in Cholon. Ron Nessen, cameraman Dennis Moore, and soundman White were in on the early fighting in the old imperial city of Hue as the North Vietnamese seized the former capital, which they then held for almost a month. Most important to me, and to everyone else in the bureau, was the return of Detlev Arndt from Ban Me Thuot. Pinned down for many hours in an American compound under fire, he had filmed every aspect of the story. Because he was also a soundman, he managed to get good natural sound of the fighting to accompany his dramatic silent pictures.

Detlev had arrived in Vietnam from Berlin five months before the Tet Offensive. He had been the only man available when I had the chance to cover the heavy fighting in Ban Me Thuot. The trip was supposed to have lasted only a few hours. Others in the press corps made it back to Saigon the same day, but not Detlev. He had with him the Bell & Howell Filmo—a small silent camera—and ten rolls of film. He also carried a small audiotape recorder and a few tape cassettes. He wore civilian clothes, as all the crews did, and had no change of clothing. When he arrived in Ban Me Thuot, the GIs, for reasons unknown to Detlev, told him to put his camera down. They gave him an M-16 rifle and showed him how to use it. It frightened and confused him. He was there to take pictures, not to fight. In the ride from the airfield, a bullet hit his jeep. Fortunately, no one was hurt. Detlev never used his weapon, but instead filmed as much of the action as he could. Rather than feeling safe with a rifle, he felt threatened. He later said, "When they're shooting at you, you know they're in there but you can't see anything. I was more comfortable with my small camera."

Over his three days in Ban Me Thuot, he made every effort to call us in the bureau so we would know he was all right. Finally, he got a call through on a military line. Lutz Gruebnau, also a German, picked up the phone. They were so excited to hear each other that they began speaking in German until the military operator cut in and screamed at them to speak in English. They thought they might have created a security problem, but did that mean the Viet Cong spoke German? It made no sense. Detlev finally returned to us with the only film of the fighting in Ban Me Thuot and its aftermath.

We shipped his film to Yakota Air Base on an Air Force AirEvac flight. I told New York the tail number on the plane, that our film bags were in the crew luggage compartment, and that a Seventh Air Force information officer would meet the plane. With so many MedEvac flights in the air carrying seriously wounded Americans, it was necessary to relay the most information I could, including where the plane would park. It was the only way to make sure our material got to where it had to be. One wrong number, one misplaced or misspelled name, could mean a lost story and the loss of our competitive edge. Amazingly, once shipped, nothing ever went astray.

I notified the desk that George Murray had arrived but that, as I suspected, he could not get into town. He would have to stay overnight in a bunk at Tan Son Nhut and come to Saigon the next day with an armed escort.

Coming to the end of three days of nonstop war coverage, we were starting to wear down fast. None of us had any time to think. I could only react to the tired faces, the dull eyes, the sagging bodies. The pace had become too much to bear. I made a hard decision to swallow my pride and sent the following cryptic message to Reuven Frank in New York:

12–2, JOHNSON PROREUVEN ITS RATHER IMPORTANT YOU MEET THE TELEX
SOONEST FOR A DETAILED MESSAGE AND POSSIBLE DISCUSSION WITH ME RE
A FEW PROBLEMS. LET ME KNOW WHEN TO START SENDING.

20

Fatigue

IT WAS A DIFFICULT message to send, one that I long agonized over. After three days of intensive, brave, and remarkable coverage from the entire bureau, often in the face of danger, the mental and physical fatigue of everyone had become my overriding concern. The conditions we were working under were threatening to overwhelm us. I feared that attrition would win the battle for survival, not a pleasant thought. My pride and my good sense were at war over whether to admit we needed help.

We had received continuous and flattering praise from around the world for our dramatic coverage. New York had lovingly massaged my ego and the ego of everyone in the bureau. But in rare quiet moments, I realized anew that New York, though appreciative of our effort, did not understand what we were up against covering the war. I knew that we had gone as far as we could on spirit, drive, and guts. After running the bureau for more than twenty months, instinct kicked in and signaled that we needed help quickly if we were to survive as individuals, as a bureau, as a network.

No one in the bureau knew I planned to meet Reuven on the telex and ask for his support. I asked him to go to the wire room on the seventh floor, two floors above his office, where all incoming messages arrived. We talked to each other over the very slow telex that ran at sixteen characters a minute. Later, he released to the press a small part of what we had discussed. Here, for the first time, is most of our exchange.

I wrote the following message to Reuven:

> WE HAVE SOME MAJOR PROBLEMS THAT MUST BE SOLVED AS SOON AS POS-
> SIBLE OR ELSE WE WILL BE IN SERIOUS TROUBLE. AT THE START OF THE VIET
> CONG OFFENSIVE IT LOOKED LIKE HIT AND RUN. NOW ITS BECOME HIT AND
> HOLD AND HARASS AND STAY AND FIGHT. IN THE TWO WEEKS BEFORE THE

OFFENSIVE OUR CREWS OF MOORE AND POLLAK IN EYE CORPS HAD BEEN
UNDER ALMOST CONSTANT FIRE. POLLAK AT KHE SANH, DANANG AND HUE.
MOORE AT PLEIKU, KHE SANH, DANANG AND HUE. THEY ARE EXHAUSTED
PHYSICALLY AND MENTALLY AND SPIRITUALLY. IT WOULD BE IDEAL IF I
COULD SWITCH CREWS AND GIVE THEM SOME FRESH PEOPLE. BUT THAT IS
IMPOSSIBLE. OUR SAIGON PEOPLE: HUYNH, NGHIA, SUU, DINH, GIAC, ARNDT,
AND ROSS HAVE BEEN PUSHING JUST AS HARD. THEY HAVE BEEN UNDER
FIRE DAILY AND AT LENGTH. I CANT MOVE THE VIETNAMESE STAFFERS FROM
THEIR HOME CITY. SOUNDMAN DINH MOVED HIS FAMILY TWICE TODAY.
THERE WAS FIGHTING AROUND HIS HOUSE AND LATE THIS AFTERNOON IT
WAS MOSTLY DESTROYED. IT STILL STANDS BUT ONLY AS A BROKEN SHELL.
CAMERAMAN NGHIA MOVED HIS FAMILY ONCE OUT OF DANGER TODAY.
GRUEBNAU AND ARNDT ARE STAYING AT THE CARAVELLE BECAUSE OF FIGHT-
ING IN THEIR NEIGHBORHOOD. ALL HAVE AVERAGED PERHAPS ONE HALF
DECENT MEAL A DAY SINCE TUESDAY SAIGON TIME. WE AVERAGE LESS THAN
FOUR HOURS SLEEP EACH DAY. THERE IS A THREAT OF A FOOD SHORTAGE IN
SAIGON AND THE REST OF THE COUNTRY. TUCKNER, HALL, BEL, AND RUS-
SELL HAVE BEEN DOING YEOMAN LIKE DUTY IN SAIGON, BIEN HOA AND GIA
DINH. NESSEN DITTO IN DANANG, NAM O AND HUE. EVERYTHING ELSE WE
HAVE EVER DONE HERE WAS LOW CALORIE BY COMPARISON. EXHAUSTION IS
STARTING TO SET IN. SOME OF OUR GUYS WILL DEFINITELY START TO FOLD
UNDER PRESSURE, FATIGUE, HUNGER. WE WILL BE UNABLE TO CONTINUE
TO COVER THIS PHASE OF THE WAR CONSISTENTLY UNLESS WE GET SOME
HELP IN THE FORM OF CORRESPONDENTS, CAMERAMEN AND SOUNDMEN.
IT COULD END IN THREE DAYS OR THREE WEEKS. SO WE NEED HELP. GETTING
INTO SAIGON IS A PROBLEM BUT MURRAY MADE IT TODAY VIA BANGKOK BY
HITCHING A RIDE ON A MILITARY AIRCRAFT. CAN PAUL CUNNINGHAM TRY
THE SAME ROUTE? CAN YOU GET ME TWO CAMERAMEN AND TWO SOUND-
MEN TO RELIEVE SOME OF THE PRESSURE ON MY CREWS?

STEINMAN EXREUVEN I AM ANSWERING BEFORE YOURE FINISHED. OBVI-
OUSLY YOU NEED HELP AND WE WILL GET TO IT IMMEDIATELY. CAN YOU HIRE
ANYBODY LOCALLY? YOU HAVE FULL AUTHORIZATION. ANYBODY WE FIND
WILL TAKE TIME TO GET TO YOU. REPEATING THIS WRITTEN WHILE YOUR
MESSAGE MOVING.

REUVEN EXSTEINMAN I WILL TRY TO FIND IF ANYONE ELSE AVAILABLE
HERE IN SAIGON. I DONT THINK I WILL HAVE MUCH LUCK. ONE IDEA I HAVE

IS LETTING FREPPEL AND ARNDT SHOOT SILENT. I KNOW THAT CUTS DOWN ON NATURAL SOUND BUT IT WILL GIVE US MORE MOBILITY IN CERTAIN AREAS, MAYBE I'VE LOST PERSPECTIVE. IT COULD BE OVER IN A WEEK AND THEN WE MIGHT, I SAY MIGHT, ROUND BACK INTO SHAPE IF SOMETHING LIKE KHE SANH DOESNT BLOW WIDE OPEN.

STEINMAN EXREUVEN I HOPE WE HAVE MADE IT OBVIOUS TO YOU HOW MUCH WE APPRECIATE EVERYBODYS EFFORTS TO THE POINT THAT IT SEEMS FRIVOLOUS TO SINGLE OUT ANYBODY AT A TIME OF BREATHTAKING PROFESSIONAL DEVOTION. BUT CONGRATULATORY MESSAGES DONT SOLVE YOUR PROBLEMS AND MY PROBLEM IS WHAT DOES? I THINK I CAN GET THE TWO SOUND CREWS YOU ASK BUT FROM HOW FAR AWAY AND WHEN WOULD THEY ARRIVE? I MUST GO DOWNSTAIRS FOR HUDDLES AND PHONE CALLS AND WILL GET BACK TO YOU SOONEST AND AT THE RISK OF SOUNDING FOOLISH I HOPE SOONEST IS SOON BUT I CANT GUARANTEE. MEANWHILE USE TRAVIS WHO IS MURRAYS CAMERAMAN WHENEVER AND HOWEVER HE ARRIVES AND THE KIKER CREW INCLUDING KIKER LIKEWISE. THE LONGER RANGE NEEDS MUST BE SECONDARY AT THIS TIME AND I KNOW YOU WILL TAKE CARE OF THEM AS YOU CAN WHEN PEOPLE GET SOME SLEEP SOME FOOD AND SOME RELIEF FROM CURRENT ATMOSPHERE. LET ME PUT IT IN WRITING SO THERE IS NO QUESTION. ESPECIALLY IN THIS TIME YOU MUST BE IN ABSOLUTE CHARGE OF EVERY NNBBCC BODY IN VIETNAM MAKING ALL ASSIGNMENTS AND SETTING YOUR OWN SCALE OF PRIORITIES FOR ALL REQUESTS. CORRIGAN AND I WILL ENTERTAIN APPEALS ONLY FROM THOSE WHO FOLLOW YOUR ASSIGNMENTS AND APPEAL LATER. I HAVE CHECKED THIS WITH SHAD. NOW I GO DOWNSTAIRS TO THE BODY BANK AND I HOPE WE ARE NOT OVERDRAWN. MEANWHILE BEST WISHES AND FOR WHAT ITS WORTH FELICITATIONS AND GRATITUDES. ON THE OTHER HAND MY ADVICE ABOUT BREAKING SOUNDMAN AWAY FROM CAMERAMAN TO COVER MORE LOCATIONS IS RECONSIDER. THE NUMBER OF LOCATIONS TAKES SECOND PLACE IN MY MIND TO THE QUALITY OF COVERAGE SO I WOULD DO THIS ONLY WHEN YOU STRONGLY FEEL LEAVING ONE LOCATION UNCOVERED IS DAMAGING BECAUSE ITS UNIQUE AS WELL AS IMPORTANT. I SHOULDNT PUT THIS IN WRITING BUT IF YOU SHUT DOWN YOUR FILM OPERATION FOR TWO DAYS BRANDEX COULDNT CATCH UP TO THE LEAD YOU PEOPLE HAVE ALREADY GIVEN US.

REUVEN EXSTEINMAN YOU ARE RIGHT ABOUT THE NUMBER OF LOCATIONS AND THE SOUNDMEN WILL STAY TIED TO THEIR CAMERA. WHAT I

MIGHT DO IS USE A SOUNDMAN AS A RELIEF CAMERAMAN BUT I WONT
SPREAD THIN TO GET MORE STORIES FROM MORE AREAS. REGARDING EVERY-
THING ELSE YOU SAID, I CANT SAY MUCH MORE THAN THANKS. I AM GOING
TO GET SOME SLEEP AND WILL BE BACK IN THE OFFICE AROUND 2200 GMT OR
5 PM YOUR TIME. AGAIN THANKS.

With a stroke of his pen, Reuven gave me what I wanted, told me what I wanted
to hear. My worst fears disappeared. Maybe good works do lead to heaven. Reuven
resolved the potential morale problem, gave the bureau back to me and my hardworking, dedicated staff, and started help our way. I wanted to say, bless you, boss,
but being a hardened newsman, I contained myself and only said, thanks.

When I awoke, there was a message on the telex from Bill Corrigan. It was the
one we were waiting to see.

YOU AND YOUR TIRED FRIENDS DID IT AGAIN. AABBCC WAS OUR CLOS-
EST COMPETITION. WE WERE ALONE WITH THE EXECUTION AND NUMEROUS
PROTESTING PHONE CALLS ATTEST TO THE IMPACT OF IT ALL.

As promised, help was on the way. Cameramen Jim Nickless and Earl Wells
and soundman Tom Cosgrove were coming in from the States. Cameraman Joe
Oxele and soundman Hannes Peschke were on the way from Germany. From New
York, correspondents Paul Cunningham and Tom Glennon were trying to get to
Saigon, as was producer Frank Donghi, who would help run the bureau.

Despite their weariness, the teams kept running and producing. Wilson Hall
covered another firefight near the An Quang Pagoda. Ron Nessen continued covering the battle for Hue. He told me it was the best street fighting footage he had
ever seen or been in. Hue would soon become the major focus of the Tet Offensive. Along with the fighting in Saigon, it brought the war to the streets for the
first time, and it was a battle we covered well. We shipped the obligatory President Thieu news conference in which he said very little that was illuminating.
Howard Tuckner and Phil Ross had another strong story of fighting on the outskirts of Saigon, with helicopter gunships firing rockets at enemy positions, a brief
firefight, and a burning gas station to round out the action.

As always in combat, especially when journalists were close to the action, it became a photographer's war. Phil Ross had been there when the South Vietnamese
marines again assaulted the An Quang Pagoda, and he gave me an example of
what his eye had seen and what his camera recorded: "There was this Vietnamese

kid with the recoilless rifle jumping out into the alley and firing down the alley. He stands up in the middle of the gutter and mows the street with his machine gun. The fact that he is attacking a highly religious area, the pagoda, where there may be a conflict between his religious upbringing and his job at that moment—that's the story."

When the Tet Offensive started, Vo Huynh had been with NBC News for more than seven years, covering more combat than anyone else, including the rash of coups and attempted coups in the Vietnamese leadership that occurred in the 1960s. "This time it was really worse than a coup," he said. "Then you knew where to go. But now you didn't. In many sections of the city, we'd pass by in the morning and nothing happened. In the afternoon, there was firefighting all over. What's worse, you didn't know where the enemy was. You didn't know where our troops were. As for myself, I know Saigon very well and in case something happened I could get away easily. What about the rest of the crew? What about the foreign correspondent? I wondered how to help."

All our correspondents were "foreign" to Huynh, who always felt he had to take care of the crew. They were his responsibility. During the fighting, he said, "I learned that every hundred meters you must get out of the car, talk to the people, and find out what's going on in the next block." At one point, his crew was following a convoy into an area of the city where bitter fighting raged. South Vietnamese troops guarded the roadblocks. About a hundred meters away, Huynh suddenly saw an Airborne trooper pointing his gun and yelling at them not to make another move. Huynh said, "I screamed at our driver to stop the car. We found out that on the other side the VC had captured some American and South Vietnamese military police vehicles and the Vietnamese army guards couldn't tell who was friendly, who was not." An ARVN commander told Huynh that he did not always recognize all the men in his own company and that if he told them to stop and they did not, he'd open fire on them, too. That nervousness accounted for many civilian casualties—innocent people who ran in fear when a jittery soldier shouted at them to halt.

Another day, Huynh found himself fighting a different enemy. He and Wilson Hall were covering an attack on the ARVN Joint General Staff Headquarters in Saigon. The Viet Cong were using portable grenade launchers and Huynh had to be cautious. Grenade launchers are not accurate weapons. The grenades often land anywhere but on target. Huynh was filming the action from a safe position. However, he did not know he was standing on top of an ant colony. "Soon they were creeping all over me. Red ants, the worst kind," he said.

Wilson wanted to do his on-camera stand-up, but it had become too dangerous to do it in the middle of the street. Huynh's corner was safe from fire, so Wilson decided to move there. While he was talking into the camera, the ants found him, too, and started moving over his clothing and onto his body. Huynh said, "I told him I didn't worry about the bullets because the ants were much worse." They did the stand-up and moved to another position, brushing at their clothing with little success and taking the ants with them.

On February 3, the fourth day of the fighting, Howard Tuckner and Huynh filmed a story that ran on *The Huntley-Brinkley Report*. While roaming the Saigon streets looking for action, they shot a complete piece about security, with young men searched and arrested as Viet Cong sympathizers when their only crime was their youth. They also told the story of refugees, closed markets, scarcity of goods, and garbage piling up, with, fittingly, discarded yellow flowers left over from Tet. It was a story about the people of Saigon trying to rise from the rubble of war.

Earlier in the day, Wilson Hall and his crew were also on the Saigon streets, accompanying ARVN paratroopers as they advanced on enemy positions in an attempt to wipe them out. The action became very heavy as the VC counterattacked and pushed the paratroops back. Our crew retreated with the South Vietnamese, running and crawling and ducking, getting away as fast as they could. They made it, and with good film. All were glad to return to the bureau in one piece. It proved no one was ever safe anywhere on the streets of Saigon.

That same day, I needed fresh air. I had not seen daylight, except from my windows, since the start of the Tet Offensive. My life centered on my desk, my little-used apartment on the floor above, the ever-clattering telex machines, my tired and hungry crews, and my throat, raw from too many packs of Camels. Occasionally I emptied my heaping ashtray as I opened yet another pack of cigarettes. Sometimes I had as many as three cigarettes burning at once.

The twenty-four-hour curfew had been cut back to 2 P.M. to 8 A.M., meaning people could move around between eight in the morning and two in the afternoon. Perhaps this was a hint of a return to what passed for normalcy. I needed some freedom from running the bureau. All the teams were in the field on stories. I decided to breathe some real air, even if polluted, instead of the unnatural, air-conditioned air of the office. So I walked the four flights to the street. I stood in front of the Eden Building on the corner of Nguyen Hue and Le Loi, blinking my eyes, trying to get them used to being outside. The day was unusually quiet. The street vendors and food stalls were nowhere in sight. There were no motorbikes or scooters, trucks or cars—it had become too dangerous to move through the streets. I felt like I was in a B movie about the end of the world. Only the buildings remained. There were no people anywhere. So I thought. Occasionally the sound of distant rifle fire broke the silence, American jets flew overhead, and helicopters swooped and dipped over the horizon looking for targets.

I leaned against the building, my hands behind my back against the stone fa-cade, the ever-present cigarette lying hot between my lips. I relaxed, for the mo-ment. Somewhere in the distance I heard the faint chug of a Vespa motor scooter. I ignored it, but the sound grew louder until I could see the scooter moving slowly down the middle of the street toward me, or at least toward the Eden Building. As the scooter came within a football field's length from where I stood, I did not believe what I saw. Driving the Vespa was Tu Hong Phat, Josephine's father. On the back sat Josephine with her two arms wrapped tightly around her father's waist. The wig I bought her in Hong Kong to cover her healing wound was held firmly in place with a colorful kerchief.

My first reaction, other than pure surprise, was a negative one. The possibility of an ambush everywhere, behind every tree, out of every window, made it dan-gerous to drive in Saigon. What were they doing? And, now that they were here, I thought, what did they want? Specifically, what did Josephine want?

As it turned out, they did not want much. Josephine and her family had decided she would be safer with me in my apartment and in the bureau than at home on Phat Diem Street. Every day the Viet Cong fired rockets at National Police Headquarters less than a mile away; the rockets passed over their house from the other side of the Saigon River. Worse, they awoke that morning to find a Viet Cong flag planted in the middle of their street. Usually all they saw were potholes filled with dirt or mud. Viet Cong sympathizers—from the men who worked in the adjacent market to the local cyclo drivers—were always in front of their home. Josephine saw four Viet Cong with rifles and grenades sitting in the alley outside her house, calmly eating soup and rice. After a hasty meeting, Josephine and her family decided she should stay with me.

Tu Hong Phat and I smiled at each other as he helped Josephine from the scooter and unloaded her small overnight bag. He and I bowed and then I took her upstairs as he chugged back to his home. Later that day everyone greeted her effusively, including her friends at the Associated Press. She enjoyed a steady stream of well-wishers who came by to pay homage to her survival and courage. She stayed with me in the apartment but spent most of her time in the bureau, smiling, sometimes laughing, and, though she could not work, relishing her role back in the world. Four days later, when much of the fighting in Saigon had ended, Josephine returned to her family.

On the fifth day of our coverage came word that the curfew would not start until 7 P.M. I made sure the staff would be safe in their hotel rooms and in their homes. I had heard that the National Police planned a sweep in areas where there were unconfirmed reports of Viet Cong attacks. I arranged a military police escort for anyone in the bureau who went out after curfew, even if they had to cross only one street.

As suddenly as the war had come to the streets of towns and cities across the country, it just as quickly began to abate. Viet Cong and North Vietnamese losses had been stunning. South Vietnamese losses, including civilians, were staggering. The numbers of American dead and wounded were also reaching record highs. The political damage in America was incalculable and would be felt more in the coming months. Demonstrations against the war increased and President Johnson would soon stun the world by announcing he would not run for a second term.

We still covered everything we could and I used everyone on staff to maximum efficiency. But the bloom on the story had started to fade. One piece began to look like another. Reuven Frank decided to use the Tokyo satellite sparingly, only in specific cases depending on the strength and value of our offering. Although I wanted our stories on the air every day in every news broadcast, I knew we would continue to have more than our fair share of air time. I understood Reuven's decision and I did not disagree. For the moment, there was no further discussion.

But there were nagging problems. Howard Tuckner had been investigating a story about the attack on the embassy that had been floating around Saigon. He had fresh information that American marines and the South Vietnamese police guarding the embassy contended that the seizure had in part been an inside job. Tuckner said that a few South Vietnamese accredited as embassy drivers were really Viet Cong. They hid in the compound the night of the attack and killed two American marines, thus making it easier for the suicide teams to penetrate the walls.

Realizing the potential of the story, Reuven and Bill Corrigan requested my advice on how strongly they should play it. They would give it good play if we were absolutely sure of what we had. It turned out that I was not as certain as I was when I first read Tuckner's copy and passed on it. After looking over the copy a second time, I sent the following message about this and other matters.

AHH, FOR THE VIRTUE OF SLEEP. I READ THAT COPY ORIGINALLY AND PASSED ON IT. ON SECOND THOUGHT, I WOULD HOLD IT BACK NOW. IT CAME FROM AN MMPP LIEUTENANT BUT THERE IS NO OTHER CONFIRMATION, AND WITHOUT A SECOND SOURCE IT OPENS AN UNHOLY CAN OF WORMS. THUS, I WOULD DROP THAT PARAGRAPH. I AM SURE THERE WILL BE AS MANY THEORIES ABOUT HOW THE EMBASSY WAS ATTACKED AS THERE ARE ABOUT WHO KILLED JFK. WE MAY HAVE A SENSATIONAL BEAT BUT WITHOUT SOME HIGHER SOURCE, I WOULD DROP THAT WHOLE PARAGRAPH FROM THE NARRATION. IN RESPONSE TO A SERIES OF OTHER QUERIES, HERE ARE MY THOUGHTS. CASUALTIES ARE SUPPOSED TO BE COUNTED BY TROOPS AND BATTLEFIELD OFFICERS IN THE FIELD. EACH NUMBER SHOULD REPRESENT ONE KILLED OR ONE WOUNDED. THE PROBLEM IS IN COMBAT, OFFICERS AND MEN ALWAYS SEEM TO WANT TO PLEASE HIGHER OFFICERS AND SOMETIMES EITHER ESTIMATE OR PAD THE COUNT TO MAKE EVERYONE LOOK GOOD. NATURALLY THERE ARE SOME ACCURATE AND RELIABLE BODY COUNTS. IT IS DIFFICULT TO KNOW HOW MANY VVCC DIED AND HOW MANY DEAD CIVILIANS ARE VVCC. THE FIGURES AREN'T ALL IN AND WHEN THEY ARE, THEY STILL MAY NOT BE CONCLUSIVE. IF BY LIBERATION FRONT YOU MEAN THE VIET CONG CALL TO ESTABLISH NEW GOVERNING BODIES WHERE THE PEOPLE ARE SUPPOSED TO HAVE RISEN AGAINST THEIR OPPRESSORS, THERE IS NO EVIDENCE THEY HAVE ANYWHERE. THE MAJOR CONTINUING ACTION IS HUE. I HAVE IT FROM ON HIGH THAT HUE IS A LIKELY SPOT WHERE THE NORTH VIETNAMESE HAVE HAD VERY GOOD COOPERATION FROM PARTS OF THE POPULATION. SENIOR AMERICAN OFFICIALS SAY THAT HUE AND SAIGON ARE THE TWO PLACES WHERE THE VVCC RECEIVED THE MOST COOPERATION. ITS OBVIOUS TO SEASONED OBSERVERS, THE VVCC HAD TO HAVE LOTS OF COOPERATION TO ENTRENCH THEMSELVES SO DEEPLY. TERROR AND THREATS ARE ONE THING AND CAN LAST JUST SO LONG. BUT THE ELEMENT OF SURPRISE WAS SO SWIFT THAT IN THOSE SECTIONS OF THE CITY WHERE THE VVCC SUDDENLY EMERGED IT BECOMES OBVIOUS THE PEOPLE HAD TO KNOW THEY WERE THERE. IF THE VVCC HOLD IN THOSE AREAS WAS NOT COMPLETE, WORD WOULD HAVE LEAKED OUT. THE VIETNAMESE CANNOT KEEP A SECRET.

Problems of every kind continued, not the least of which was the unavailability of flights in and out of the country. It hampered the movement of my crews because Tan Son Nhut was also where we boarded military helicopters that took us into the field. No Vietnamese were being allowed on the base. Vietnamese civilians regularly employed on the base stayed home. Even the Vietnamese working for us and known to security had difficulties. Ground crews who handled airplanes could not work and commercial passenger airplanes were not landing. Immigration and customs officials were not working. However, some Pan American cargo flights continued to depart, and we shipped two stories on Pan Am 876 to Tokyo. After a long wait, we finally sent a team aboard a helicopter to the Mekong Delta with a military escort.

Khe Sanh started seeing more action. We assumed Hanoi might be taking a breather with different tactics, because of its heavy losses in most of the country, and would now concentrate on the northern tier of South Vietnam. When I had a free crew, I sent it in that direction. Wilson Hall went to I Corps to help cover Hue and Khe Sanh.

Though the Tet Offensive was changing, the war was still with us. Fighting in Cholon had become mostly the flush-and-shoot variety. Cameraman Nghia's home in Cholon was in the same neighborhood as a recent firefight, so I gave him permission to move his family to safety. While he was moving his family, we had no cameramen available to cover the action near his home.

Phan Bach Dang, a Saigon native and a trained artist, also lived in what had become a dangerous neighborhood. At NBC News for more than three years, he was a maintenance and engineering assistant, soundman, and sometime cameraman. He was married with two children and, like the other Vietnamese staffers, the welfare of his family came first. It was usually quiet around his home, generally considered in a secure area. Six days after the attacks started, he awoke to find a Viet Cong flag hanging on a home near his house. No place was safe.

By February 5, the sixth day of the Tet Offensive, we started working on stories that illustrated how people were suffering. One such piece was about the Mekong Delta town of My Tho, where enemy attacks had destroyed more than half the town, killing hundreds of civilians and wounding many more. According to Howard Tuckner and his cameraman, Vo Huynh, the destruction had been needless, the killing indiscriminate. In an interview, an American doctor said he had to amputate limbs butcher-style, without anesthetics, the way they did in the Civil War. He went on to say there were no antibiotics and many would die of infection, others from tetanus. Angry with the Vietnamese doctors who did not come to work, he openly wondered why we were fighting the war. Huynh shot a moving sequence in a graveyard showing mass burials by Vietnamese soldiers wearing masks to block out the stench of the dead. We coupled this with other film of crowded hospitals everywhere in the country, including Saigon, and we agreed we had a telling story. In Saigon, My Tho, and elsewhere, three wounded soldiers would often share one bed and many lay on the floor in crowded hallways. I thought we had a significant piece about the wantonness of war.

I recommended the satellite for this story and a story we had on food distribution and the growing refugee problem in Saigon. I felt both pieces would make a very strong package, showing the terrible results of war in the cities. In a sense, these stories showed the completion of phase one on the road from war to destruction. But the *Huntley-Brinkley* producers turned my idea down because, so I heard, the stories did not involve American troops. I wondered what had happened to their news judgment.

The same dilemma prevailed as before Tet. I was on the ground, making fast, often instinctive judgments daily. However, the dynamic of the story had changed. We were still covering the fighting but I had also decided to cover the effect of the war on the Vietnamese and how it disrupted their lives. Hanoi clearly staged the Tet Offensive to show America it could not win the war. I thought I had the responsibility to explain the effect of the offensive on the innocent, the average Vietnamese who wanted to be left alone by everyone, Americans and Viet Cong. The Vietnamese people would never have been in such a terrible situation if America had kept its troops at home. The war might have ended years before. But that was not the situation in February 1968. I wanted to split the coverage to somehow send a wake-up call to anyone who doubted the horror of war and how it always affected the noncombatant. I suspect that some in New York never understood what I was trying to do. I had no trouble with most of my correspondents and crews when I assigned them coverage other than hard combat. Combat was exciting and dangerous, but it was often the same. Stories with content, though not as dangerous or exciting and with potentially less air time, gave them a chance to do more than count the dead and wounded and hear bullets and rockets flying over their heads.

But New York was unhappy with my recommendation. They thought me frivolous and the stories we had prepared not strong enough for the expensive satellite. NBC News had spent a great deal of money to get exciting pieces on the air from the Saigon bureau. These new stories were more thoughtful than exciting. Money was always a consideration. I never disagreed with that. I did try to comply with management's wishes by carefully recommending only what I considered important for immediate air, but I reserved the right to suggest what I believed the American audience deserved to see. Judging from the undercurrent of crisp-ness and anger in our discussions, management obviously did not see things the same way. Our small battle ended in a stalemate. I knew that some news editors "back in the world," as American soldiers referred to the United States, realized that war was not always dead soldiers and destroyed cities and countryside. Too often, war was as horrible for those left behind, the living. I hoped my message would eventually get through.

During my dispute with New York over the satellite, the news desk sent me another message about Howard Tuckner's embassy story. It referred to *New York Times* correspondent Charlie Mohr's piece about the "supposed" inside job that made it possible for the Viet Cong to so easily attack the Saigon embassy. I did not know Mohr's sources, but knowing the sources we had, I stuck by the recommendation I had made to not use the information. Howard became furious with me when he learned that the well-respected Mohr, in his words, "verified my story." I told Howard that his sources were not good enough and that I would not use another journalist as a source. I said if he got me another source I would go with his story. The blood rose in his face and he stomped out of the office. I stood by my decision then and still do. Howard never came up with another source and to this day the inside-job theory is just that, a theory without verification.

I advised the news desk of some coming phases of the Tet Offensive, each in the form of a question. When and how would there be an end to the battle for Hue? Would North Vietnamese troops continue to mortar, then attack and overrun the marine base at Khe Sanh? American military intelligence now thought of Hanoi's action as what it described as a phased plan. If Khe Sanh in its earlier stages seemed to have been a diversion for the massive attack on the cities, then in turn, in a byzantine way, the attack on the cities may have been a diversion for the North Vietnamese attack on Khe Sanh. Hue might be a holding action, an attempt by Hanoi to secure a major city and a prelude for the attack on Khe Sanh. American intelligence thought there would be another massive attack on the cities, or, at the very least—and most possible in the thinking of Hanoi and the old Viet Minh— another large-scale attack on Saigon, which was still reeling and trying to recover from the rubble and demoralization of the first attack. I told New York I would probably recommend the satellite depending on what stories we had. It did not mean they would go with my recommendation.

21

Reinforcements

IN THE FIRST five days of the Tet Offensive, I had perhaps a total of five hours of uninterrupted sleep. I exaggerated when I told Reuven that I averaged four hours each night. I probably spent four hours every night alone in my apartment, but I was never far from the problems of covering the story. My staff did no better with sleep. Problems emerged with eating as well. All the Vietnamese restaurants closed during the fighting. The military PX and commissary, where we bought our American goods, closed, as did all the food stores in Saigon. The U.S. officers' mess halls around the city were running out of food. More often than not, Saigon and all the major cities were under twenty-four-hour curfew. Fortunately, the bureau had stockpiled a small amount of food and many cartons of C rations, but it went quickly with some two dozen people in and out of the bureau all day, grabbing whatever they could to sustain themselves. We soon ran out of coffee, tea, Coke, beer, sugar, tuna fish, soda crackers, peanut butter, and condensed soup. Over the first three days, each of us Westerners ate perhaps one decent meal a day. Vo Huynh, who lived one floor above the office, fed the Vietnamese and occasionally me with rice he had stockpiled in case of an emergency.

We were also running out of cigarettes. I think the average smoker went through three packs a day—with bullets flying everywhere, cancer was an incidental worry. The water pressure was low, and baths and shaves were kept to a minimum. Many staffers could not go to their homes, so they bunked together in extra rooms at the Caravelle Hotel diagonally across the square from the office. In a way, covering the war was easy. It was like springtime, but with buds of fire instead of flowers popping out wherever you chanced to turn your head. It was all the other problems that made our lives difficult. But in time we solved these. Food came from one source or another. Cigarettes appeared. Instant coffee and tea bags showed up. We could live in spotty luxury, at least until the next firefight.

One source of food was Jan Moorehead, a twenty-three-year-old woman from Scottsdale, Arizona, and a graduate of Arizona State University. Jan worked for the USO in Saigon and had met some of our correspondents in the Rex BOQ mess hall after the Rex extended dining privileges to the press. She knew that during the crisis our men were running around covering stories all day, and she thought they were sure to be hungry. On the third day, she showed up at the bureau and took orders for hamburgers. Within an hour, she returned to the bureau with steaming food, our only meal of the day. The next day, she took orders for steaks. She knew the sergeants at the mess hall. The three soldiers who guarded the USO's long-distance telephones helped her with the cooking. Jan stayed busy doing the same for others who needed help. She had been in Vietnam for two years, first with the Red Cross and then with the USO. After a short home leave, she planned to return for another two years, if possible. She said her father told all his kids they owed something to their country. Each had an obligation, and she was fulfilling hers. Without Jan, we would have been hungrier than we could have imagined.

By the end of the seventh day of the Tet Offensive, though additional correspondents and camera crews were converging on the bureau, most had not yet arrived. They were scattered throughout Asia, trying their best to get into the country and relieve our tired people. From Hong Kong, I expected Hugh Vannes, a Dutch soundman. The Berlin bureau had sent cameraman Peter Dehmel and his younger brother, Klaus, a soundman. Many other staffers were stuck in Tokyo and Bangkok. Each carried his own camera and sound equipment, including sorely needed film stock, fresh batteries, and audio cassettes. Our expected arrivals faced further delays because of renewed fighting at the northwest edge of Tan Son Nhut Air Base. Two Viet Cong battalions were causing havoc with incoming flights and aiming to knock out low-flying helicopters. I sent Paul Cunningham, one of my veteran reporters, to the base along with cameramen Nghia and Suu and soundman Dinh. Jack Russell went to cover for radio. It was Paul's first action since his return, and he took the assignment like a trouper.

During the Tet Offensive, our driver-couriers were unsung heroes who never received enough praise. They arrived in the bureau at first light, drank their coffee or tea, talked and argued, and smoked their cigarettes. They sat around in the narrow outer office and played cards while waiting for their assignment—to drive a crew into the action, or me to a meeting at the embassy or MACV. They used their own beat-up American-made automobiles and complained about never making enough money. Often fearless, perhaps mad, they were mostly reliable beyond the call of duty. One of these men, a quirky driver, was named Mai Van Ngoi. Nick-named "Ut," he was a recent addition to the staff. One week into the fighting, Ut took Howard Tuckner and a crew to Cholon, the Chinese district of the city, where entrenched Viet Cong troops were a danger to everything. Once out of the car, Howard and the crew told Ut to stay behind and started searching for the South Vietnamese troops. Not knowing the neighborhood, they carefully made their way through the streets looking for friendly troops. The crew, as often happened, wandered into enemy territory, but they were lucky. Instead of the Viet Cong, they met a South Vietnamese patrol and, with it, they moved safely through the area.

Ut became nervous waiting for the crew to return. He parked his car on the side of the road, locked it, and began looking for them. While on his search, he stumbled onto the Viet Cong position. He was taken to the unit commander, ter-ribly frightened, and his interrogation started immediately. Asked where he was born, Ut told the commander he came from Long An, a province west of Saigon. The Viet Cong commander had also been born there, and he recognized Ut's ac-cent. He decided to free Ut if he quit working for the Americans, which Ut readily agreed to do. Shaken but unharmed, Ut returned to his car. Soon the team reap-peared, having finished their filming, and Ut drove them back to the bureau. He did not quit as he promised, and remained working for NBC News in Saigon.

As the fighting settled in, Nguyen Cao Ky, now vice president of South Vietnam, again forced his way onto center stage. He held a news conference at which he said he would create a new security force to help restore order, to pass out food, and to aid refugees pouring into the safe portions of the city. He discussed a plan to arm the people so they could help in their own defense in any future engagements. Ky said he would severely punish anyone caught hoarding illegal supplies. When the camera was turned off, he explained that he had to arm the people because he lacked enough government troops. Before he gave weapons to anyone, there would be a loyalty check. Ky said he would show the people how to use the guns and that distribution could begin within the next seven days. During the crisis, Ky was everywhere, and always the fashion plate, wearing his flak jacket and air force uniform. In contrast, President Thieu rarely made a public appearance. Ky's bizarre idea of arming the civilian population was never carried out. It was typical of his grandstanding, especially when he saw TV cameras.

I informed New York that Earl Wells, Jim Nickless, and Tom Cosgrove had ar-rived and would be safe at Tan Son Nhut until we could get them to the bureau under an armed escort the next day. I said I did not think I needed another correspondent and that I would let them know when I did. I felt more secure and in control now that the first week of coverage had ended, but once the gate was opened, it was impossible to close. Bill Corrigan sent the following message:

> NATBROCAST SAIGON STEINMAN EXCORRIGAN APPRECIATE THE STAMINA OF ALL CONCERNED IN YOUR SAYING NEED DOES NOT EXIST FOR ADDITIONAL CORRESPONDENT. OUR CONCERN WAS THAT CORRESPONDENTS HAVE THE LUXURY OF DAY OR TWO RESPITE FROM HORRORS OF PAST WEEK IN SAME FASHION AS CAMERA STAFF WHICH HAS BEEN BEEFED UP. ALSO WITH MAJOR OFFENSIVE STILL THREATENED DID NOT WANT TO BE CAUGHT BY RR AND RR NOR DO I FEEL THEY SHOULD BE DELAYED UNLESS ESSENTIAL. YOU HAVE ALL HAD A RATHER ROUGH TIME OF IT AND SOME RELIEF FROM THE STRAIN WOULD PROBABLY HELP. WE HAVE OLD SAIGON HAND DAVID BURRINGTON IN TOKYO READY TO COME IN FOR ONE MONTH TOUR. PLEASE ADVISE IF THIS FACT AND MY STATEMENT OF FEELING ABOVE RESULTS IN ANY CHANGE IN YOUR INITIAL OPINION.

When I received that note, I honestly felt we did not need another correspondent, although I welcomed David Burrington, who had already served more than a year in Saigon. He had experience, a mature approach, and good skills. I agreed with Bill that our correspondents could use a rest, but there was only so much we could cover, and the news shows could handle only so much material. Though we enjoyed thinking about more coverage, we knew—though we did not like the idea—that there were other worthy stories elsewhere in the world vying for air time. In a few days, however, there would be an event that would change my mind on the need for another correspondent.

On February 6, the seventh day of Tet, Frank Donghi arrived from New York as my second assistant bureau chief. I worked out a schedule that had Frank on in daylight with me on at night to handle message traffic and all the small battles with New York. I was around all the time anyway, because there was noplace else to go. Frank would read morning copy, prepare a news budget, monitor breaking events, man the phones and telex, and call me if there was a question he could not answer but otherwise allow me to sleep. I would be in better shape to plan and assign. Frank's schedule would change if the curfew changed. But we foreigners were still under a strict curfew between the hours of 7 P.M. and 8 A.M. and the Vietnamese from 2 P.M. until 8 A.M. The American military and its Vietnamese government employees had twenty-four-hour curfews but that was meaningless because they were always on permanent alert.

Radio, ever hungry, wanted longer pieces and I said we could finally take care of them. There were also inquiries from editors in New York regarding the exact number of casualties and other nuances. I sent them the following:

> MACV, UNITED STATES MILITARY ASSISTANCE COMMAND VIETNAM, IS THE SOURCE OF CASUALTY FIGURES. THEY ARE NOT USING THE WORD, ESTIMATE. WE ALWAYS TRY TO LAY OFF ANY QUOTE FIRM UNQUOTE FIGURES ON THEM. THE ENEMY CASUALTY FIGURES ARE HARD TO BELIEVE BUT THERE HAS BEEN A LOT OF DEATH AND DESTRUCTION. THE VIET CONG AND NORTH VIET-NAMESE HAVE BEEN HURT VERY BADLY WITH MANY DEAD AND WOUNDED. WE SHALL CONTINUE TO CITE THE SOURCES FOR ALL FIGURES. WATCH THE NEWSPAPERS AND WIRES AND US BECAUSE THE COMING STORY IS THAT OF CIVILIAN CASUALTIES. BY THE LOOK OF THINGS THOSE ARE GOING TO BE PAINFULLY AND TEARFULLY HIGH. SOURCES ON THOSE WILL BE EVEN MORE IMPORTANT AND EVEN MORE DIFFICULT TO CITE BUT WE WILL DO OUR BEST. ITEM: THE VIET CONG HAVE BEEN IN ALL THE TERROR ATTACKS. IN SOME PLACES THEY HAVE BEEN AIDED BY NORTH VIETNAMESE COMMANDOS OR SAPPERS. IN HUE, THERE ARE OR WERE AT LEAST FOUR OR FIVE NORTH VIET-NAMESE BATTALIONS. BATTALION SIZE IS DIFFICULT TO JUDGE. IN SAIGON THERE ARE OR WERE ELEMENTS OF THE 7TH NORTH VIETNAMESE REGIMENT. NORTH VIETNAMESE REGULARS WERE FIGHTING IN THE CENTRAL HIGH-LANDS. THE REASON WE REFER TO THE ATTACKS AS VIET CONG IS THAT THE VVCC HAVE BEEN IN THE LEAD. GENERALLY GUERRILLAS WOULD COME FIRST, FOLLOWED BY THE NORTH VIETNAMESE ONCE THEY ESTABLISH A BRIDGE-HEAD. SOMETIMES THE VVCC AND NORTH VIETNAMESE WENT IN TOGETHER. IN HUE, THE NORTH VIETNAMESE OBVIOUSLY HAD THE SUPPORT OF SOME PEOPLE OTHERWISE THEY COULD NOT HAVE INFILTRATED THE WAY THEY DID. THERE ARE NORTH VIETNAMESE EVERYWHERE, EXCEPT THE DELTA.

On the ninth day of the Tet fighting, we had our first casualty. I sent the following to New York:

> 3–8, JOHNSON PROCORRIGAN ETREUVEN HOWARD TUCKNER WAS VERY FORTUNATE TODAY. TUCKNER WAS SLIGHTLY WOUNDED WHEN A VIET CONG B-40 ROCKET WAS FIRED AND EXPLODED AT THE POINT WHERE HE, VO HUYNH, NGHIA, VI GIAC AND JACK RUSSELL WERE COVERING MORE OF

THE ACTION IN CHOLON. TUCKNER IS WELL. HE TOOK AT LEAST SIX SMALL PIECES OF SHRAPNEL IN HIS LEFT THIGH. HE WAS IMMEDIATELY TAKEN TO THE 17TH FIELD HOSPITAL WHERE HE WAS TREATED AND RELEASED. SEVERAL PIECES REMAIN IN THE THIGH, EMBEDDED IN THE MUSCLE NOT REPEAT NOT NEXT TO THE BLOOD VESSELS. I REPEAT HE IS WELL, WALKING AND IN VERY GOOD HUMOR AND FRAME OF MIND. HIS SPIRITS ARE EXCELLENT. TOMORROW HE WILL GO BACK TO THE HOSPITAL FOR ANOTHER CHECK ON THE WOUND AND WILL KEEP DOING SO UNTIL SUCH TIME ITS NO LONGER NECESSARY. HE WANTS HIS FAMILY NOTIFIED SOON. BUT HIS SISTER AND NOT HIS MOTHER SHOULD BE CALLED. HIS SISTER WILL INFORM HIS MOTHER. I SAW HIM IN THE OFFICE A FEW MINUTES AGO. HE IS WELL, IN NO PAIN. IF THERE ARE ANY OTHER DEVELOPMENTS I WILL TELEX YOU IMMEDIATELY BUT EVERYONE SHOULD REST EASY. FINALLY, THIS HAPPENED AT THE END OF THE AFTERNOONS FILMING. FROM WHAT I CAN GATHER THEY HAVE A VERY GOOD PIECE THAT WE WILL BE SHIPPING MIDDAY FRIDAY. IT CAN GO TO TOKYO IF YOU WANT. IT HAS THE FIREFIGHT AND SHOTS OF TUCKNER AFTER HE TOOK THE PIECES OF SHRAPNEL. WHEN YOU HAVE NOTIFIED HIS SISTER PLEASE LET US KNOW. AAPP IS DOING A STORY THEY HAVE HELD UNTIL TUCKNER'S KIN HAVE BEEN NOTIFIED. THEY WILL RELEASE IT WHEN I TELL THEM TO. IN THE SAME INCIDENT A VIETNAMESE PHOTOGRAPHER FOR THE AAPP NAMED PHUOC WAS WOUNDED IN THE HEAD, BUT NOT SERIOUSLY. OUR OTHER PEOPLE ESCAPED INJURY.

THE ACTION TAKES PLACE TWO BLOCKS FROM THE AN QUANG PAGODA, SCENE OF MUCH FIGHTING IN THE HEART OF CHOLON, THE HOME OF THE MILITANT BUDDHISTS. IT IS THE AREA WHERE THE VIET CONG ARE DEEPLY ROOTED IN SAIGON. THERE WAS THE USUAL FIREFIGHT, INCLUDING VIET CONG SUSPECTS BEING BEATEN WITH RIFLE BUTTS, ALL STRONG STUFF. AFTER THE B-40 ROCKET EXPLODES, WE SEE THE WOUNDED, INCLUDING THE AAPP PHOTOGRAPHER BEING CARRIED TO A MEDICAL VAN. TUCKNER, AFTER BEING WOUNDED, STARTS DOING HIS CLOSER. JUST THEN, A VIETNAMESE MEDIC RUNS INTO THE FRAME AND STARTS WORKING ON HIS LEG BY CUTTING HIS TROUSERS AND APPLYING TOURNIQUET. TUCKNER DID TWO VERSIONS OF THE CLOSER. ONE CLOSER HAS THE WORD DAMN AND ONE DOES NOT. IT'S UP TO YOU WHICH ONE YOU USE.

Jack Russell was a tough, aggressive radio reporter who was everywhere in the field with his tape deck recording the sounds of war. He was with the crew when

Tuckner took the shrapnel in his thigh. AP still photographer Dang Van Phuoc, as he often did, also went with our team. On that day, the war was a ten-minute drive from the office. The men arrived in Cholon late in the afternoon. Saigon policemen, in their usual white shirts and gray slacks, crouched behind and hugged a wall near a police station. Armed with .38 caliber revolvers, carbines, and a few light machine guns, they were outgunned and no match for the Viet Cong less than a block away. Firing was sporadic. Hardened South Vietnamese marines arrived to help the police. The rapid bursts of their M-16 automatic rifles responded to the slower, heavier, explosive beat of the enemy's AK-47s. Jack said the crew dodged around two marine armored cars and worked their way up a wide street to where the two forces were engaged. The Viet Cong were in alleys, inside flimsy wooden shops and homes. There was a sudden lull in the fighting: The South Vietnamese had captured several Viet Cong suspects. They bound their arms behind them and threw them into a truck. Refugees began to flee during the pause in the battle. Howard, Huynh, and Giac moved closer to get pictures of the refugees, but Jack stayed in place and squatted down on the sidewalk. Next to him was Nghia, the other cameraman. Jack said, "I had just turned on my tape recorder to complete a radio narration when a tremendous explosion shook the street. There was no doubt about what caused it, an enemy B-40 rocket. I reported that two and possibly three persons had been wounded." Nghia thought he had taken some shrapnel in the shoulder; Jack could not see the others in the NBC crew. He rolled back Nghia's shirt and saw where he had been struck. His skin was red and inflamed, but there were no tears or rips. Nghia felt relieved, thinking that perhaps he had been struck not by shrapnel but by rocks kicked up by the rocket blast. Jack said, "Tuckner and the AP photographer were not so lucky. They had been hit simultaneously, Tuckner in the back of the leg and Phuoc on the head by shrapnel. Ten minutes later, they were in the 17th Field Hospital." Shortly after, Russell and the rest of the NBC crew were back in the office.

The offensive had settled into its own rhythm. When there was action, we covered it and shipped. With reinforcements now in place, we finally had the chance to do the softer stories, the so-called think pieces in which we tried to explain the Tet Offensive. But the New York producers still wanted only the most exciting war footage. Nothing "marginal"—New York's word—would do. Our early coverage had spoiled them.

Still, by the tenth day of the offensive, the battles never stopped. There was no letup for the correspondents. Paul Cunningham, now working out of Danang, found himself in the middle of any number of big stories. He filed a piece about a North Vietnamese tank attack against the Lang Vie Special Forces camp west of Khe Sanh, near the Laotian border, where there were only a few survivors. Oddly, it was the only time Hanoi used tanks until 1975, when it sent hundreds of tanks into the South to finally end the war. Cunningham also sent in a story about a battle outside Danang that included close air strikes. From Hue, Wilson Hall had a strong piece about the never-ending fighting to take back the city from the North Vietnamese. Hue was shaping up as the end piece of the Tet Offensive, and I worried how to watch over it without being there myself.

In concert with New York, I established a subbureau in Danang to handle shipments, transportation, and communications and to be the liaison on the scene with the U.S. Marines. By February 9, day ten, Frank Donghi was on his way to Danang to run that operation. That meant I needed another manager equal to Donghi's experience and I told New York that if they could send someone, he would not want for work.

As if by design or some unknown factor, attrition—the biggest enemy of my regular staff—started to take its toll. Bill Corrigan and I had the following meeting, which I initiated, over the telex about personnel.

14–9, JOHNSON PROCORRIGAN PROBLEMS, PROBLEMS. I AM RECOMMENDING HOWARD TUCKNER HAVE SEVERAL WEEKS OFF TO FULLY AND PROPERLY RECOVER. THE WOUND IS NOT SERIOUS BUT IT IS OPEN AND PRONE TO INFECTION. HE WAS DUE FOR RR AND RR AND IT WOULD BE PERFECT TO SOLVE TWO PROBLEMS. THIS IS MY IDEA. I WENT TO TUCKNER AND HE BOUGHT IT, ALTHOUGH HE DID SAY HE CAN WORK AND WANTS TO WORK. HE SAYS HE COULD HELP US OUT AS MUCH AS POSSIBLE UNDER THE CIRCUMSTANCES BUT WE AGREED THAT ITS FOOLISH. I PREFER THAT HE HEALED PROPERLY AWAY FROM VIETNAM WHERE HE COULD GET GOOD CARE AND A LOT OF REST SOMEPLACE HERE IN THE ORIENT. HE CAME UP WITH ONE BETTER. HE ASKS IF HE COULD POSSIBLY RETURN TO NEW YORK ON NNBBCC'S MONEY FOR A COUPLE OR THREE WEEKS. THAT WAY HE COULD SEE HIS FAMILY AND GET EVEN BETTER CARE AND TREATMENT. WHEN WELL AGAIN RETURN TO HIS ASSIGNMENT IN VIETNAM. I TOLD HIM I WOULD OFFER IT TO YOU AND AWAIT YOUR DECISION WHETHER THE COMPANY WILL BRING HIM TO THE STATES FOR REST AND RECUPERATION IN LIGHT OF HIS WOUND. PLEASE DONT ONPASS TO HIS SISTER THE POSSIBLE INFECTION PROBLEM. ITEM PROBLEM NUMBER TWO. ONE OF OUR CAMERAMEN THREW IN THE TOWEL TODAY. HE CAME

TO ME AND TOLD ME HE HAS HAD IT, THAT HE CANT TAKE IT ANYMORE. HE FEELS ITS NOT WORTH IT TO GO OUT THERE DAY AFTER DAY AND FACE WHAT HE HAS TO FACE. I ASKED HIM IF HE NEEDS A REST AND HE SAID NO. HE SAID IF HE GETS A REST HE WILL HAVE TO FACE HIS PROBLEM AGAIN WHEN HE RETURNS. I MADE NO EFFORT TO CHANGE HIS MIND BECAUSE I KNOW MY PEOPLE AND ONCE THEIR MINDS ARE SET THERE IS NO RECIRCUITING THEM. THUS, I GO ALONG WITH HIS WISH. I TOLD HIM HE WOULD LEAVE THE BUREAU WITH NO PREJUDICE AND THAT HOPEFULLY NNBBCC WOULD REACT THE SAME WAY. HE HAS BEEN HERE FOR OVER EIGHT MONTHS. HE WOULD LIKE TO DEPART AS SOON AS POSSIBLE REALIZING THAT IT MAY BE IMPOSSIBLE UNTIL THE FLIGHT SITUATION EASES. HE SAID HE WILL TAKE ASSIGNMENTS UNTIL SUCH TIME WE CAN GET HIM OUT. HE ASKS NOTH-ING FROM NNBBCC EXCEPT CONSIDERATION FOR POSSIBLE EMPLOYMENT IN THE FUTURE. ITEM PROBLEM NUMBER THREE IS ANOTHER STAFFER WHOSE TOUR IS UP ON MAY 11. PRIOR TO CURRENT CRISIS HE WAS GOING TO EX-TEND TO EIGHTEEN MONTHS. HE HAS FIRMLY DECIDED THAT ONE YEAR HERE IS ENOUGH. I SUGGEST WE COMPLY WITH HIS WISHES. HE WILL HAVE FULFILLED HIS OBLIGATION. THE RECENT TEN DAYS MADE THAT DECISION FOR HIM. WE WILL NEED A REPLACEMENT AT LEAST ONE MONTH BEFORE HE DEPARTS. ITEM PHIL ROSS WAS ON THE VERGE OF BEING LET GO (AND KNEW IT BASED ON TALKS WE HAD) BUT I FEEL HIS RECENT WORK IN SAIGON DURING THE HEAVY FIGHTING SAVED HIM AND I WOULD LIKE TO KEEP HIM AROUND UNTIL HIS TOUR RUNS OUT. ITEM IF NO OTHER BODY IS AVAILABLE THIS MIGHT BE TIME TO TURN JACK RUSSELL LOOSE FOR TELEVISION TO SEE WHAT HE CAN DO. HE IS A GOER AND CERTAINLY MORE THAN WILLING TO TRY.

STEINMAN EXCORRIGAN ON THE CAMERAMAN I SEE NOTHING TO DO BUT PERMIT HIM TO LEAVE. MUST POINT OUT HIS AGREEMENT WAS FOR YEAR AND SINCE HE NOT STAYING FULL TERM WE WILL NOT PAY HIS FULL RETURN FARE. WE WILL PAY TWO THIRDS HIS AIR FARE TO WHATEVER POINT HE MAY BE GOING AND HE WILL BE RESPONSIBLE FOR REMAINING ONE THIRD. THIS WAS PART OF AGREEMENT WITH HIM AND ALL OTHERS WHO HAVE GONE SAIGONWARDS SINCE TWO MEN LEFT EARLY LAST YEAR. SORRY AS YOU TO LOSE ANYONE RIGHT NOW BUT AGREE THAT NOTHING ELSE CAN BE DONE. SINCE WE GOT CAUGHT NOT QUITE READY FOR THIS. ITEM ON OTHER STAFFER, THERE IS NOTHING TO DO EITHER EXCEPT WISH HIM WELL. WE WILL HUSTLE UP A REPLACEMENT AND ADVISE YOU ON THIS. NATURALLY

WE WILL MEET THE SCHEDULE YOU PROPOSE. ITEM USE JACK RUSSELL AS
YOU SEE FIT BUT HE IS NOT REPEAT NOT TO BE CONSIDERED ANYTHING BUT
AN EMERGENCY TYPE REPLACEMENT. ITEM I AM GOING BACK DOWN STAIRS
AND WILL ANSWER ANY QUERIES WHICH YOU RAISE AS QUICKLY AS THEY
COME. KEEP PLUGGING AWAY AND DONT LOSE HEART.

New York allowed Howard Tuckner to return and, once there, he received high
praise for his reporting and courage. It was what he wanted and it kept him happy
for the moment. The cameraman left as quickly as we could get him on a plane
out of Saigon. He was unhappy with the part of the airfare he had to pay but
he understood the agreement he had made with NBC. A replacement came on
schedule for the staff person who wanted out at the end of his year. Phil Ross
stayed on. Jack Russell, though a terrific reporter, simply did not have what New
York wanted in a television correspondent. He continued working in the bureau
as the radio reporter and did television only in emergencies.

As the war changed, the Vietnamese increasingly did odd things. One night,
they walked off the job at the PTT and went home. None of our messages got
through. I understood they had had no pay for the last ten days. I tried to devise
a plan to bribe them to stay on, but my go-between said they were too afraid of
the government to take my offer.

The war had noticeably slowed in Saigon and other parts of the country. The
fighting had shifted more quickly to the northern frontier than I had thought.
In Danang, Frank would be very busy. With the curfew being cut back each day,
we were returning to something of a normal schedule in Saigon. Gary Bel would
start the day in the bureau around 6 A.M. Because the bureau's phones rang in my
apartment, I was always there to take local calls and military calls, at least those
that got through. The additional crews were making life easier and I started to
give the Vietnamese staffers time off so they could get their disrupted lives together. Looking ahead to week three of the Tet Offensive, I hoped to have Danang
staffed with Frank, two correspondents (one of which would possibly be Jack
Russell), three cameramen, and three soundmen. Naturally, this could change
depending on the whim of Hanoi and the Viet Cong. I planned to staff Saigon
with two correspondents and at least three cameramen and three soundmen. I
knew there would be other assignments for other staffers, depending on how the
story developed.

Thirteen days into the coverage, a new set of rules governing satellite transmis-
sions came from New York. NBC Tokyo had released staff for other duties and

sent others home. Flights from Tan Son Nhut were almost back to normal, and the *Huntley-Brinkley* newscast wanted our film sent to the West Coast so it could transmit it immediately, if warranted. New York would still order the satellite every day. On days when it wasn't needed, they would have to cancel it by a certain time or the network would incur a costly penalty. The message said:

OUTSTANDING OR UNUSUAL MATERIAL CAN STILL ALWAYS BE SATELLITED. WE ARE DEPENDENT ON YOUR ADVISORY THAT MATERIAL IS SPECIAL OR URGENT AND THAT SHIPPING NOT AVAILABLE TO THE WEST COAST. PLEASE BEAR WITH US UNTIL WE CAN FEEL THAT SITUATION MORE NORMAL. EARLIEST ADVISORIES ESSENTIAL IF SYSTEM TO WORK.

I did my best to comply with New York's instructions, but the war would not go away. There was more heavy fighting in Cholon, and I sent correspondent Tom Glennon, with Peter Dehmel, Vo Huynh, and Vo Suu. During a lull after the Viet Cong started burning several buildings, an ARVN officer charged inside a house and dragged out a prisoner. General Loan, continuing his personal crusade, almost killed in cold blood again. He walked up to the suspect and put his pistol to the man's head. He said in Vietnamese, "If you are lying, I will kill you." But, to the relief of Huynh and Suu, who had been there before when Loan had pulled the trigger, he never did.

On the fourteenth day, we had another casualty, but it was not because of enemy fire. Cameraman Phil Ross was filming a story on navy boats ferrying refugees from Hue to Danang. After completing the story, Phil, belowdecks with the crew, decided to go topside for some much needed air. As he came up, the steel hatch slipped from its lock and slammed down on the three middle fingers of his right hand, cutting his middle finger to the bone and cutting and bruising his index and third fingers. The doctor said he fortunately had no broken bones. I planned to keep him out of action for at least a week.

Then, fifteen days into the Tet Offensive, I sent the following message to Shad Northshield, executive producer of the *Huntley-Brinkley* show:

9–14, JOHNSON PROSHAD HERE IS THE EXPECTABLE REPORT FOR THURSDAY SHIPPING. NOTHING FROM THE SAIGON WAR FRONT. IT WAS QUIET AND WE BLANKED.

Those were the key lines of a much longer message. It was the first time in fifteen days that we did not have a story for New York. Historians officially end the Tet Offensive on or about February 28, 1968, when control of Hue went back into the hands of the South Vietnamese. There would be more action, more death and destruction. There would be more stories. Nothing, though, would compare with the first exhilarating, exciting, uncertain days of our coverage.

The life of the bureau had changed when the reinforcements arrived. Those good people were temporary, there to relieve us, offering solace and respite for our battered bodies and psyches until they departed in March and April. Then we returned to normal again in that most abnormal of activities, covering a war.

I wrote the following lines sometime after the first week of the Tet Offensive. They were true then and are true now. They remain always with me:

Our staffers went to cover the war repeatedly, exposing themselves to the incredible danger and the hostile fire of well-trained, dedicated, street-fighting Viet Cong suicide squads. Suddenly it became a different war than the one we had been covering. These reporters wore no jungle fatigues. They had no early morning helicopter rides. There were no long patrols with well-armed American troops. My crews went to war in civilian clothing. They drove to a certain street and parked their car. Their ears, and the sight of fleeing refugees, guided them to the action. These newspeople were in the open most of the time. There were not many trees to kneel behind, just an occasional wall or armored car or tank. Snipers were everywhere, in buildings in front of them, behind them, to their left and right. I told them to go and they went. I kept them going, repeatedly, and their response is something that I will never forget.

22

Life Would Never Be the Same

AFTER THIRTY DAYS, the Tet Offensive was coming to an end. For those who covered the story, it would never be over. The Tet Offensive had become the major event of the war. At the height of the fighting, I found myself running NBC's largest foreign bureau in the world. When the offensive started, twenty-four people were working in the bureau. After three weeks, there were more than sixty of us covering the biggest, longest, fiercest battle in the Vietnam War. Years later, those who had been there and returned to London, Paris, Berlin, San Francisco, New York, Atlanta, and Miami told me they relived and remembered their experience not always fondly, but always deeply. On staff, I had two assistants, as many as eight correspondents for television and one for radio, nine cameramen, eight soundmen, and the necessary cars and drivers to get them into battle or, when available, to the nearest helicopter pad at Tan Son Nhut. In addition, there were visiting NBC staff and freelancers. With the battle raging, we had the people we needed to cover the war. Even when it was quiet, we had to be prepared because there was always the possibility of more attacks. We were ready for anything and lived for those moments when we would prove to ourselves and to our peers the consistency of our reporting, the strength of our journalism, our commitment to the story. Through it all, we never forgot our prime mission: to provide the audience with what it needed to make an informed decision.

After midnight on February 29, bright white flares still lighted portions of the city, mainly over the Saigon River, a major crossing for North Vietnamese troops hoping to infiltrate Saigon. I heard firing, as usual, in every direction. U.S. and Vietnamese artillery were shelling the enemy on the outskirts of Saigon. A strict curfew remained in place. Nothing moved on the streets except the ever-present American MP jeeps, mounted with machine guns and filled with men wearing helmets and flak jackets and carrying M-16 rifles. They patrolled the city's cramped alleyways and narrow back lanes, looking for trouble and hoping not to find any. They had had their fill of war and there was only so much fighting each soldier could handle without a break from combat. Tension remained high. It felt like another attack would come. I knew the Viet Cong never attacked until one or two in the morning. Then they had more freedom of movement and the important cover of darkness. I would be up in my office at my desk because . . . because I was always up, always, it seemed, at my desk. I would be there when new action happened and I would hear more heavy firing.

Josephine had been improving slowly since the day she walked out of the hospital on my arm before the Tet Offensive. She still had no feeling on her right side and little use of her right arm and hand. That would probably not improve. Part of her face had no feeling, but she could speak, though with difficulty. She told me her family thought she now spoke Vietnamese like a child. Considering the extent of her brain injury, it was remarkable that she could speak at all.

Josephine had been undergoing physical therapy at the Third Field Hospital at Tan Son Nhut, but that ended during Tet when the air base came under daily enemy attack. Between the curfew imposed on the Vietnamese and the danger of traveling anywhere in the city, Josephine suffered a major setback in her recovery. To heal, she needed constant care and therapy. Hong Kong loomed as the only possibility, but getting her an exit visa to leave Vietnam and then an entry visa into Hong Kong would be a major challenge. The war worked against us. The Hong Kong authorities were usually anti-immigrant, and it had a special bias toward South Vietnamese, believing that once a Vietnamese landed on the island, a safe sanctuary, she would stay forever, which was probably true. Through friends and colleagues in Hong Kong, I started working on that first. Grant Wolfkill, an NBC cameraman, and his wife Barbara agreed to take her in. They offered to care for her and see that she had physical therapy and met with a psychiatrist to help her adjust to the different life she now faced.

Despite the turbulent weeks of heavy war, I visited and talked to everyone I knew in the South Vietnamese government about the need to get Josephine out of Saigon. They said they could not help, telling me that what I wanted, even with Josephine's serious injuries, was impossible. Negative responses did not stop me. Then, as happened so often in Vietnam, one day everything changed. A well-connected Vietnamese I knew who worked for a wire service walked into my office to tell me he knew how to get Josephine to Hong Kong. It would not be illegal, but it would cost money—some in dollars, some in Vietnamese piasters, and all in new bills for good luck. My Vietnamese friend, out of his affection for Josephine, would be the go-between with the fixer. Enter Black Flower. I never met him, but I did talk to him once over the telephone and explained what we needed. He listened, asked some questions, and decided he could handle the job.

Josephine already had a passport from a trip she had made the previous year to Hong Kong. One of my drivers picked it up at her home and brought it to a prearranged location, a restaurant in Cholon. Good to his word, Black Flower delivered on his promise. When Josephine's newly stamped passport arrived on my desk, I sent Black Flower three hundred American dollars and thirty thousand piasters, all in new bills, the equivalent of four hundred fifty dollars. I contacted Hong Kong, and the NBC bureau worked to get Josephine an entry visa for three months. Once she had a visa to leave Saigon and one to enter Hong Kong, I bought her a round-trip ticket, the return ticket being part of the deception that she would return home when her therapy ended. Several weeks later, she boarded a flight to stability and peace, where the only noises at night were car horns in the streets and foghorns in Victoria Bay. I later learned that Black Flower had been at the airport the day Josephine left, there to guarantee her orderly departure.

Reflecting on the Vietnam War and the Tet Offensive, I knew there would some-day be other wars and other coverage of major, life-changing events. What we produced in the thirty days of Tet Offensive coverage, however, and the impact and excitement those stories provided for our worldwide audience, will be diffi-cult for anyone to equal in the future. In the news business, I always had difficulty reconciling our success with the plight of others. I knew the best stories were about failure, hardship, and defeat, but Vietnam had a special quality. Rarely did we do stories about triumph or success because it hardly existed. Our achievement in the bureau had an overlay of deep sadness because of the acute chaos in Vietnam. The war had been one breakdown after another, all ending in failure.

Then as now, we are unable to understand the true meaning of the war. Of course, it remains terribly sad when we stop to think how our government broke faith with its own soldiers, thus wasting their courage and betraying the trust of the American people. The defense of our country became something few wanted to take part in. The American military did not understand its enemy and how to fight him. Our government refused to understand not just Hanoi and the Viet Cong but also the South Vietnamese, their motives for living, their needs, their fears. Conversely, the North Vietnamese, the South Vietnamese, the Chinese, the Russians, and the Viet Cong could not comprehend America. And they still do not. In the bureau, we tried to tell stories that would shed light on the souls of all these people, but we failed to tell enough of them, and so the American people remained in the dark and our mission in the Vietnam War was obscured by lost opportunities.

Some say that most readers and viewers cannot recall the specifics of what journalists say in their reports—they remember an image or a word, sometimes both in combination, but not much more. That is cynical. It is not how I think. Others say that journalists provide the first draft of history, while it is the novelists and historians whose writing lasts, who permanently implant their vision in the collective memory. My fear is that what we in the bureau did, and how we did it, will have to struggle for a place in this collective memory. We did so much, alone and together, young and not so young, experienced and not so experienced, often making it up as we went along, discovering the new and recycling the old.

We had a duty, an obligation, to make our stories as accurate and realistic as possible and that, I believe, we did. We had access to all the battlefields, even those that appeared inaccessible, and we could film any combat operation we could get to. Most of the military command in Saigon and Washington hated us for our freedom but there was little they could do to prevent us from moving about the country as we wished, when and where we wanted. But they rarely refused us access. We were in Vietnam as guests of the South Vietnamese government. That did not mean they welcomed us either, but other than occasionally lifting a reporter's credentials they did nothing to stop us from covering the war as we saw fit. As the war became increasingly unpopular at home after the Tet Offensive, the American military worked hard to restrict our movements, but they never succeeded. They continued supplying transportation by helicopter or airplane and sometimes by jeep because they realized that, despite Vietnam's poor transportation system, we would manage to find our way to the battlefield. And we did.

As important as it was to get to the story, we still had to report it accurately and clearly, no small task. There were times we possessed tunnel vision, when we could not see the forest for the trees. This was far less a problem for us than for our producers and managers at home. However, the action before the camera and surrounding the team that was covering the story was sometimes so powerful that it wiped away our usually reliable reporting. I tried to guard against the common logical fallacy of making "some" into "all," especially since the combat that our crews captured usually involved fewer than a hundred soldiers, a mere handful compared to the more than five hundred thousand American troops south of the DMZ. All of us in the bureau had to guard against this problem. An ambush by the North Vietnamese troops did not imply America was losing the war. A bomb dropped in error on an unsuspecting village did not mean America was deliberately targeting the innocent. We tried to give each event, no matter how mundane, some perspective so the viewer would not wander in a maze of uncertainty. I concede that we were victims of limited information. But that came with the territory. Ultimately, we could only report what we knew, what we saw, what we learned. Even then, we had to be judicious in our approach. We tried to the best of our ability never to give the public a sanitized version of the war. It was not perfect reporting. But then, no coverage ever is.

Our freedom to move where and when we wanted, though we assumed it to be our right, never went to our head. It led, however, to the Pentagon clamping down on war coverage after Vietnam. In this way, our unlimited access to the war hampered the ability of future generations to cover subsequent wars. Many call this payback for the press's undermining of America's effort in Vietnam, but this is a foolish belief. Yes, what we reported and how we reported it—bringing sometimes graphic, even horrifying, images into people's homes, images true to the film emulsion they were part of—clearly contributed to the American public's turning against the war. Why support something that is bound up in futility and the waste of young lives? But when our reporting is considered in light of the harsh reality of Washington's dismal management of the war and its consistent pattern of lies, it is unfair to blame television for America's inability to win what had become unwinnable. The White House and the Pentagon consistently mangled the truth and were caught in one lie after another. Today there are those who sing the same tune, not accepting reality. Blame them for America's failure, not the worthy messengers who brought the news home. Keeping television from the front in any war undermines the meaning of the open society we cherish and seek to protect.

It would be a disservice to the story we told, and the way we told it, if our accomplishments were forgotten. In Vietnam more than thirty years ago, we used film for the last time to cover a war. Videotape soon dominated television news and all but eliminated film. We broke new ground when we started using satellites to send our stories to the States to be broadcast on the same day they were filmed. First we fed them only from selected cities such as Tokyo, then, as the war continued, from everywhere in the world to give our stories the immediacy they deserved. We know that what we did is something no one will do again.

The life we led covering the war, and the story we covered with such intensity and passion, changed us forever. I was sometimes truculent, always tired, and often angry, fiery, combative, and driven. My mission, to provide complete, un-biased, accurate coverage, dominated me professionally and personally. Did we make a difference? I believe we did, but the quality of the reporting dominated, not the quantity. This went for everyone in the bureau. I know we succeeded. We were fiercely independent, an irrepressible collection of reporters with pen-cils, cameras, and microphones who never knew when to quit. And for that I will always be grateful.

The effect that covering the war has had on my life is powerful and omni-present. As much as I may want it to, it never fully leaves me. In many ways, I am alone with my knowledge. This book is a way of sharing that experience. In the end, though, each person's view of the war and how they covered it is different. That is the way it should be, especially in our free and pluralistic society.

Author's Note

THIS BOOK IS FOR everyone who worked in Saigon for NBC News before, during, and after my tenure. Not everyone who served on my watch appears in the book. People had different experiences and some people's stories are better and more telling than others. I had to make choices from memory, notes, logs, a seemingly infinite number of cables and messages, and, finally, emotion. Thus the story I tell is not encyclopedic, not all-inclusive. Those who failed to make the cut and are not in the book might consider themselves lucky: Each of us who recalls an event has his own take on exactly what happened. Also, in a book as in television, time and space is an important consideration, sometimes out of proportion to the subject and beyond anything reasonable. But each of you matters to me in ways that you may never realize. You were all part of the last war of its kind in modern times and probably all time to come.

I do have some special thanks for certain people who played a role in seeing the book to completion. Reuven Frank deserves thanks for first sending me to Saigon to run the bureau. I admire his strength in dealing with me through crisis after crisis in what was sometimes the best of times and sometimes the worst of times, but always incredible times. My family, especially my wife, Josephine, deserves praise for patience while watching me toil so long to see the book into print. Eileen Douglas, my partner in Douglas/Steinman Productions, contributed much by helping to organize a sometimes unwieldy manuscript and then reading the copy with a clear and critical eye. To Clair Willcox of the University of Missouri Press go thanks for believing in the book when others did not. Special thanks go to Gary Kass, my copyeditor, whose thoughtful editing and incisive questions helped make this a better book.

The words and thoughts in this book are mine, as are my conclusions, opinions, and judgments. They should not be assumed to be those of anyone else living or dead or even, for that matter, of my former employer NBC News, where I worked for thirty-five years during what I consider some of its greatest days.

Index

Page numbers in italics refer to illustrations.

DATE DUE

NOV 1 7 2003			
JAN 02 2007			
GAYLORD			PRINTED IN U.S.A.